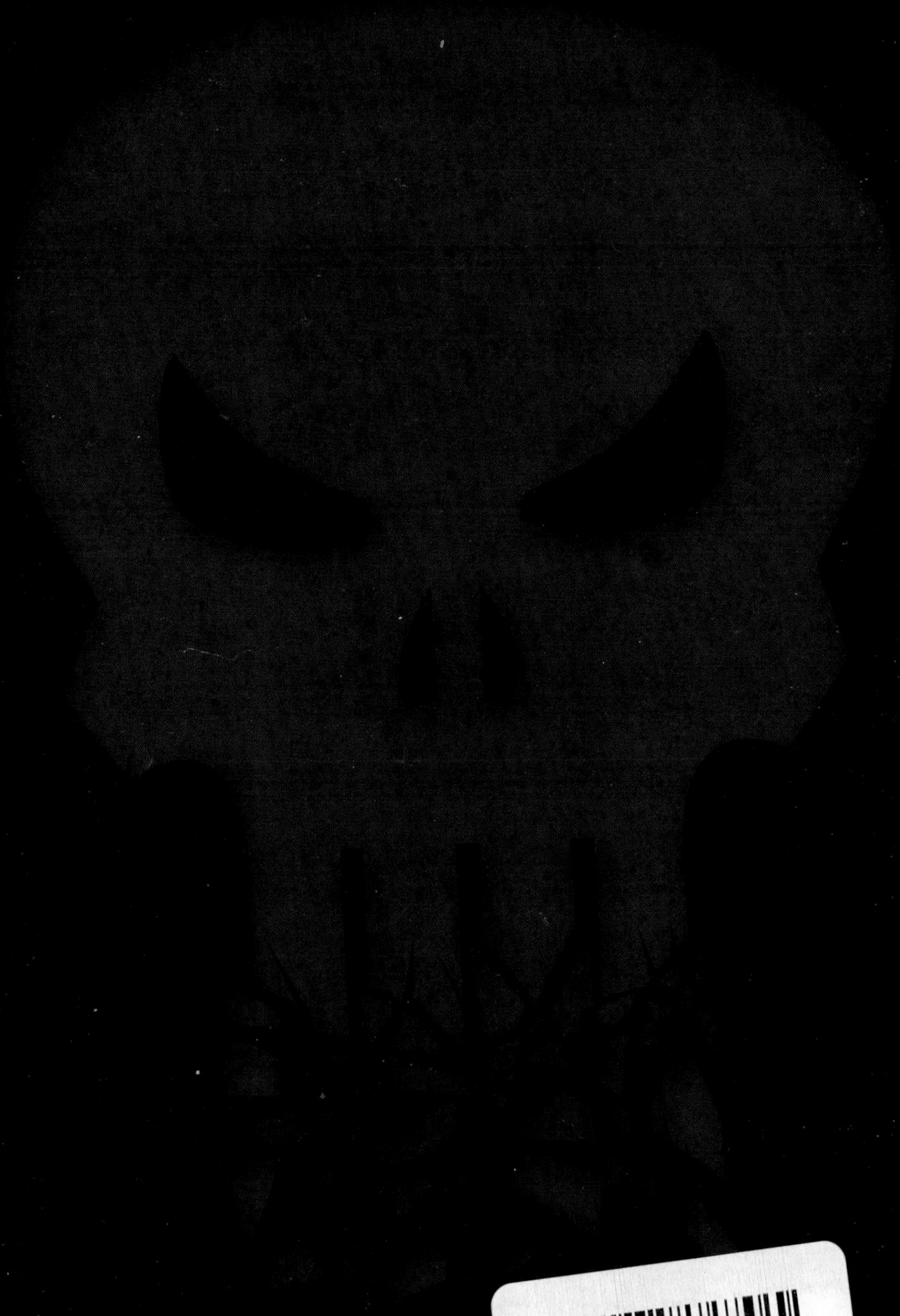

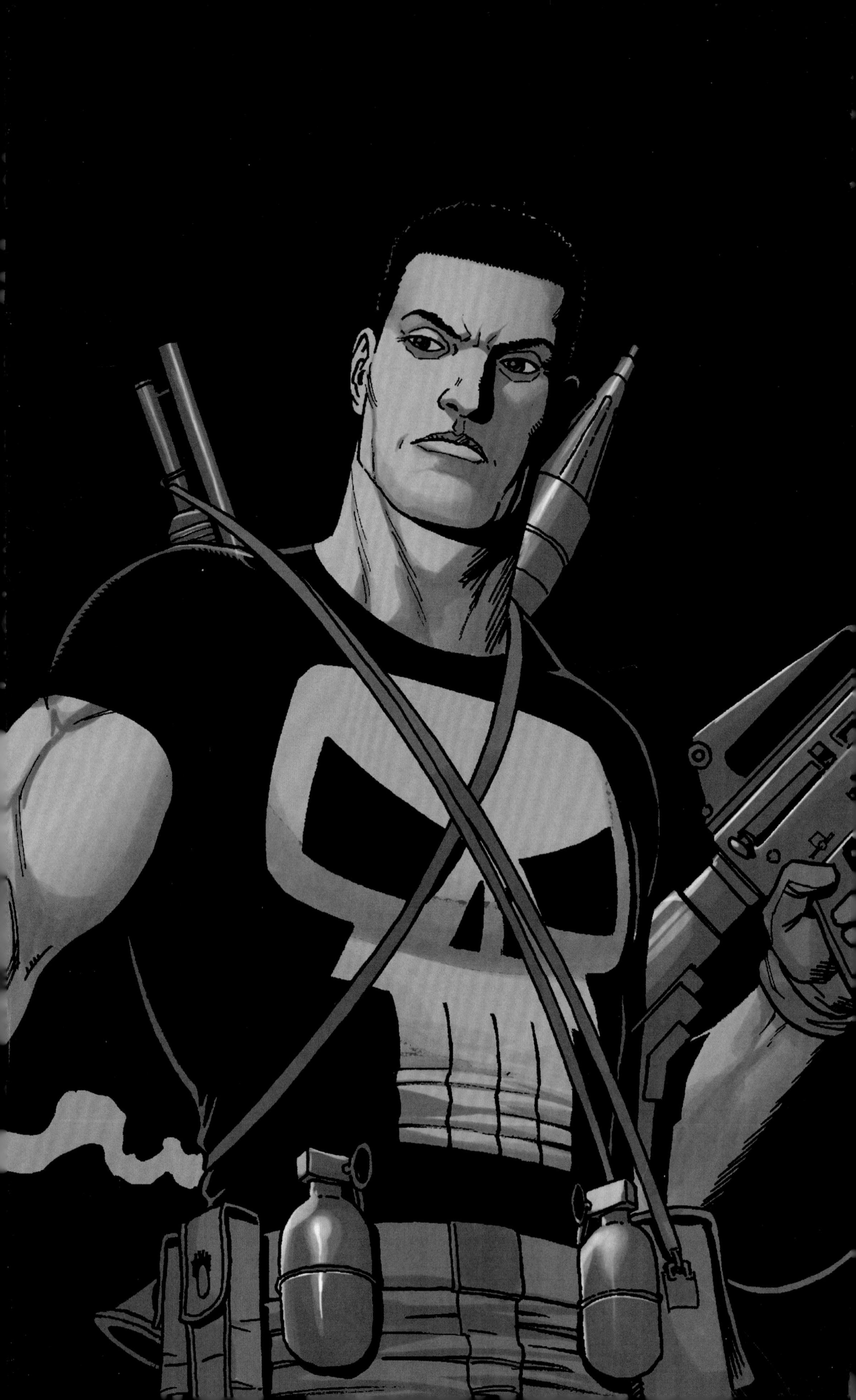

FRANK CASTLE was a decorated Marine, an upstanding citizen, and a family man. Then his family was taken from him when they were accidentally killed in a brutal mob hit. From that day, he became a force of cold, calculated retribution and vigilantism. Frank Castle died with his family. Now, there is only...

THE PUNISHER

ON THE ROAD

Becky Cloonan
writer

Steve Dillon
artist

Frank Martin with **Lee Duhig** (#6)
color artists

VC's Cory Petit (#1-2, #4-6) & **Joe Sabino** (#3)
letterers

Declan Shalvey & **Jordie Bellaire**
cover art

Kathleen Wisneski
assistant editor

Jake Thomas
editor

collection editor: Jennifer Grünwald
associate managing editor: Kateri Woody
associate editor: Sarah Brunstad
editor, special projects: Mark D. Beazley

vp production & special projects: Jeff Youngquist
svp print, sales & marketing: David Gabriel
book designer: Adam Del Re

editor in chief: Axel Alonso
chief creative officer: Joe Quesada
publisher: Dan Buckley
executive producer: Alan Fine

THE PUNISHER VOL. 1: ON THE ROAD. Contains material originally published in magazine form as THE PUNISHER #1-6. First printing 2016. ISBN# 973-1-302-90047-2. Published by MARVEL WORLDWIDE, INC., a subsidiary of MARVEL ENTERTAINMENT, LLC. OFFICE OF PUBLICATION: 135 West 50th Street, New York, NY 10020.

Printed in Canada. ALAN FINE, President, Marvel Entertainment; DAN BUCKLEY, President, TV, Publishing & Brand Management; JOE QUESADA, Chief Creative Officer; TOM BREVOORT, SVP of Publishing; DAVID BOGART, SVP of Business Affairs & Operations, Publishing & Partnership; C.B. CEBULSKI, VP of Brand Management & Development, Asia; DAVID GABRIEL, SVP of Sales & Marketing, Publishing; JEFF YOUNGQUIST, VP of Production & Special Projects; DAN CARR, Executive Director of Publishing Technology; ALEX MORALES, Director of Publishing Operations; SUSAN CRESPI, Production Manager; STAN LEE, Chairman Emeritus. For information regarding advertising in Marvel Comics or on Marvel.com, please contact Vit DeBellis, Integrated Sales Manager, at vdebellis@marvel.com. For Marvel subscription inquiries, please call 888-511-5480. **Manufactured between 10/28/2016 and 12/5/2016 by SOLISCO PRINTERS, SCOTT, QC, CANADA.**

10 9 8 7 6 5 4 3 2 1

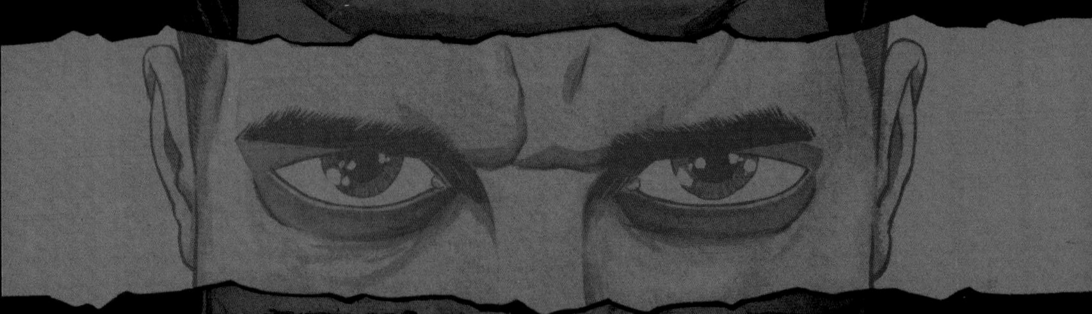

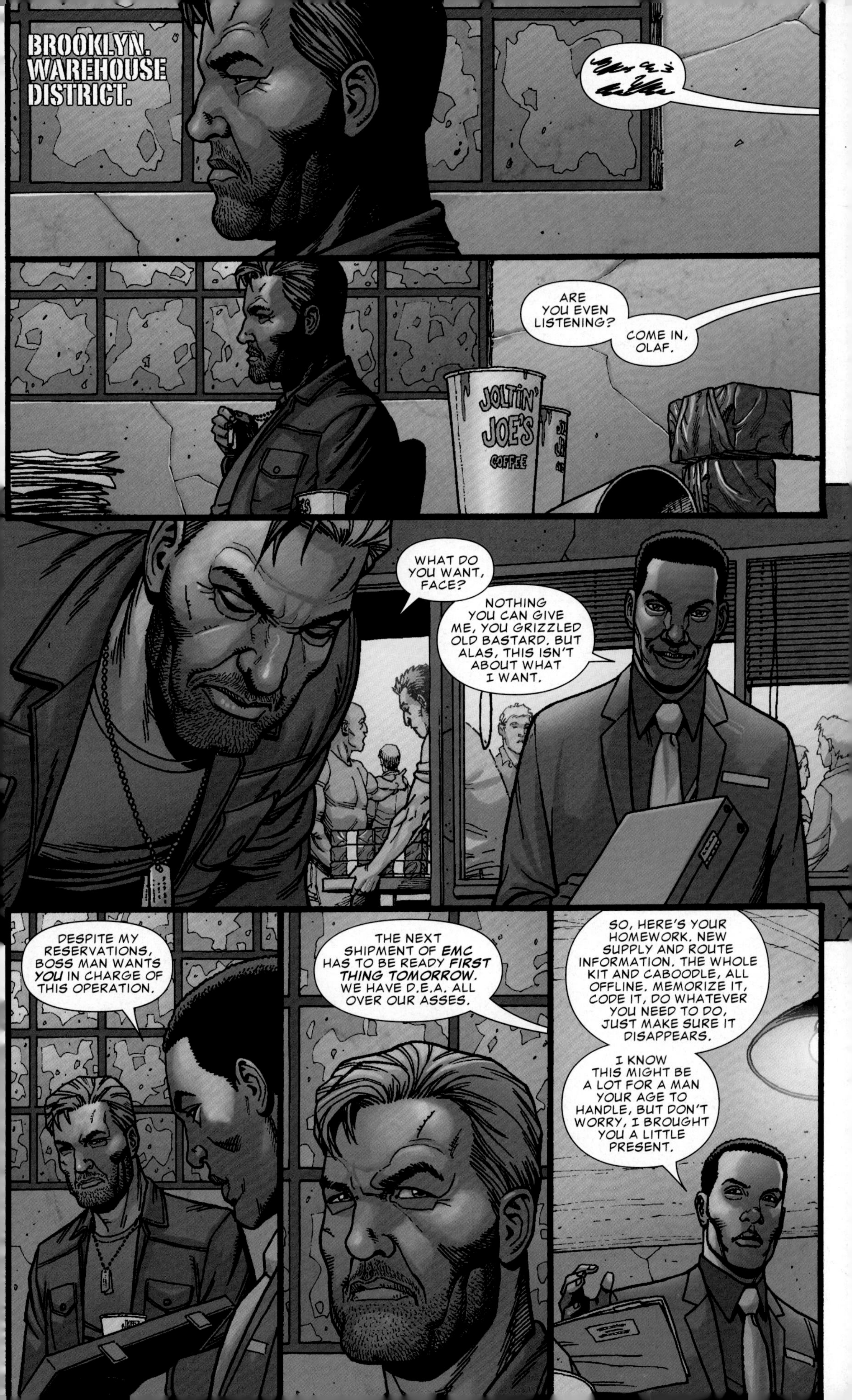
BROOKLYN. WAREHOUSE DISTRICT.
ARE YOU EVEN LISTENING?
COME IN, OLAF.
JOLTIN' JOE'S COFFEE
WHAT DO YOU WANT, FACE?
NOTHING YOU CAN GIVE ME, YOU GRIZZLED OLD BASTARD. BUT ALAS, THIS ISN'T ABOUT WHAT I WANT.
DESPITE MY RESERVATIONS, BOSS MAN WANTS YOU IN CHARGE OF THIS OPERATION.
THE NEXT SHIPMENT OF EMC HAS TO BE READY FIRST THING TOMORROW. WE HAVE D.E.A. ALL OVER OUR ASSES.
SO, HERE'S YOUR HOMEWORK. NEW SUPPLY AND ROUTE INFORMATION. THE WHOLE KIT AND CABOODLE, ALL OFFLINE. MEMORIZE IT, CODE IT, DO WHATEVER YOU NEED TO DO, JUST MAKE SURE IT DISAPPEARS.
I KNOW THIS MIGHT BE A LOT FOR A MAN YOUR AGE TO HANDLE, BUT DON'T WORRY, I BROUGHT YOU A LITTLE PRESENT.

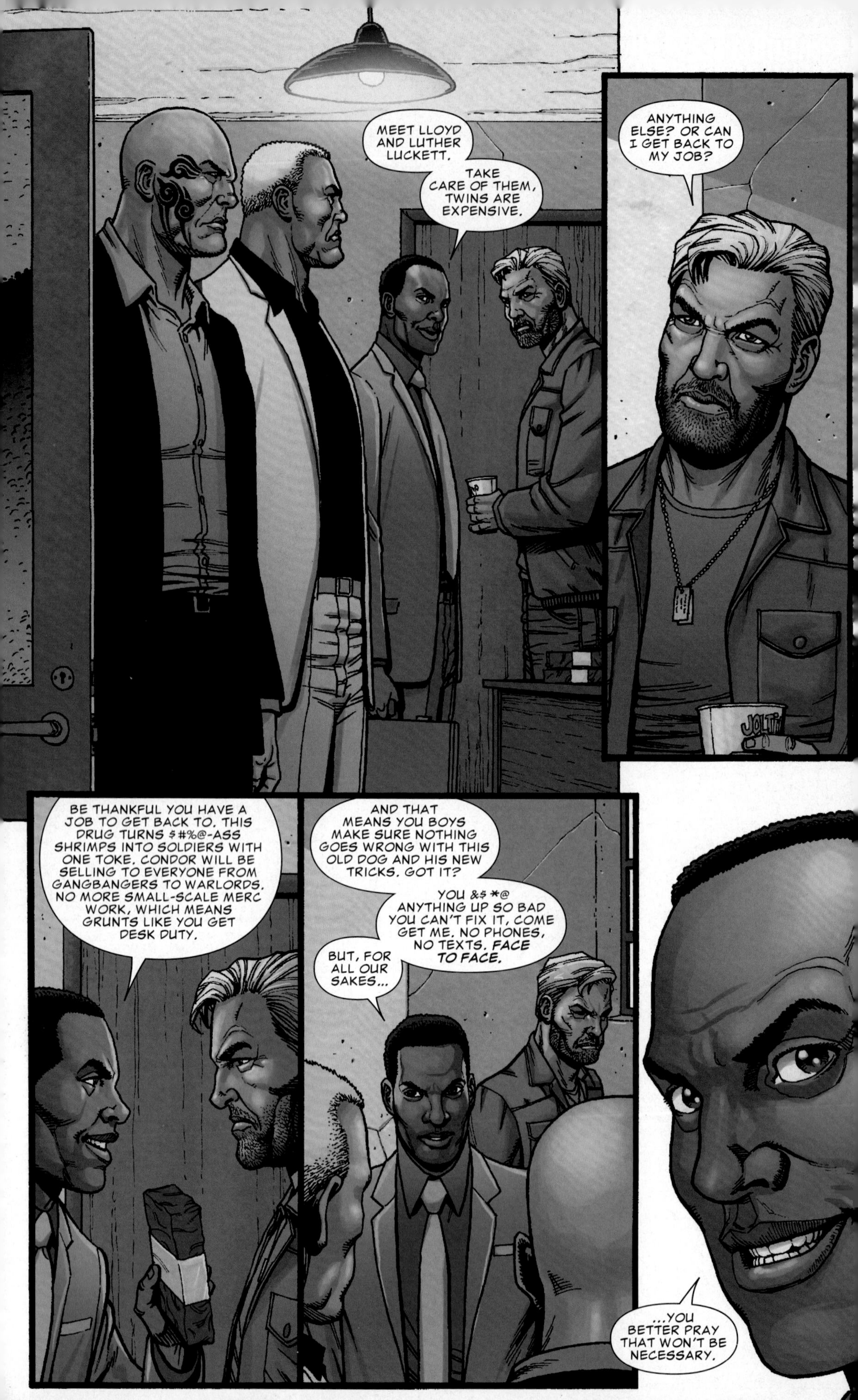
MEET LLOYD AND LUTHER LUCKETT.
TAKE CARE OF THEM, TWINS ARE EXPENSIVE.
ANYTHING ELSE? OR CAN I GET BACK TO MY JOB?
BE THANKFUL YOU HAVE A JOB TO GET BACK TO. THIS DRUG TURNS $#%@-ASS SHRIMPS INTO SOLDIERS WITH ONE TOKE. CONDOR WILL BE SELLING TO EVERYONE FROM GANGBANGERS TO WARLORDS. NO MORE SMALL-SCALE MERC WORK, WHICH MEANS GRUNTS LIKE YOU GET DESK DUTY.
AND THAT MEANS YOU BOYS MAKE SURE NOTHING GOES WRONG WITH THIS OLD DOG AND HIS NEW TRICKS. GOT IT?
YOU &$ *@ ANYTHING UP SO BAD YOU CAN'T FIX IT, COME GET ME. NO PHONES, NO TEXTS. *FACE TO FACE.*
BUT, FOR ALL OUR SAKES...
...YOU BETTER PRAY THAT WON'T BE NECESSARY.

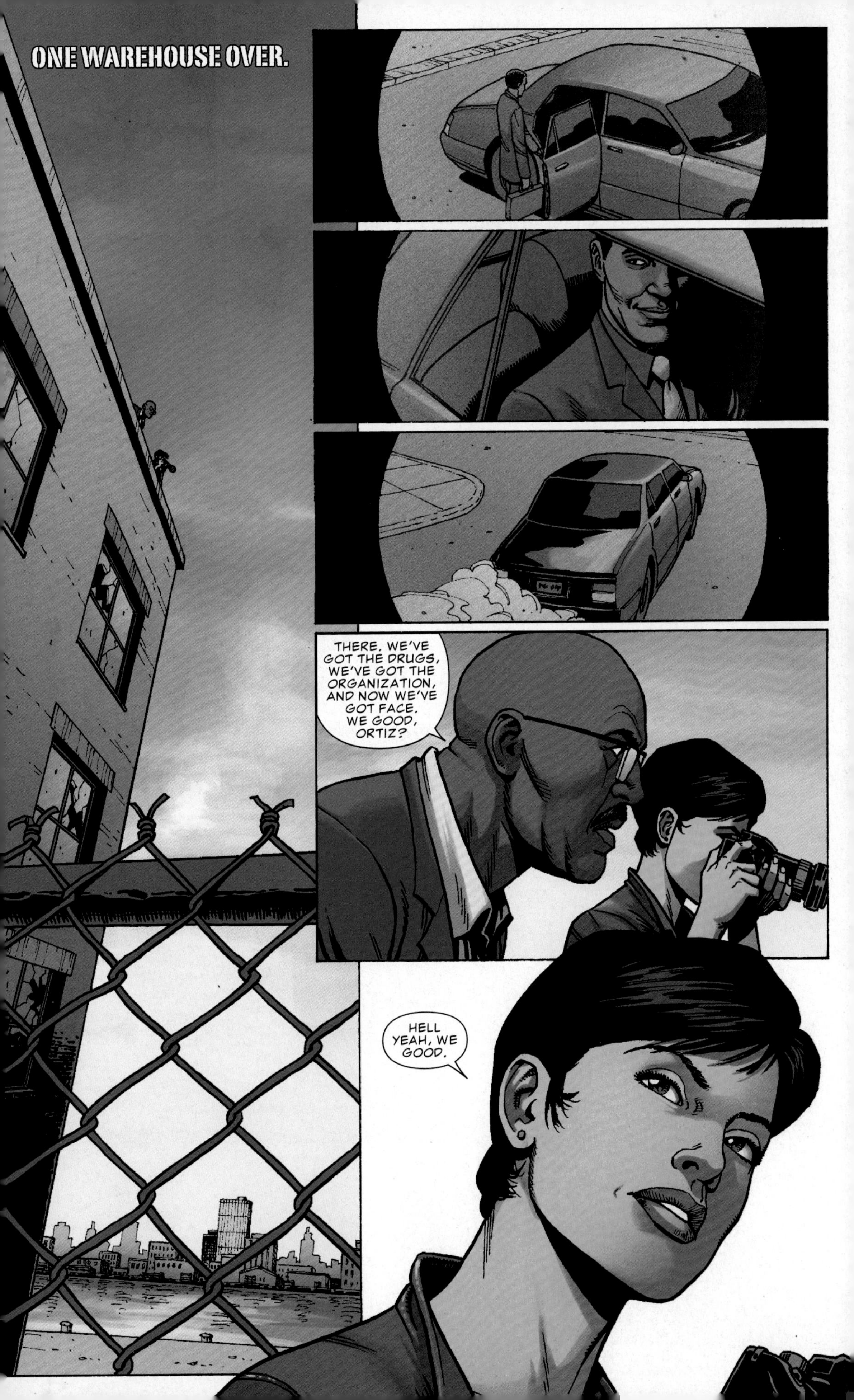
ONE WAREHOUSE OVER.
THERE. WE'VE GOT THE DRUGS, WE'VE GOT THE ORGANIZATION, AND NOW WE'VE GOT FACE. WE GOOD, ORTIZ?
HELL YEAH, WE GOOD.

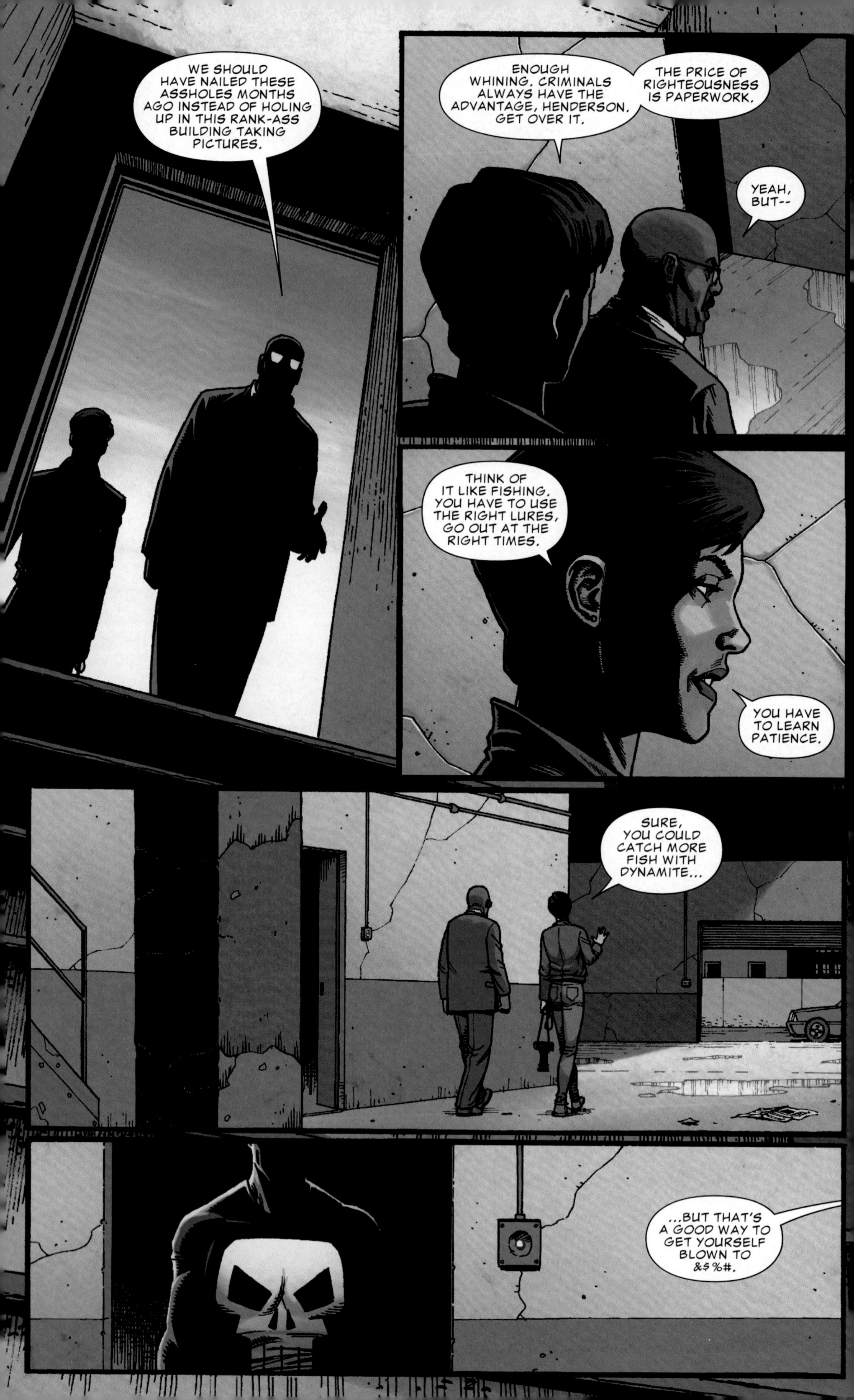
WE SHOULD HAVE NAILED THESE ASSHOLES MONTHS AGO INSTEAD OF HOLING UP IN THIS RANK-ASS BUILDING TAKING PICTURES.
ENOUGH WHINING. CRIMINALS ALWAYS HAVE THE ADVANTAGE, HENDERSON. GET OVER IT.
THE PRICE OF RIGHTEOUSNESS IS PAPERWORK.
YEAH, BUT--
THINK OF IT LIKE FISHING. YOU HAVE TO USE THE RIGHT LURES, GO OUT AT THE RIGHT TIMES.
YOU HAVE TO LEARN PATIENCE.
SURE, YOU COULD CATCH MORE FISH WITH DYNAMITE...
...BUT THAT'S A GOOD WAY TO GET YOURSELF BLOWN TO &$%#.

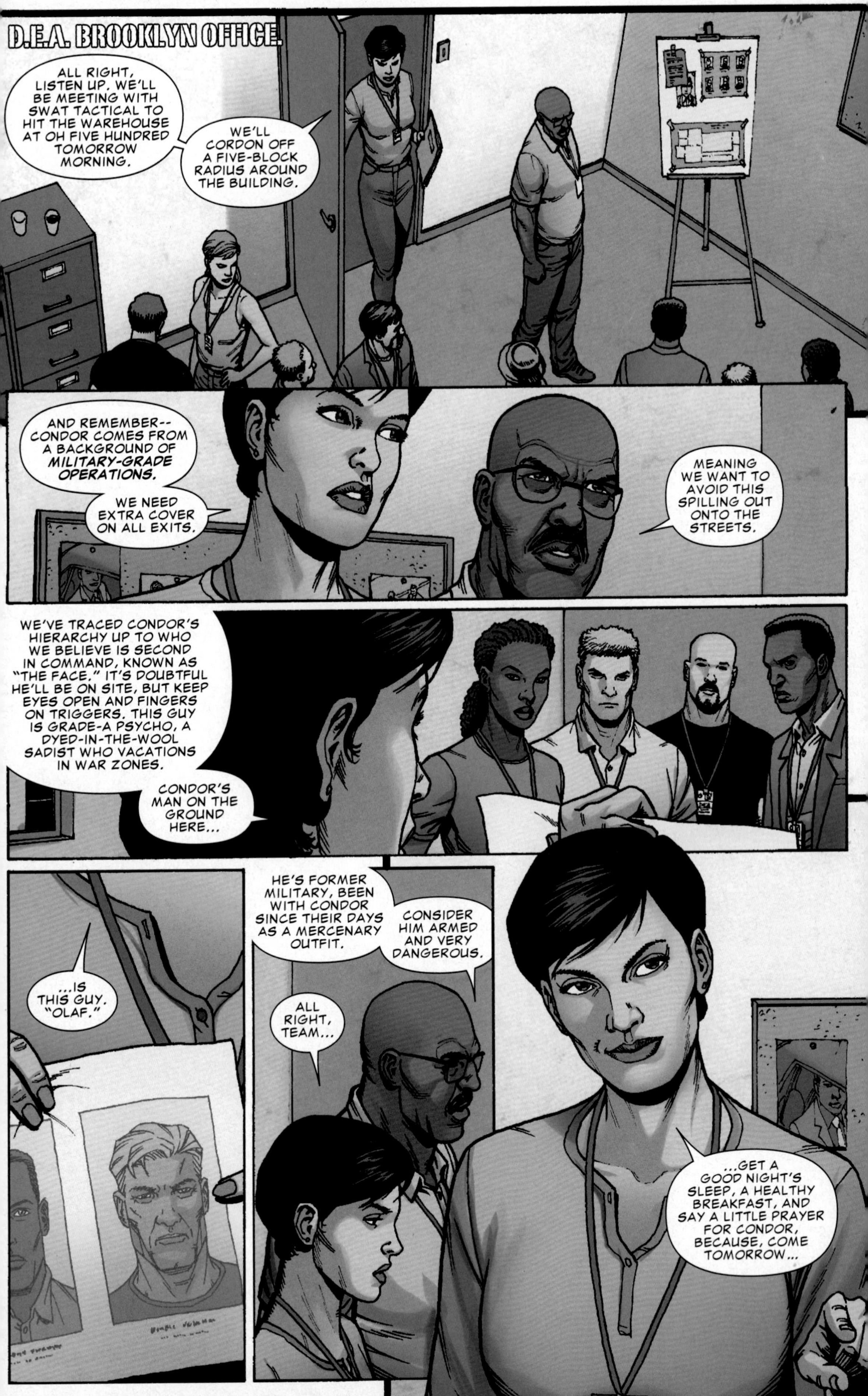
D.E.A. BROOKLYN OFFICE.
ALL RIGHT, LISTEN UP. WE'LL BE MEETING WITH SWAT TACTICAL TO HIT THE WAREHOUSE AT OH FIVE HUNDRED TOMORROW MORNING.
WE'LL CORDON OFF A FIVE-BLOCK RADIUS AROUND THE BUILDING.
AND REMEMBER-- CONDOR COMES FROM A BACKGROUND OF MILITARY-GRADE OPERATIONS.
WE NEED EXTRA COVER ON ALL EXITS.
MEANING WE WANT TO AVOID THIS SPILLING OUT ONTO THE STREETS.
WE'VE TRACED CONDOR'S HIERARCHY UP TO WHO WE BELIEVE IS SECOND IN COMMAND, KNOWN AS "THE FACE." IT'S DOUBTFUL HE'LL BE ON SITE, BUT KEEP EYES OPEN AND FINGERS ON TRIGGERS. THIS GUY IS GRADE-A PSYCHO, A DYED-IN-THE-WOOL SADIST WHO VACATIONS IN WAR ZONES.
CONDOR'S MAN ON THE GROUND HERE...
...IS THIS GUY. "OLAF."
HE'S FORMER MILITARY, BEEN WITH CONDOR SINCE THEIR DAYS AS A MERCENARY OUTFIT.
CONSIDER HIM ARMED AND VERY DANGEROUS.
ALL RIGHT, TEAM...
...GET A GOOD NIGHT'S SLEEP, A HEALTHY BREAKFAST, AND SAY A LITTLE PRAYER FOR CONDOR, BECAUSE, COME TOMORROW...

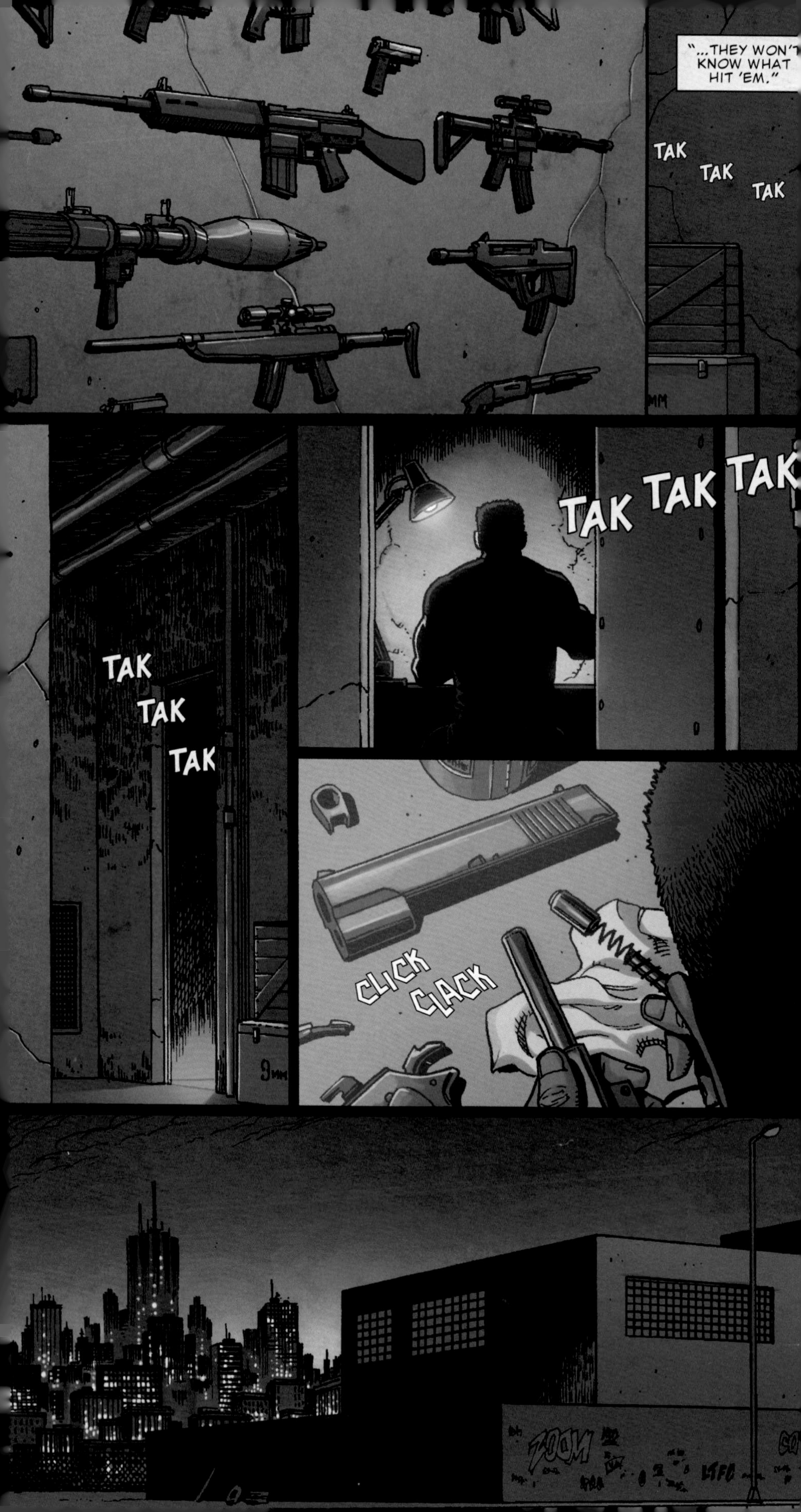
"...THEY WON'T KNOW WHAT HIT 'EM."
TAK
TAK
TAK
TAK
TAK
TAK
TAK TAK TAK
CLICK
CLACK
ZOOM

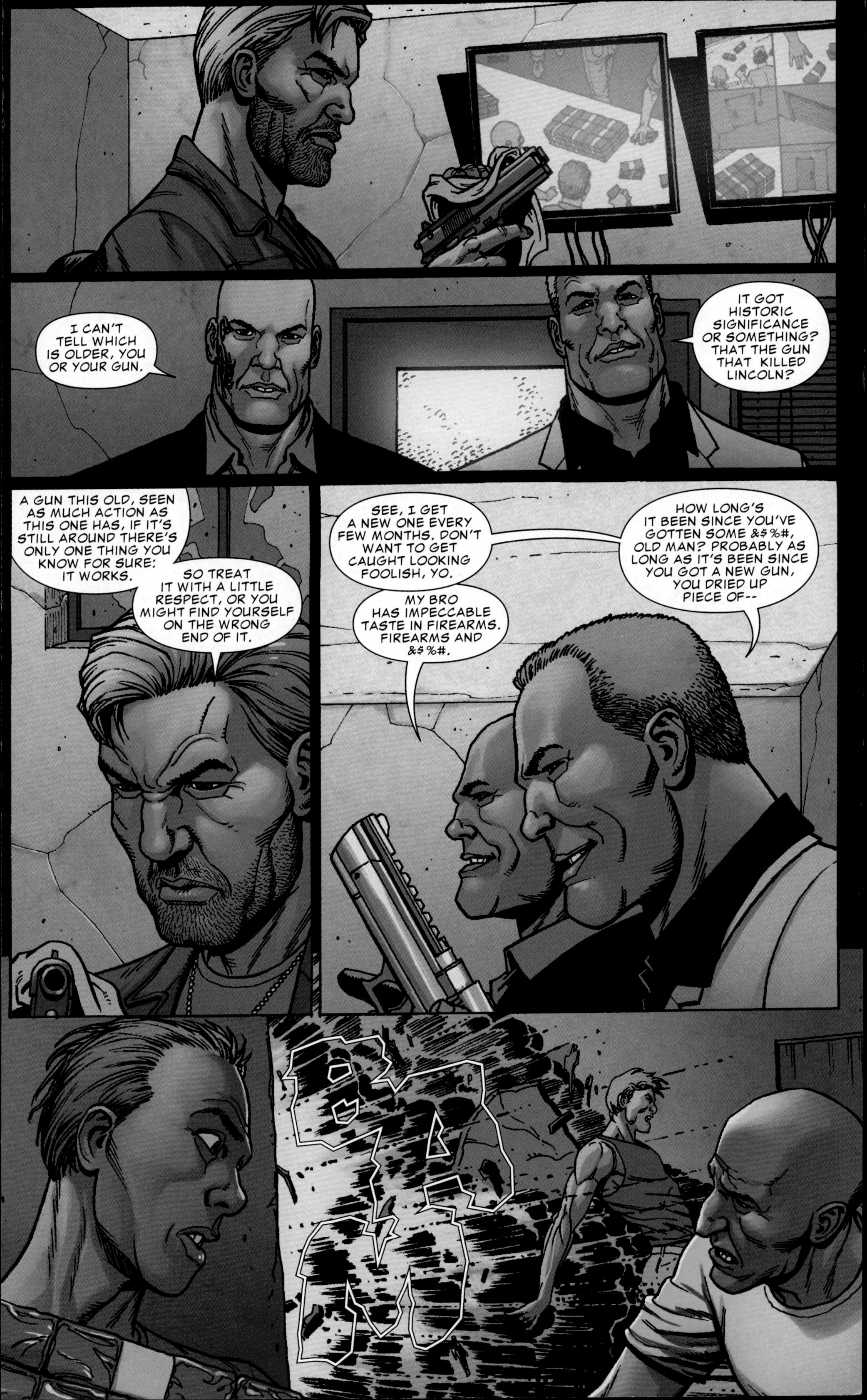

I CAN'T TELL WHICH IS OLDER, YOU OR YOUR GUN.
IT GOT HISTORIC SIGNIFICANCE OR SOMETHING? THAT THE GUN THAT KILLED LINCOLN?
A GUN THIS OLD, SEEN AS MUCH ACTION AS THIS ONE HAS, IF IT'S STILL AROUND THERE'S ONLY ONE THING YOU KNOW FOR SURE: IT WORKS.
SO TREAT IT WITH A LITTLE RESPECT, OR YOU MIGHT FIND YOURSELF ON THE WRONG END OF IT.
SEE, I GET A NEW ONE EVERY FEW MONTHS. DON'T WANT TO GET CAUGHT LOOKING FOOLISH, YO.
HOW LONG'S IT BEEN SINCE YOU'VE GOTTEN SOME &$%#, OLD MAN? PROBABLY AS LONG AS IT'S BEEN SINCE YOU GOT A NEW GUN, YOU DRIED UP PIECE OF--
MY BRO HAS IMPECCABLE TASTE IN FIREARMS. FIREARMS AND &$%#.

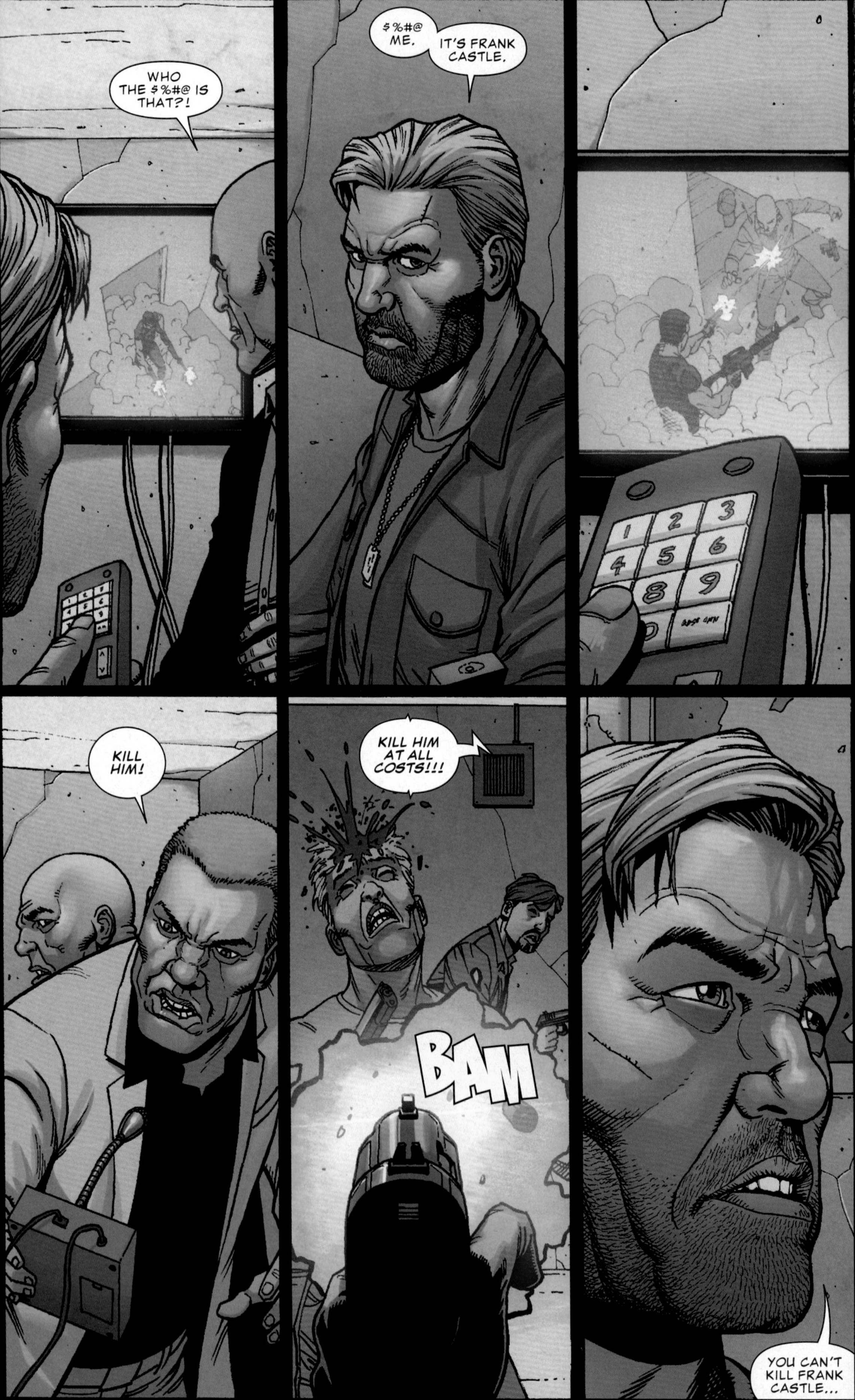
WHO THE $%#@ IS THAT?!
$%#@ ME.
IT'S FRANK CASTLE.
KILL HIM!
KILL HIM AT ALL COSTS!!!
BAM
YOU CAN'T KILL FRANK CASTLE...

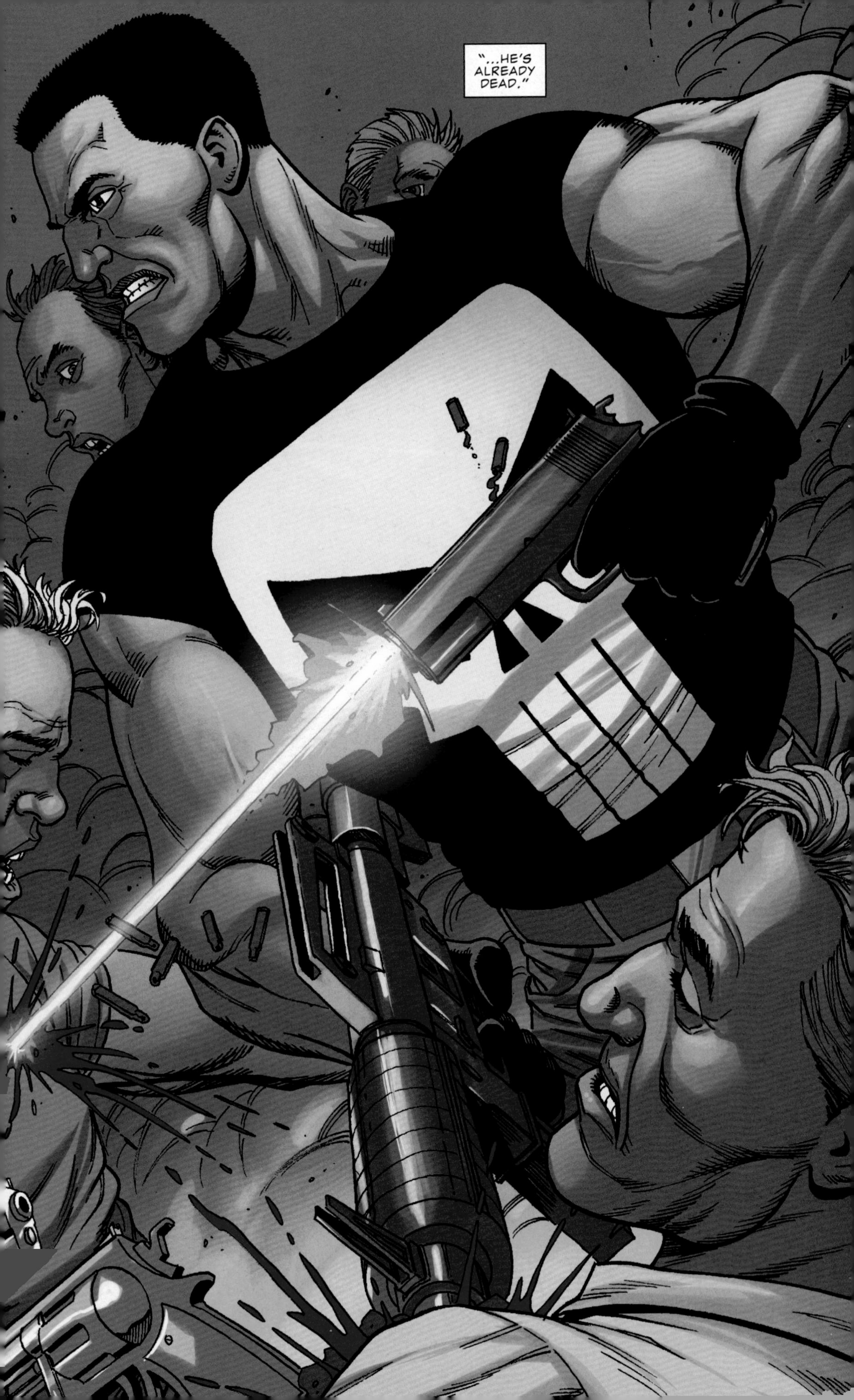
"...HE'S ALREADY DEAD."

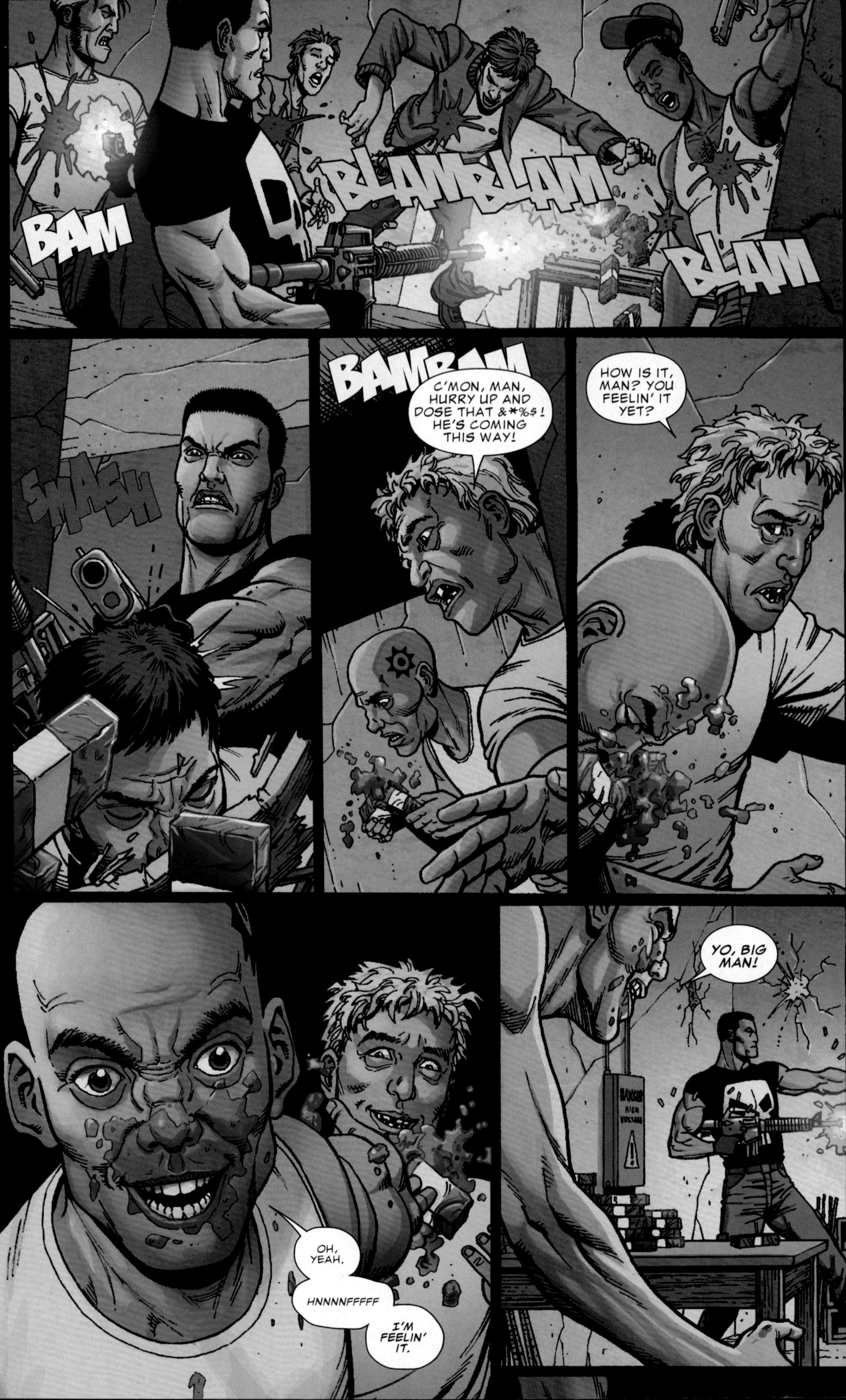
BAM
BLAMBLAM
BLAM
SMASH
BAMBAM
C'MON, MAN, HURRY UP AND DOSE THAT &*%$! HE'S COMING THIS WAY!
HOW IS IT, MAN? YOU FEELIN' IT YET?
OH, YEAH.
HNNNNFFFFF
I'M FEELIN' IT.
YO, BIG MAN!
DANGER HIGH VOLTAGE

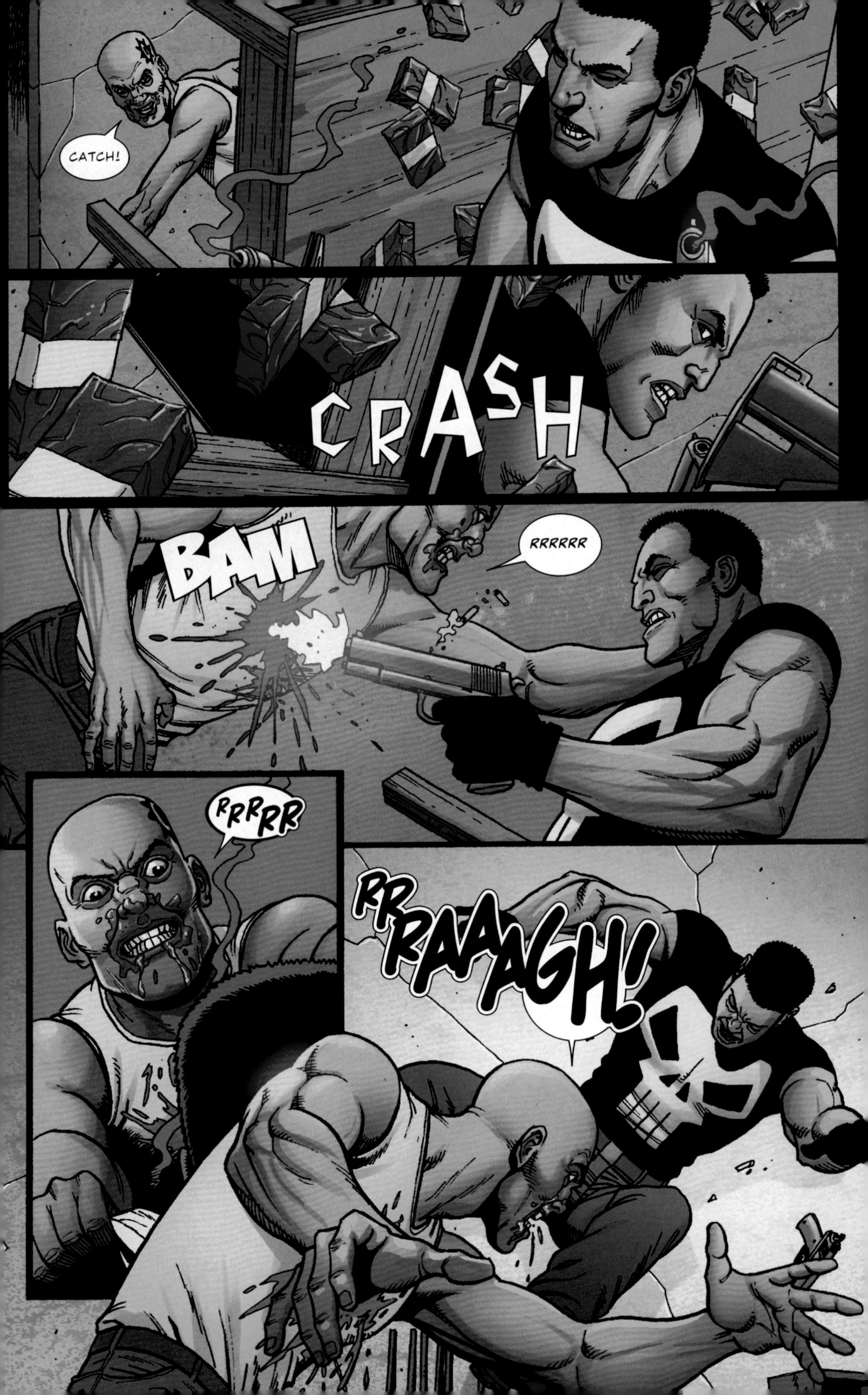
CATCH!
CRASH
BAM
RRRRRR
RRRRR
RRRAAAAGH!

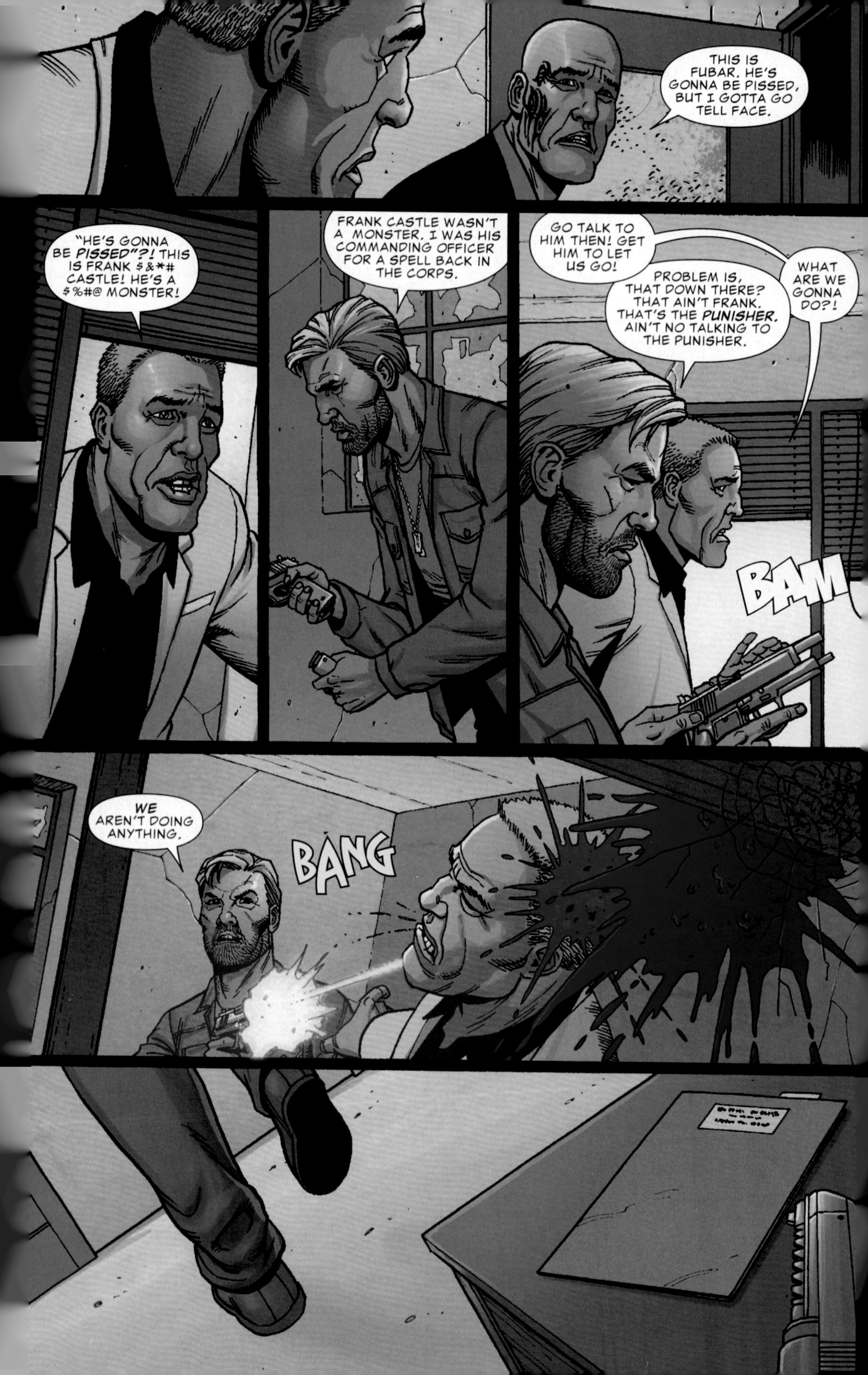
THIS IS FUBAR. HE'S GONNA BE PISSED, BUT I GOTTA GO TELL FACE.
"HE'S GONNA BE *PISSED*"?! THIS IS FRANK $&*# CASTLE! HE'S A $%#@ MONSTER!
FRANK CASTLE WASN'T A MONSTER. I WAS HIS COMMANDING OFFICER FOR A SPELL BACK IN THE CORPS.
GO TALK TO HIM THEN! GET HIM TO LET US GO!
PROBLEM IS, THAT DOWN THERE? THAT AIN'T FRANK. THAT'S THE *PUNISHER.* AIN'T NO TALKING TO THE PUNISHER.
WHAT ARE WE GONNA DO?!
BAM
WE AREN'T DOING ANYTHING.
BANG

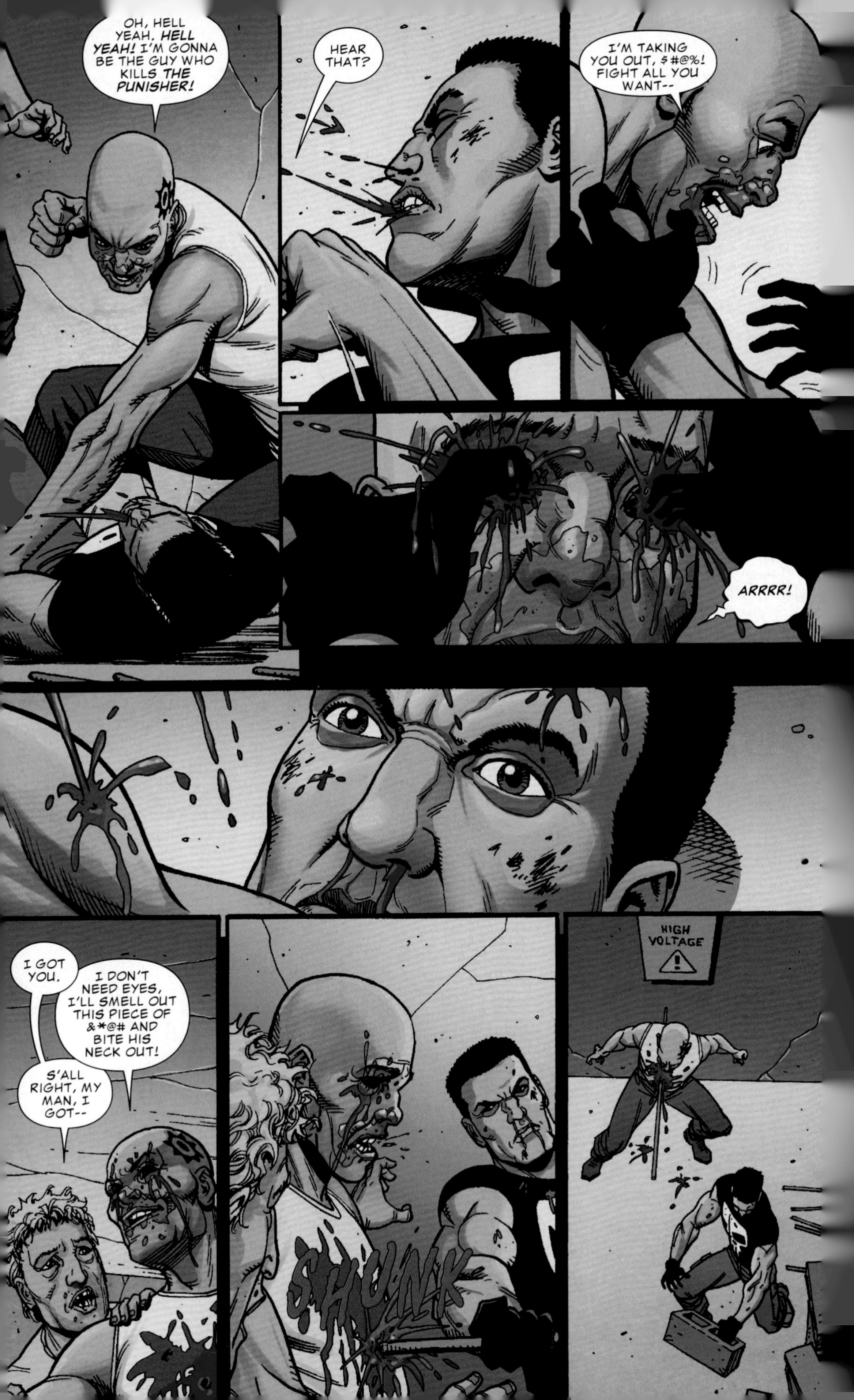
OH, HELL YEAH. HELL YEAH! I'M GONNA BE THE GUY WHO KILLS THE PUNISHER!
HEAR THAT?
I'M TAKING YOU OUT, $#@%! FIGHT ALL YOU WANT--
ARRRR!
I GOT YOU.
I DON'T NEED EYES, I'LL SMELL OUT THIS PIECE OF &*@# AND BITE HIS NECK OUT!
S'ALL RIGHT, MY MAN, I GOT--
SHUNK
HIGH VOLTAGE

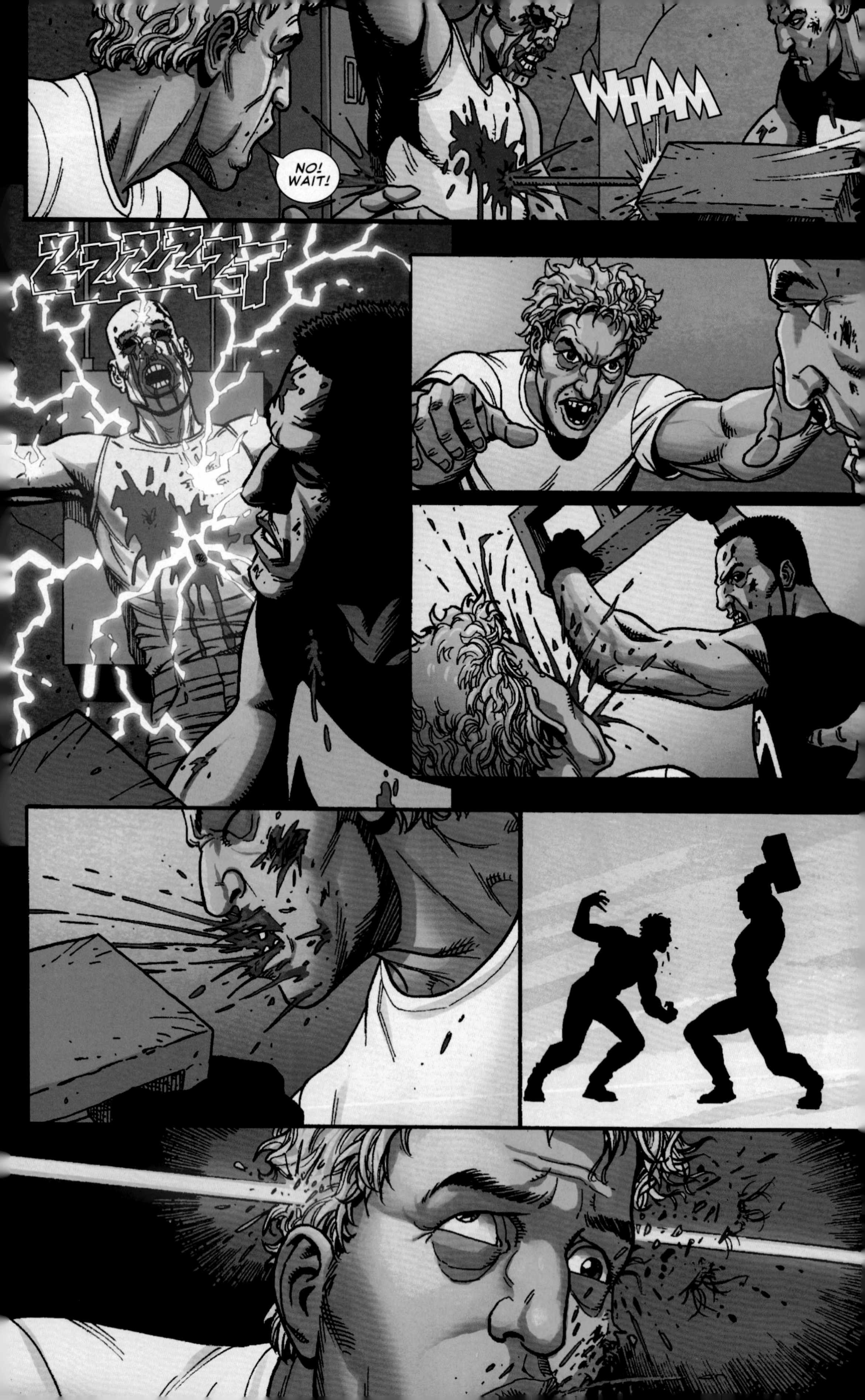

NO! WAIT!
WHAM
ZZZZZZT

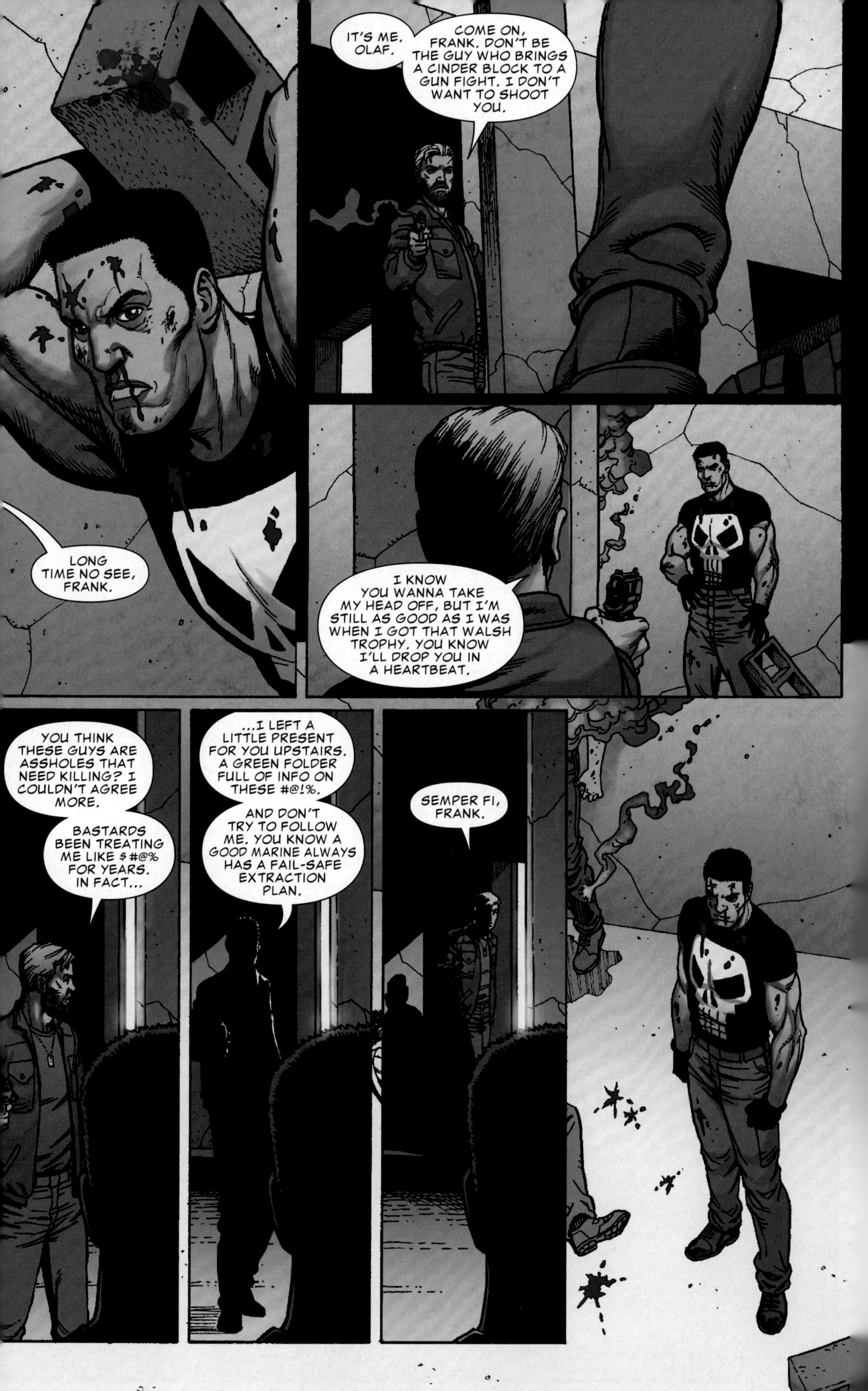
IT'S ME, OLAF.
COME ON, FRANK. DON'T BE THE GUY WHO BRINGS A CINDER BLOCK TO A GUN FIGHT. I DON'T WANT TO SHOOT YOU.
LONG TIME NO SEE, FRANK.
I KNOW YOU WANNA TAKE MY HEAD OFF, BUT I'M STILL AS GOOD AS I WAS WHEN I GOT THAT WALSH TROPHY. YOU KNOW I'LL DROP YOU IN A HEARTBEAT.
YOU THINK THESE GUYS ARE ASSHOLES THAT NEED KILLING? I COULDN'T AGREE MORE.
BASTARDS BEEN TREATING ME LIKE $#@% FOR YEARS. IN FACT...
...I LEFT A LITTLE PRESENT FOR YOU UPSTAIRS. A GREEN FOLDER FULL OF INFO ON THESE #@!%.
AND DON'T TRY TO FOLLOW ME. YOU KNOW A GOOD MARINE ALWAYS HAS A FAIL-SAFE EXTRACTION PLAN.
SEMPER FI, FRANK.

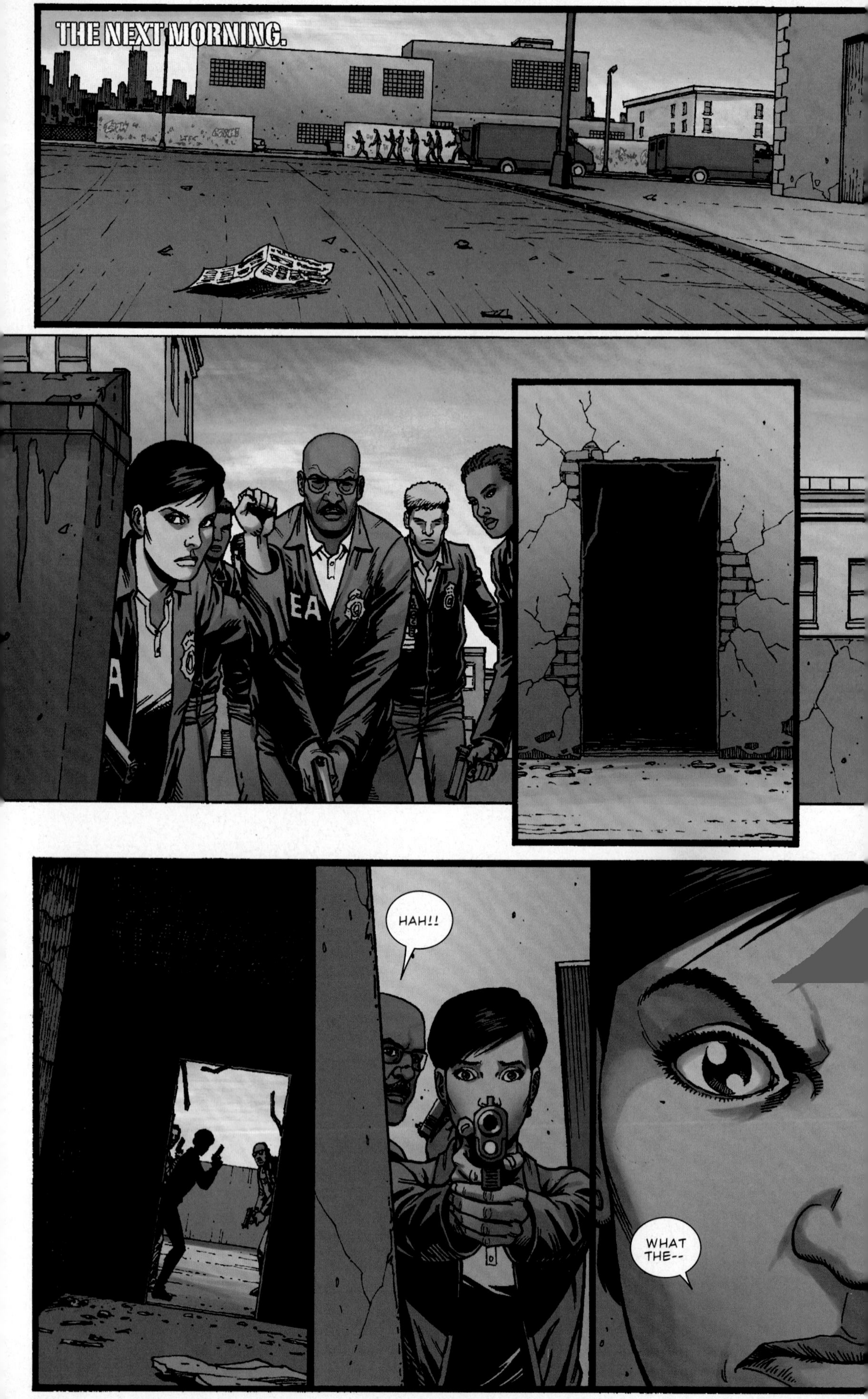
THE NEXT MORNING.
HAH!!
WHAT THE--

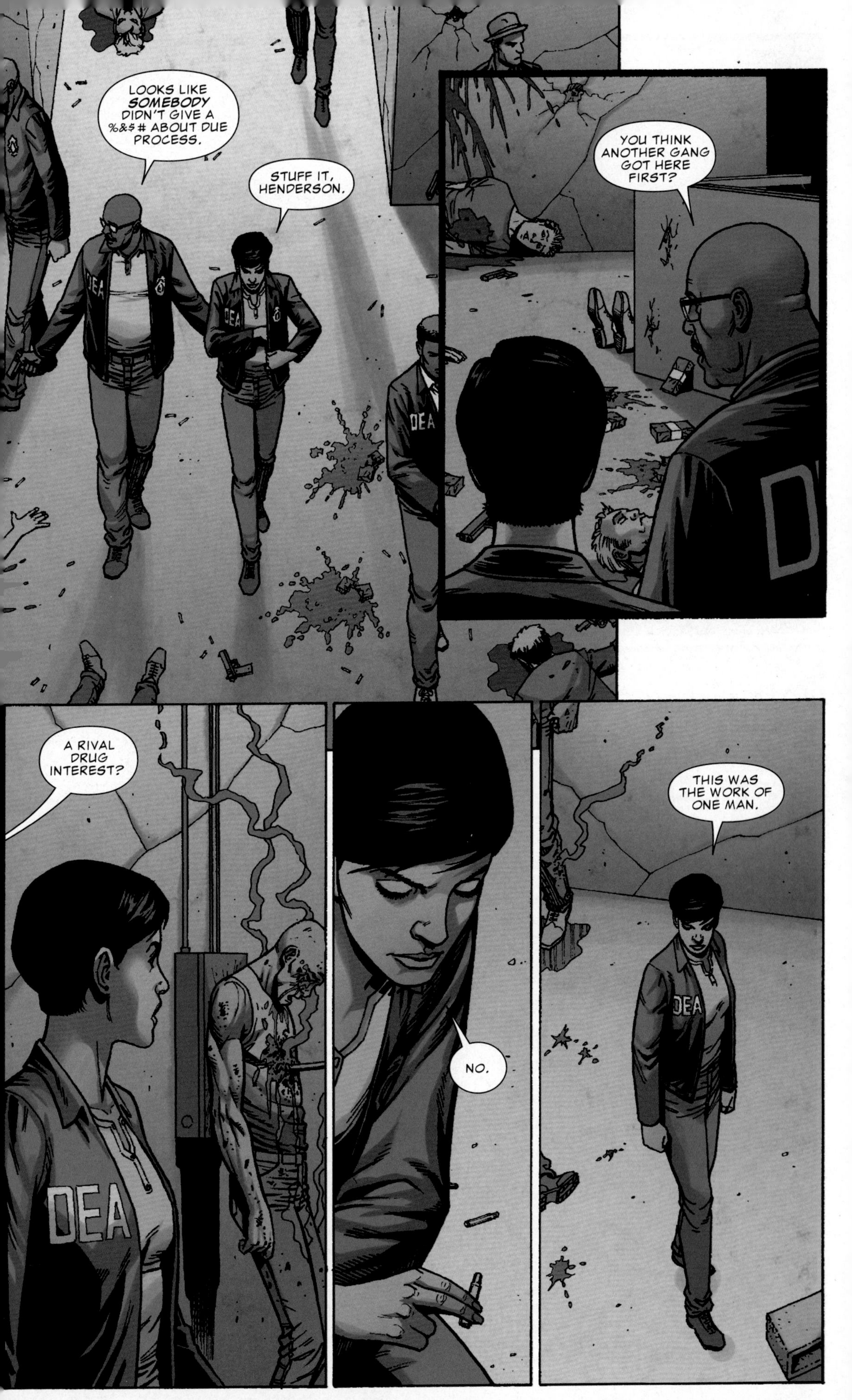

LOOKS LIKE SOMEBODY DIDN'T GIVE A %&$# ABOUT DUE PROCESS.
STUFF IT, HENDERSON.
YOU THINK ANOTHER GANG GOT HERE FIRST?
A RIVAL DRUG INTEREST?
NO.
THIS WAS THE WORK OF ONE MAN.

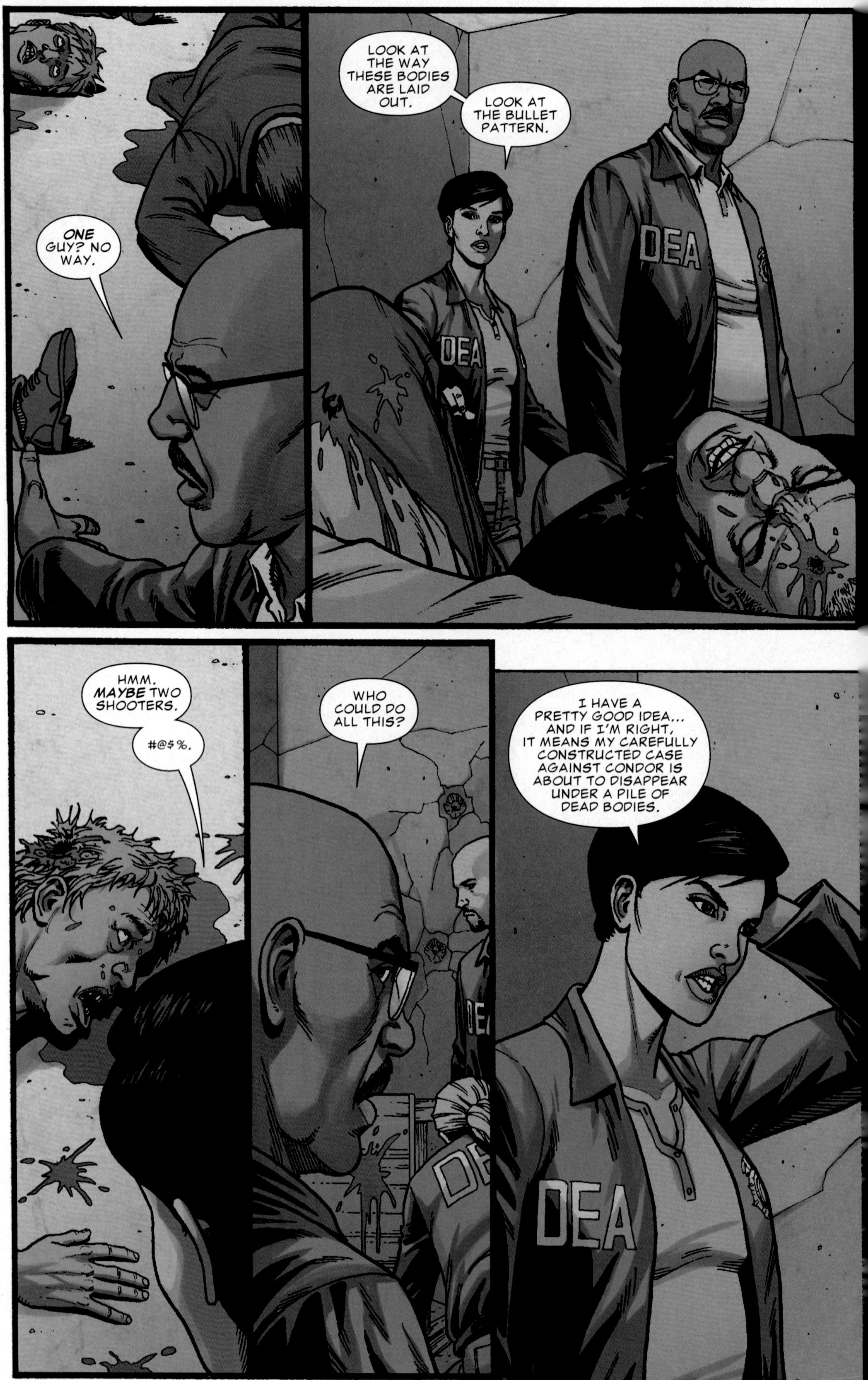
ONE GUY? NO WAY.
LOOK AT THE WAY THESE BODIES ARE LAID OUT.
LOOK AT THE BULLET PATTERN.
HMM. MAYBE TWO SHOOTERS.
#@$%.
WHO COULD DO ALL THIS?
I HAVE A PRETTY GOOD IDEA... AND IF I'M RIGHT, IT MEANS MY CAREFULLY CONSTRUCTED CASE AGAINST CONDOR IS ABOUT TO DISAPPEAR UNDER A PILE OF DEAD BODIES.
DEA

IT WAS THE PUNISHER, WE'VE CONFIRMED IT. THE WAREHOUSE IS A BUST. IT'S CRAWLING WITH D.E.A. NOW.

AND NONE OF OUR ASSETS MADE IT OUT ALIVE?

UNCERTAIN, BUT HIGHLY DOUBTFUL. THOROUGHNESS IS ONE OF THE PUNISHER'S MANY ADMIRABLE QUALITIES.

GOD HELP US. IF THAT FOLDER HAS FALLEN INTO HIS HANDS, OUR ENTIRE OPERATION IS COMPROMISED. WE'RE COMPROMISED.

TAP TAP TAP

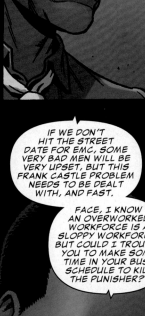

IT IS...MOST UNFORTUNATE. I TOOK THE NEWS RATHER HARD, MYSELF.

TAP TAP TAP

WHAT ARE THE ORDERS, BOSS?

IF WE DON'T HIT THE STREET DATE FOR EMC, SOME VERY BAD MEN WILL BE VERY UPSET, BUT THIS FRANK CASTLE PROBLEM NEEDS TO BE DEALT WITH, AND FAST.

FACE, I KNOW AN OVERWORKED WORKFORCE IS A SLOPPY WORKFORCE, BUT COULD I TROUBLE YOU TO MAKE SOME TIME IN YOUR BUSY SCHEDULE TO KILL THE PUNISHER?

TAP TAP TAP

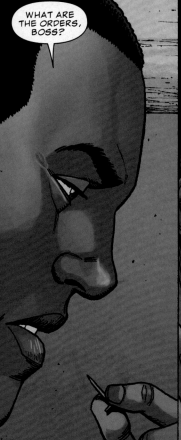

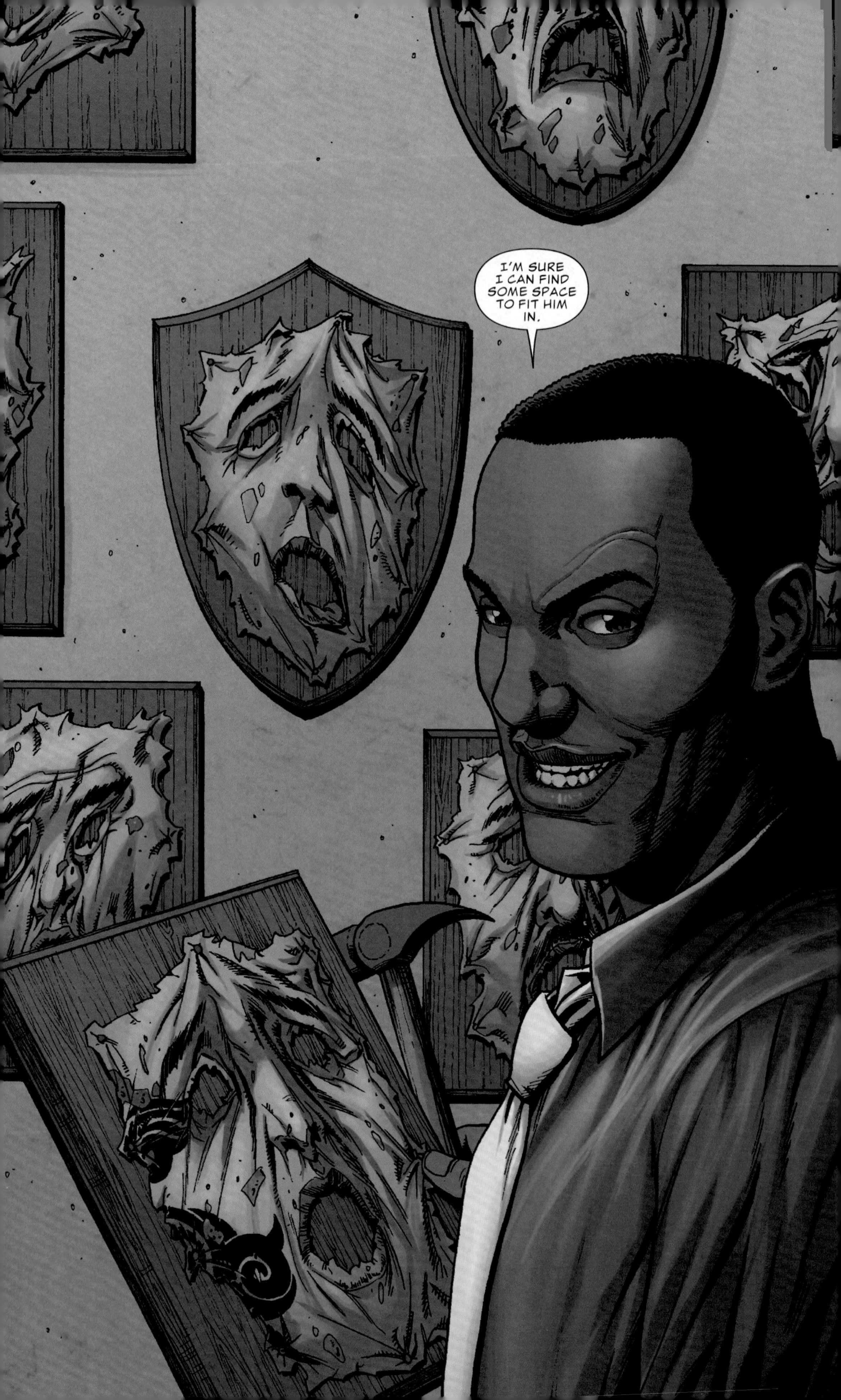
I'M SURE I CAN FIND SOME SPACE TO FIT HIM IN.

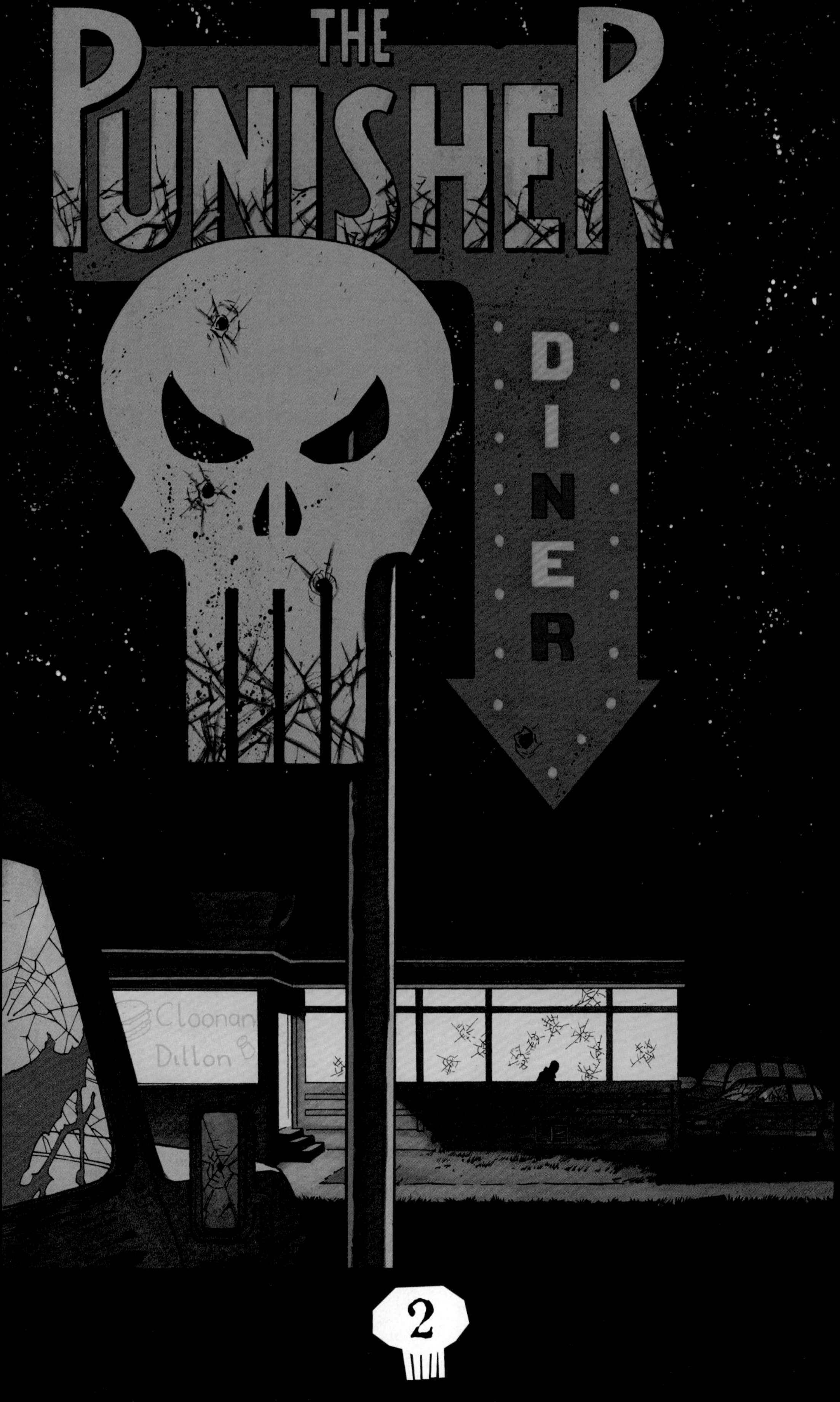
THE PUNISHER
DINER
Cloonan
Dillon
2

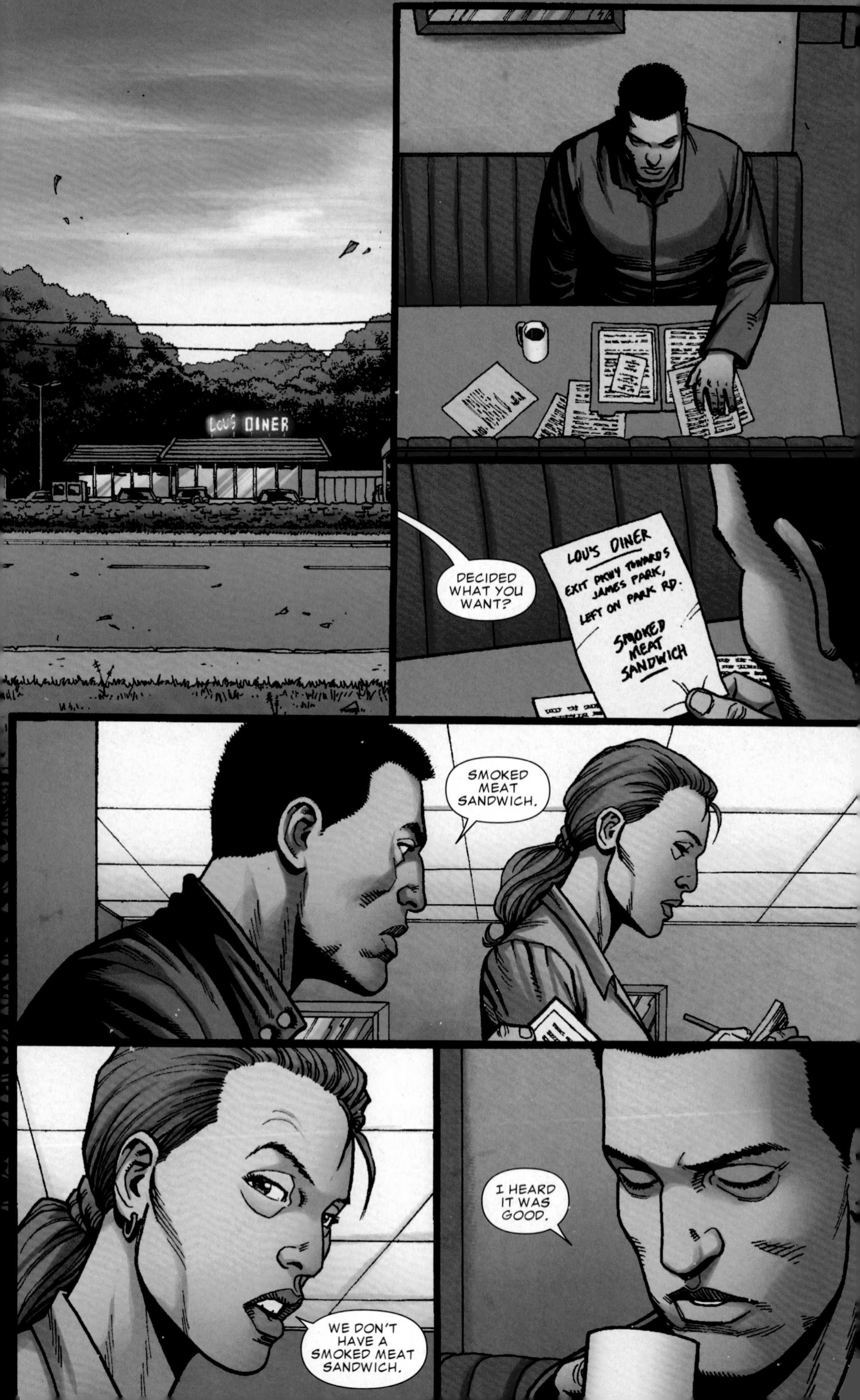
LOU'S DINER
DECIDED WHAT YOU WANT?
LOU'S DINER
EXIT PKWY TOWARDS JAMES PARK, LEFT ON PARK RD.
SMOKED MEAT SANDWICH
SMOKED MEAT SANDWICH.
WE DON'T HAVE A SMOKED MEAT SANDWICH.
I HEARD IT WAS GOOD.

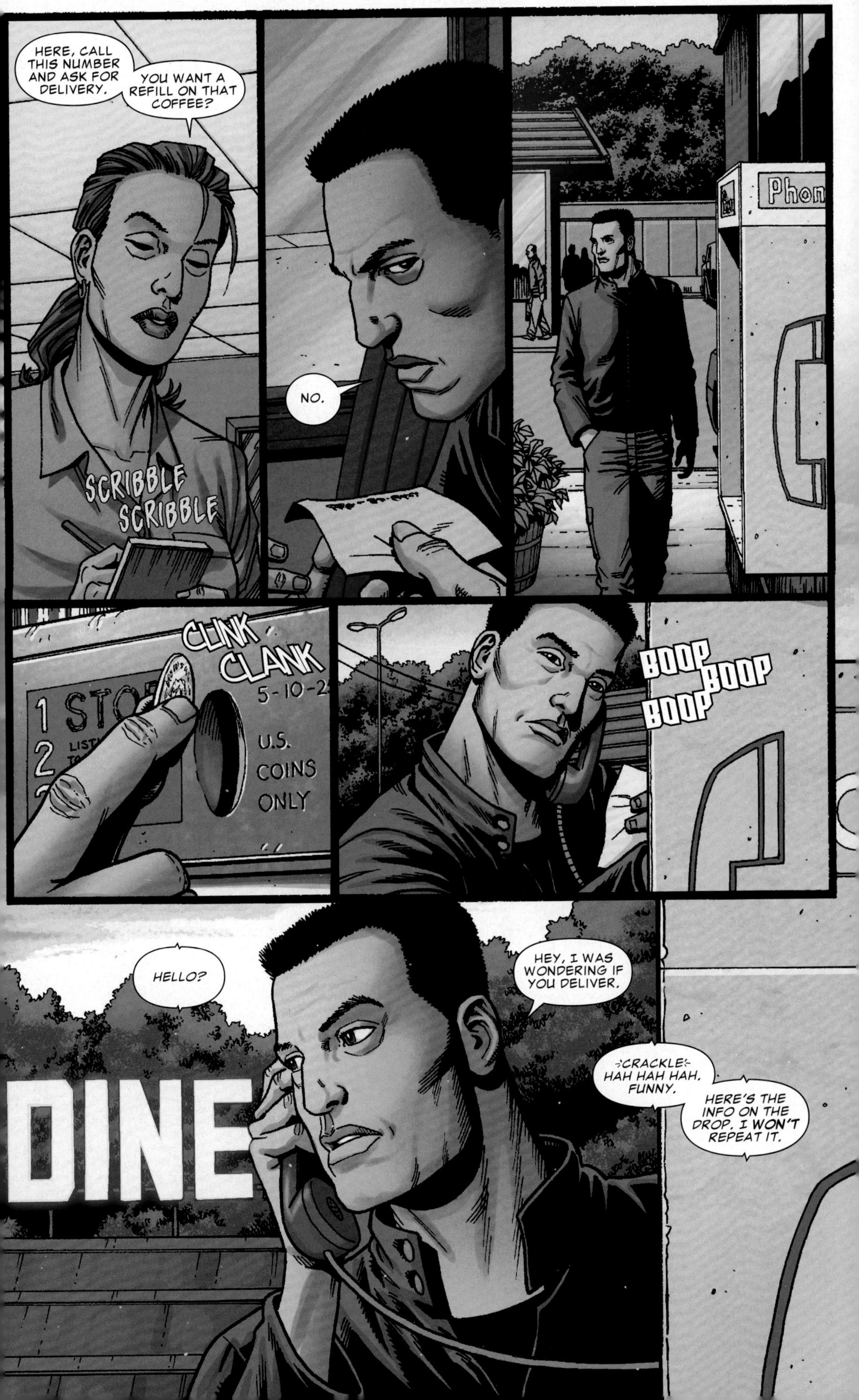
HERE, CALL THIS NUMBER AND ASK FOR DELIVERY.
YOU WANT A REFILL ON THAT COFFEE?
SCRIBBLE SCRIBBLE
NO.
Phon
CLINK CLANK
1 STO
2 LIST
5-10-2
U.S. COINS ONLY
BOOP BOOP BOOP
HELLO?
HEY, I WAS WONDERING IF YOU DELIVER.
DINE
-CRACKLE- HAH HAH HAH. FUNNY.
HERE'S THE INFO ON THE DROP. I WON'T REPEAT IT.

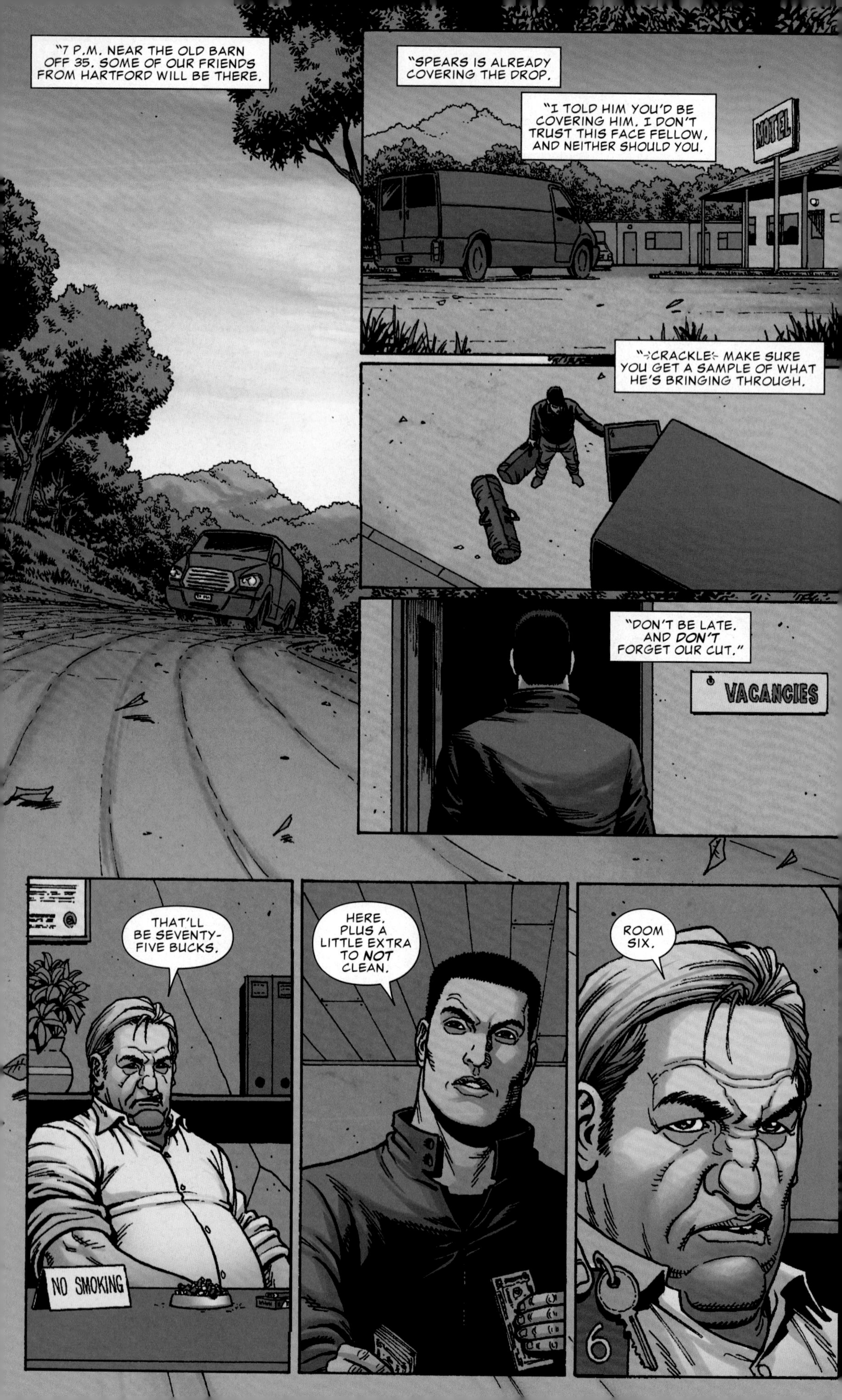
"7 P.M. NEAR THE OLD BARN OFF 35. SOME OF OUR FRIENDS FROM HARTFORD WILL BE THERE.
"SPEARS IS ALREADY COVERING THE DROP.
"I TOLD HIM YOU'D BE COVERING HIM. I DON'T TRUST THIS FACE FELLOW, AND NEITHER SHOULD YOU.
MOTEL
"-CRACKLE- MAKE SURE YOU GET A SAMPLE OF WHAT HE'S BRINGING THROUGH.
"DON'T BE LATE. AND DON'T FORGET OUR CUT."
VACANCIES
THAT'LL BE SEVENTY-FIVE BUCKS.
NO SMOKING
HERE. PLUS A LITTLE EXTRA TO NOT CLEAN.
ROOM SIX.
6

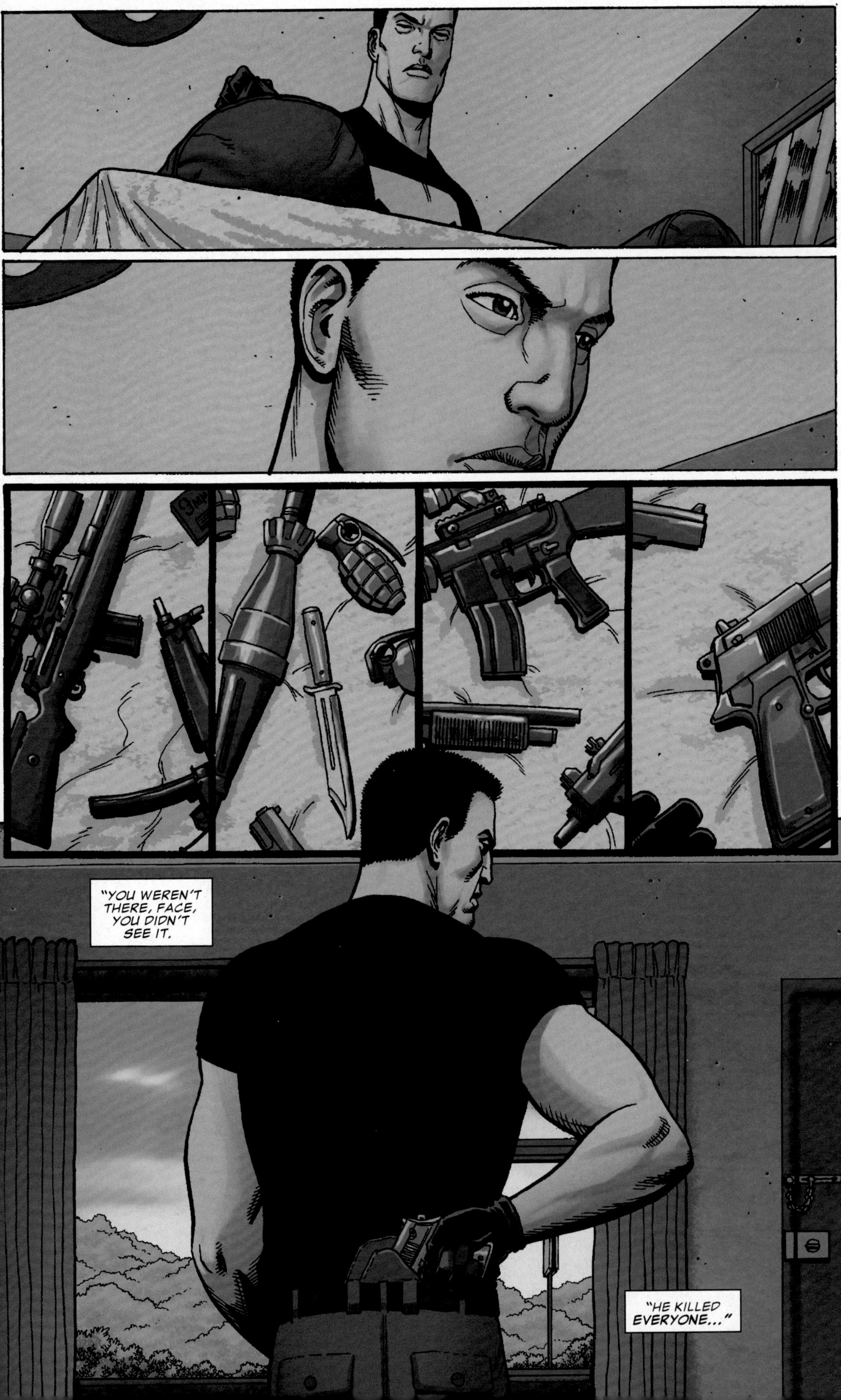
"YOU WEREN'T THERE, FACE, YOU DIDN'T SEE IT.
"HE KILLED EVERYONE..."

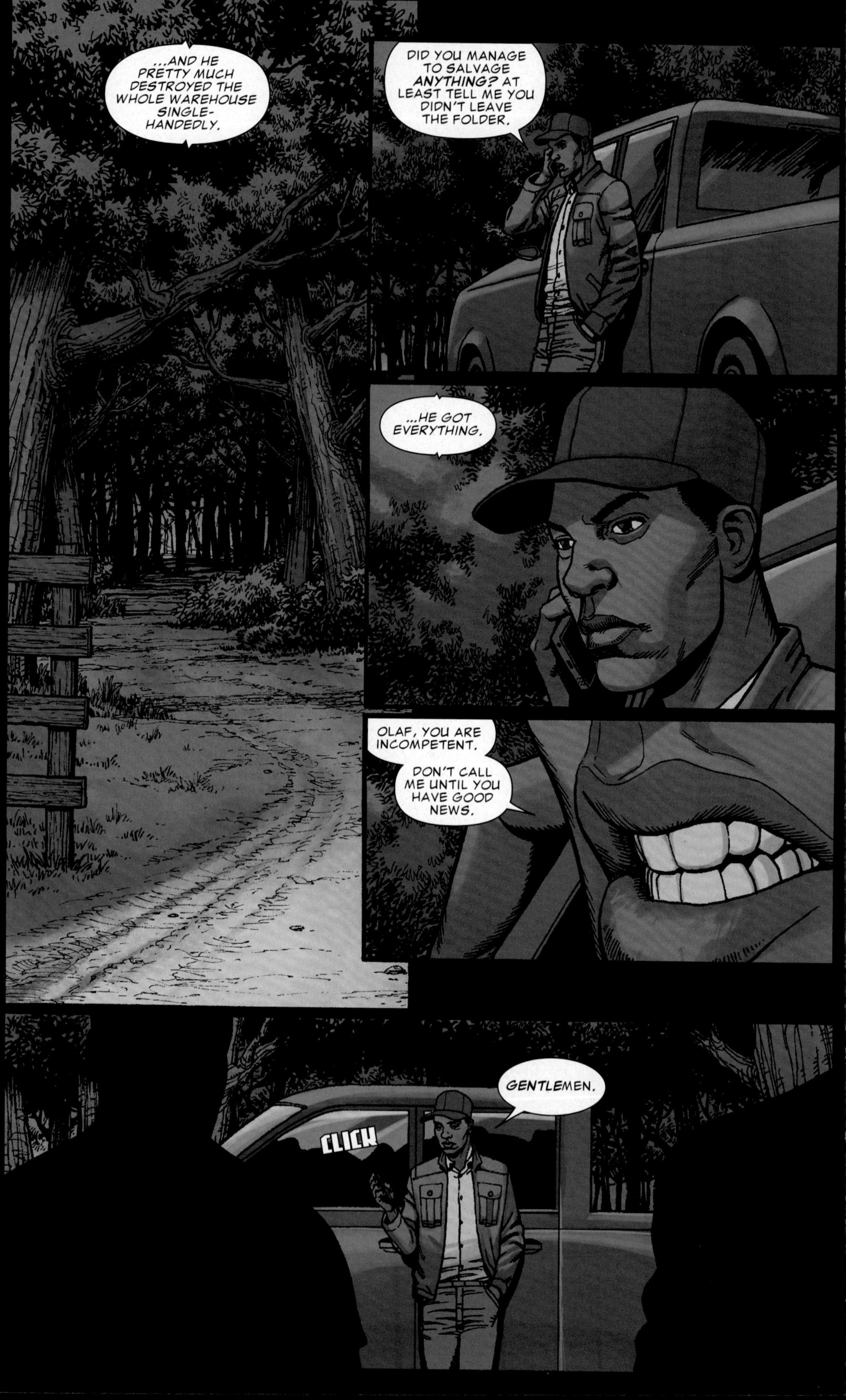
...AND HE PRETTY MUCH DESTROYED THE WHOLE WAREHOUSE SINGLE-HANDEDLY.
DID YOU MANAGE TO SALVAGE ANYTHING? AT LEAST TELL ME YOU DIDN'T LEAVE THE FOLDER.
...HE GOT EVERYTHING.
OLAF, YOU ARE INCOMPETENT.
DON'T CALL ME UNTIL YOU HAVE GOOD NEWS.
CLICK
GENTLEMEN.

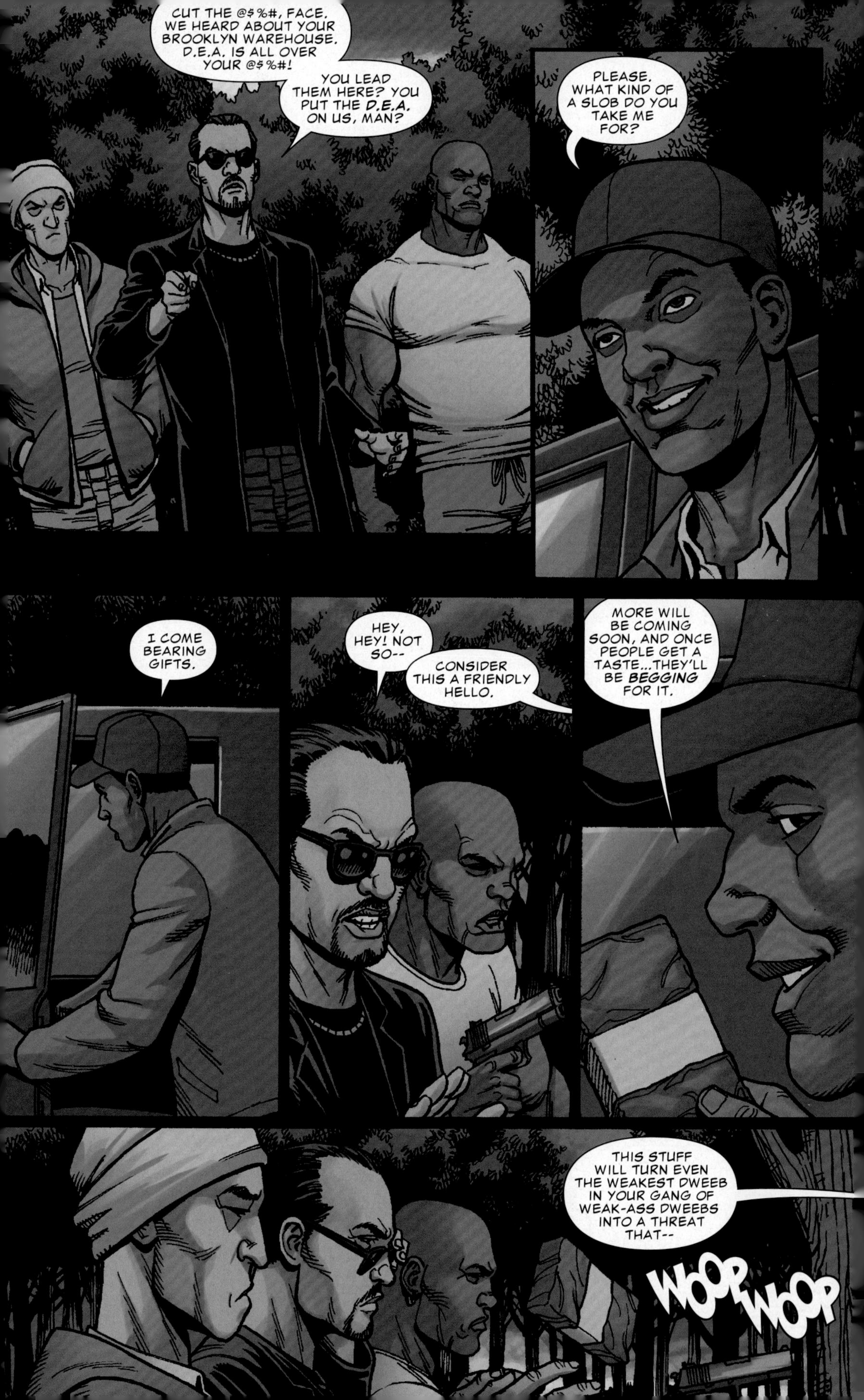
CUT THE @$%#, FACE. WE HEARD ABOUT YOUR BROOKLYN WAREHOUSE. D.E.A. IS ALL OVER YOUR @$%#!
YOU LEAD THEM HERE? YOU PUT THE D.E.A. ON US, MAN?
PLEASE. WHAT KIND OF A SLOB DO YOU TAKE ME FOR?
I COME BEARING GIFTS.
HEY, HEY! NOT SO--
CONSIDER THIS A FRIENDLY HELLO.
MORE WILL BE COMING SOON, AND ONCE PEOPLE GET A TASTE...THEY'LL BE BEGGING FOR IT.
THIS STUFF WILL TURN EVEN THE WEAKEST DWEEB IN YOUR GANG OF WEAK-ASS DWEEBS INTO A THREAT THAT--
WOOP WOOP

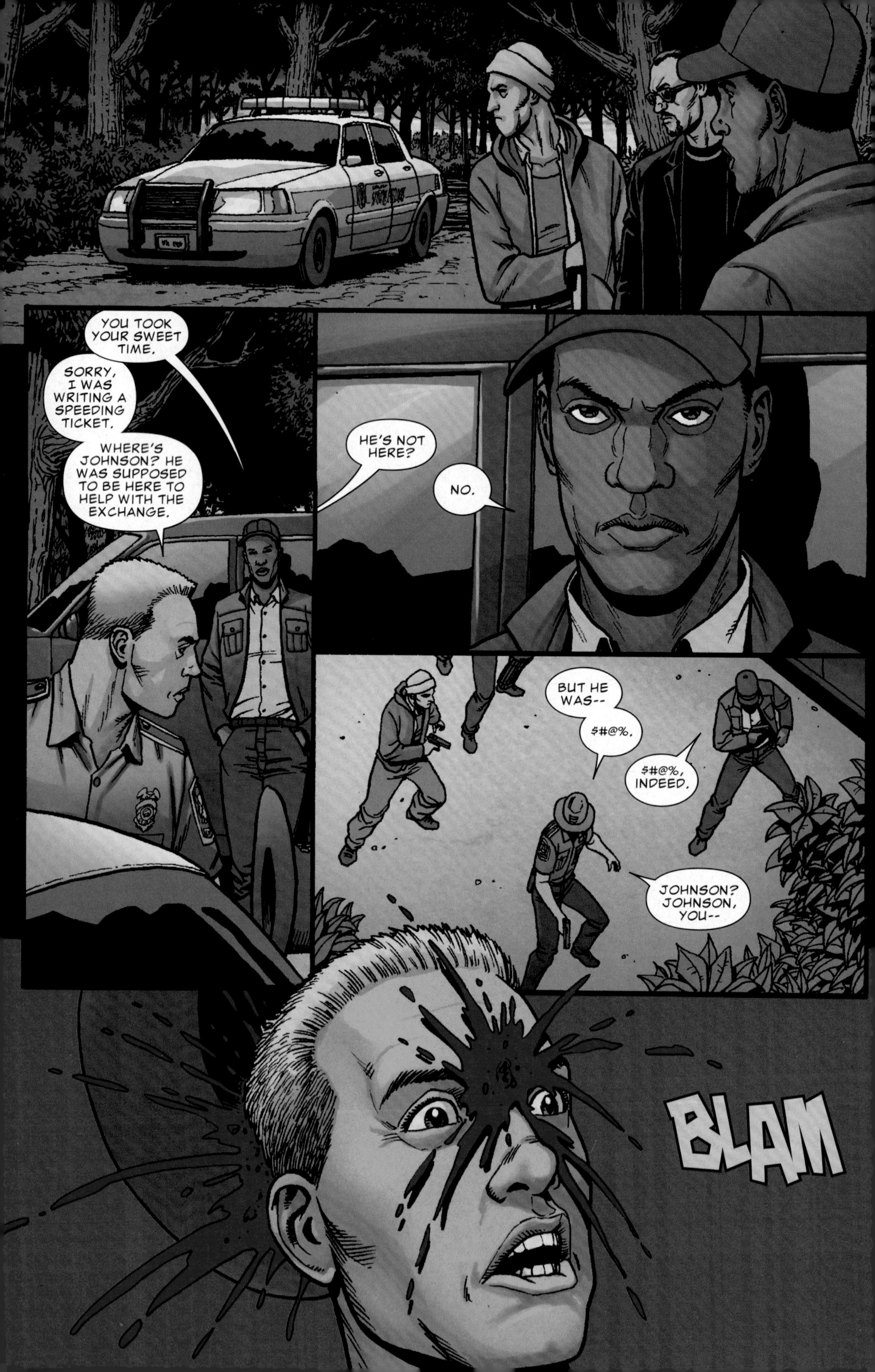
YOU TOOK YOUR SWEET TIME.
SORRY, I WAS WRITING A SPEEDING TICKET.
WHERE'S JOHNSON? HE WAS SUPPOSED TO BE HERE TO HELP WITH THE EXCHANGE.
HE'S NOT HERE?
NO.
BUT HE WAS--
$#@%.
$#@%, INDEED.
JOHNSON? JOHNSON, YOU--
BLAM

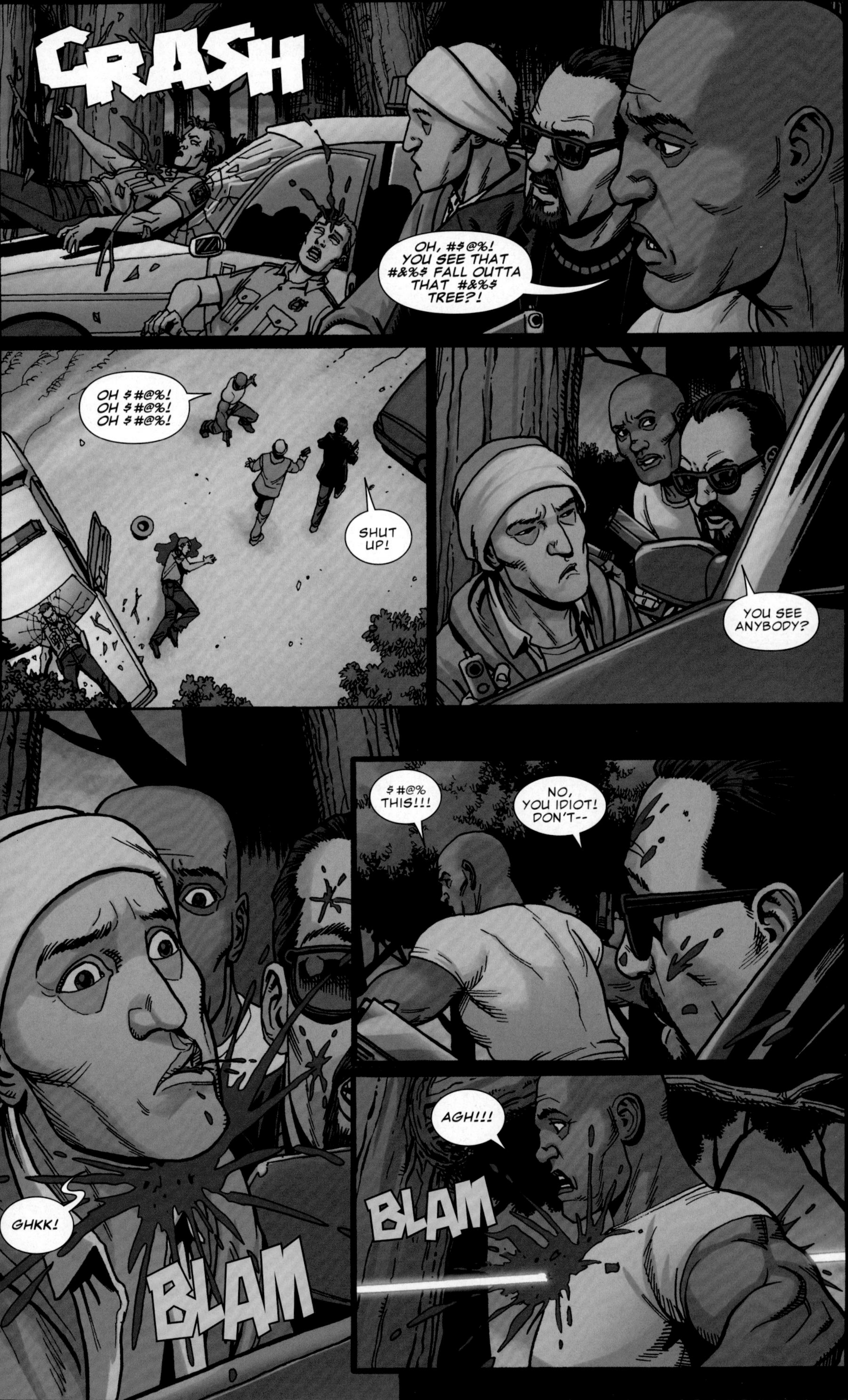
CRASH
OH, #$@%! YOU SEE THAT #&%$ FALL OUTTA THAT #&%$ TREE?!
OH $#@%! OH $#@%! OH $#@%!
SHUT UP!
YOU SEE ANYBODY?
GHKK!
BLAM
$#@% THIS!!!
NO, YOU IDIOT! DON'T--
AGH!!!
BLAM

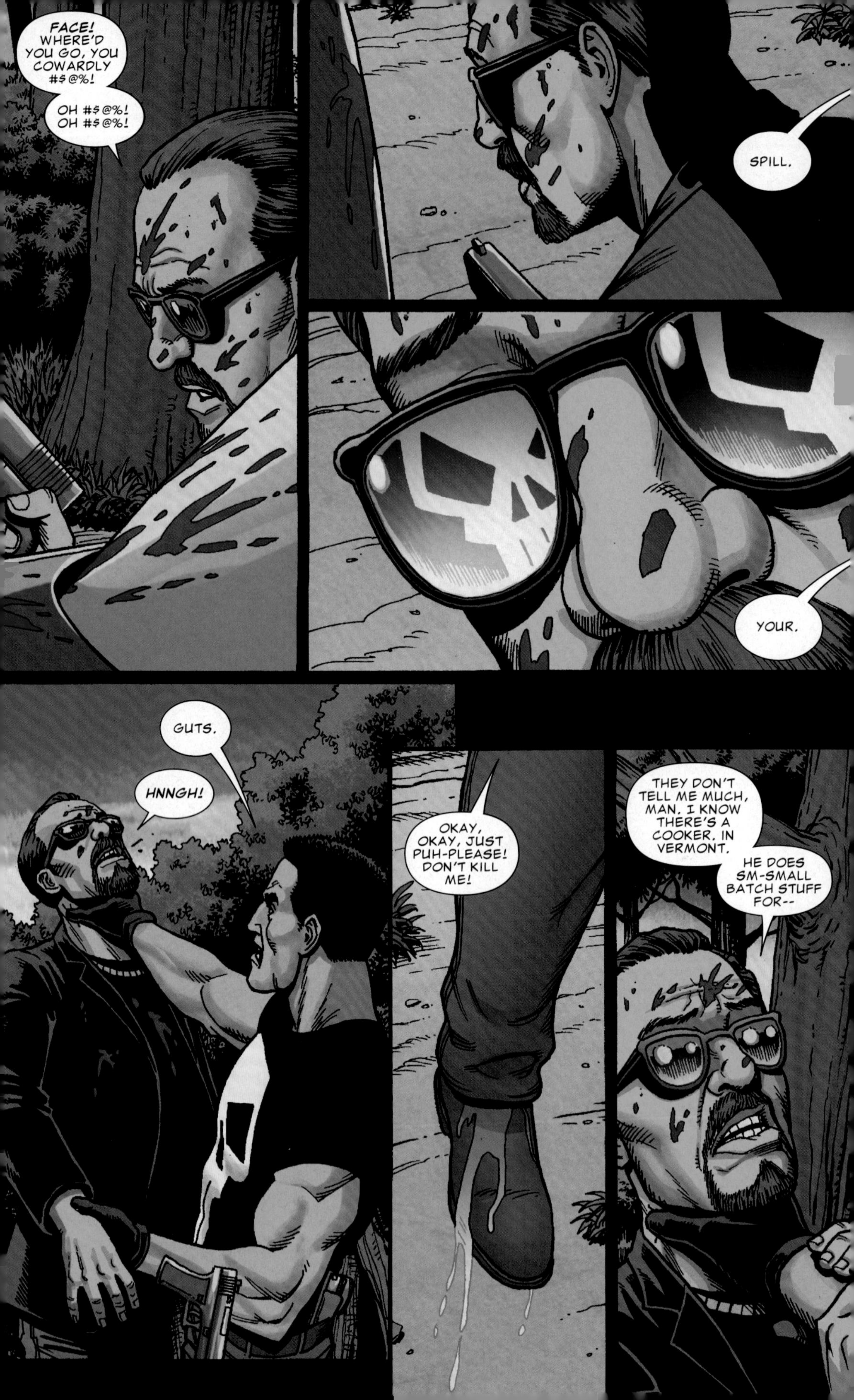
FACE! WHERE'D YOU GO, YOU COWARDLY #$@%!
OH #$@%! OH #$@%!
SPILL.
YOUR.
GUTS.
HNNGH!
OKAY, OKAY, JUST PUH-PLEASE! DON'T KILL ME!
THEY DON'T TELL ME MUCH, MAN. I KNOW THERE'S A COOKER. IN VERMONT.
HE DOES SM-SMALL BATCH STUFF FOR--

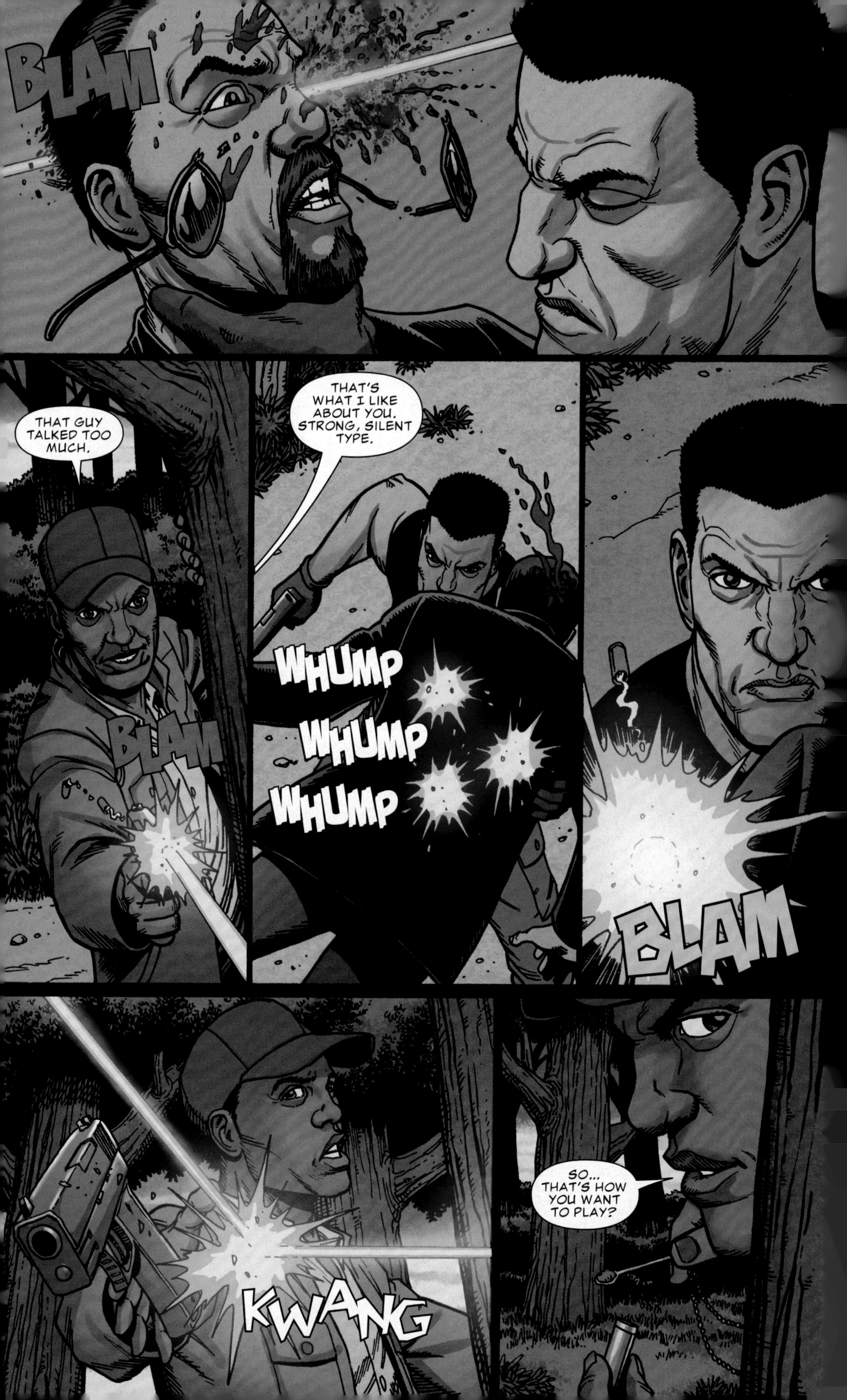
BLAM
THAT GUY TALKED TOO MUCH.
BLAM
THAT'S WHAT I LIKE ABOUT YOU. STRONG, SILENT TYPE.
WHUMP
WHUMP
WHUMP
BLAM
KWANG
SO... THAT'S HOW YOU WANT TO PLAY?

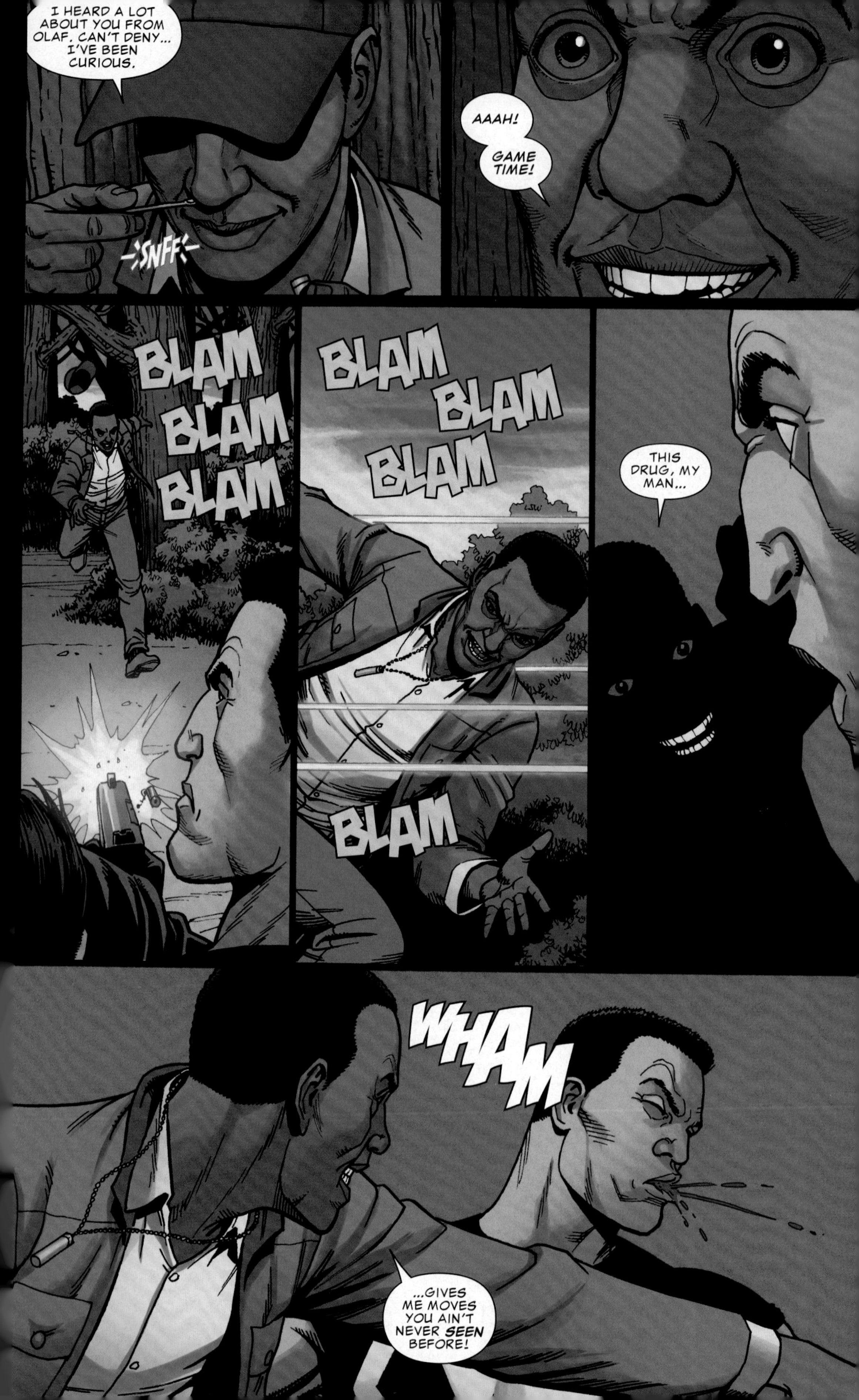
I HEARD A LOT ABOUT YOU FROM OLAF. CAN'T DENY... I'VE BEEN CURIOUS.
SNFF
AAAH!
GAME TIME!
BLAM BLAM BLAM
BLAM BLAM BLAM
BLAM
THIS DRUG, MY MAN...
WHAM
...GIVES ME MOVES YOU AIN'T NEVER SEEN BEFORE!

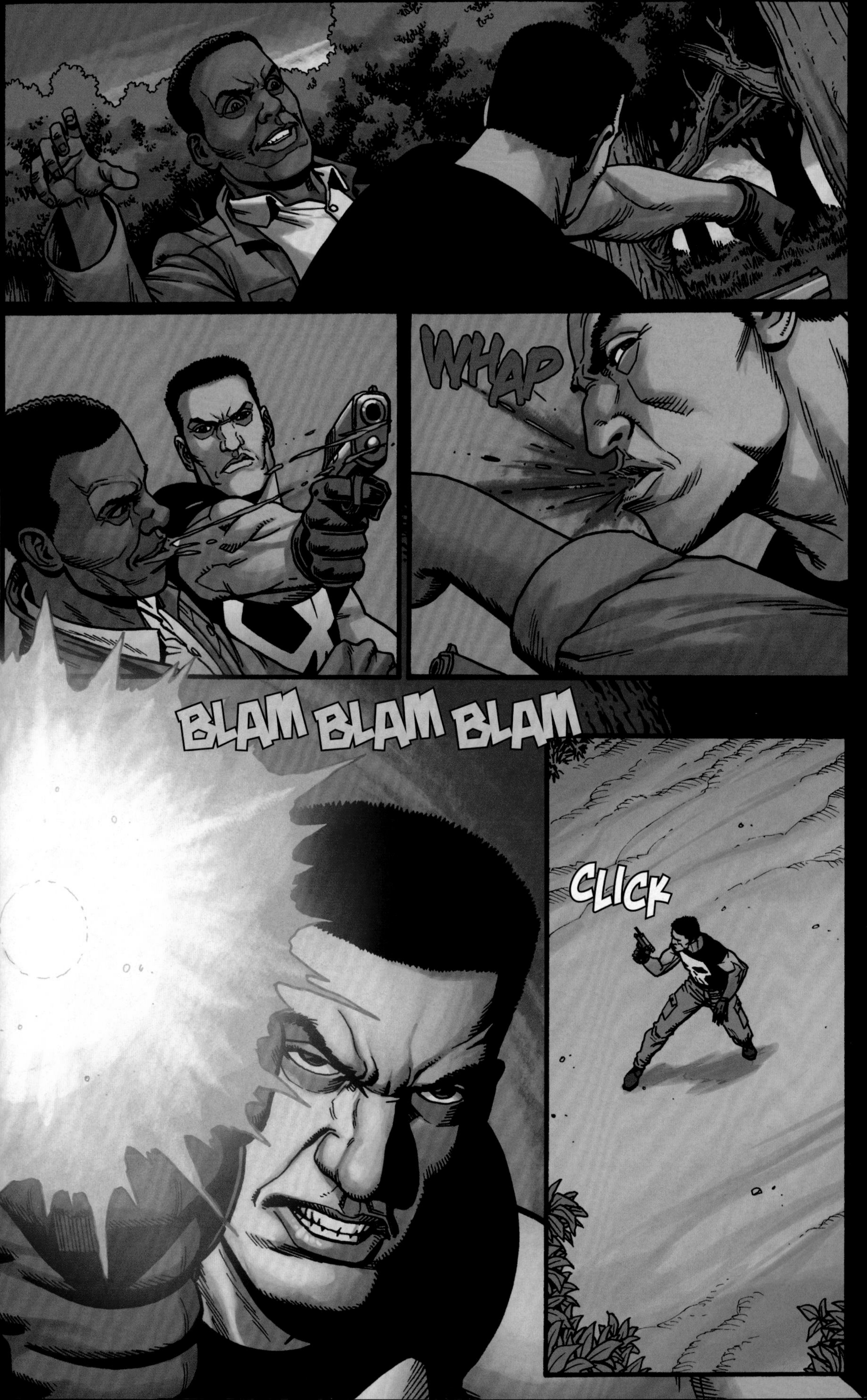
WHAP
BLAM BLAM BLAM
CLICK

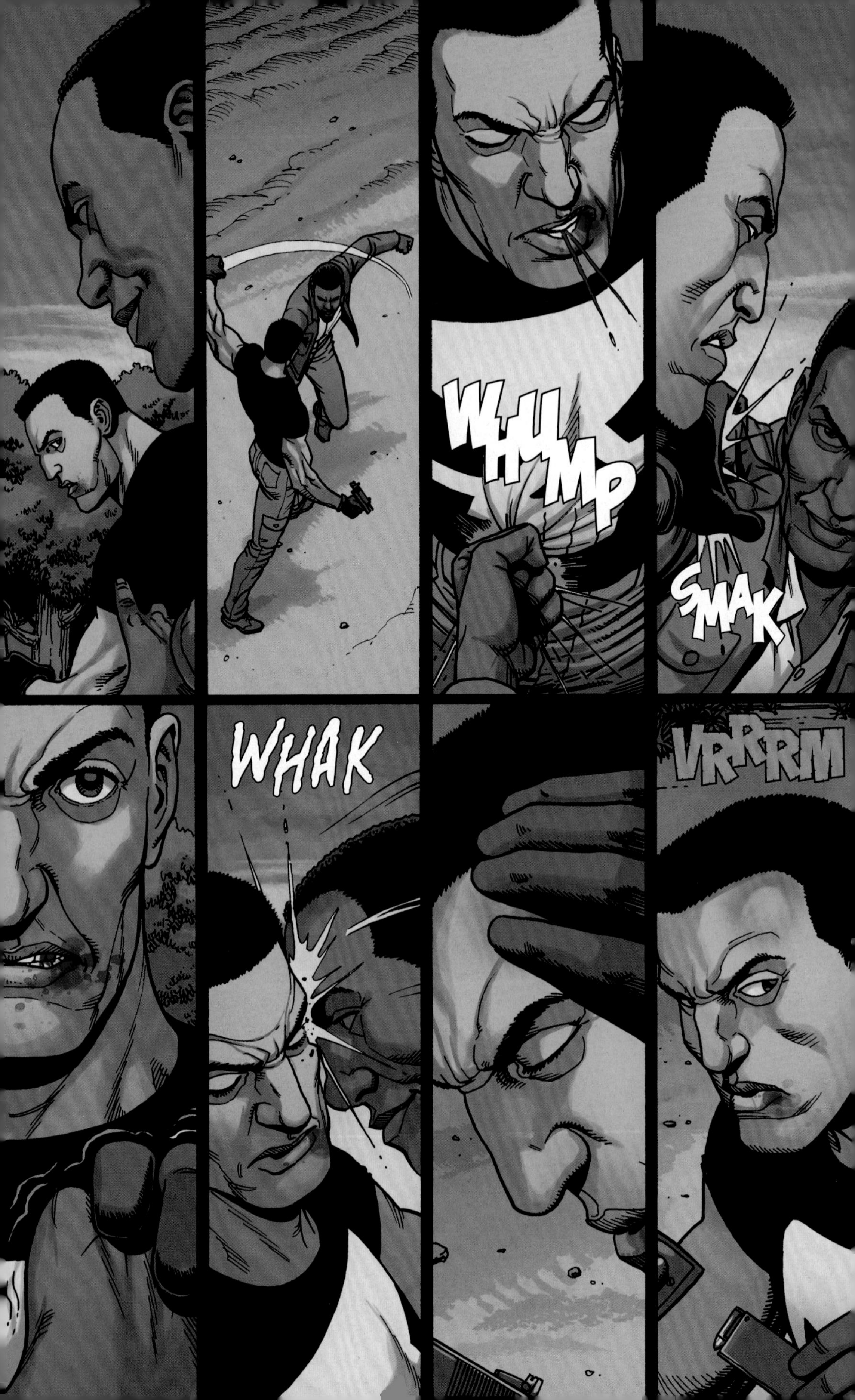
WHUMP
SMAK
WHAK
VRRRM

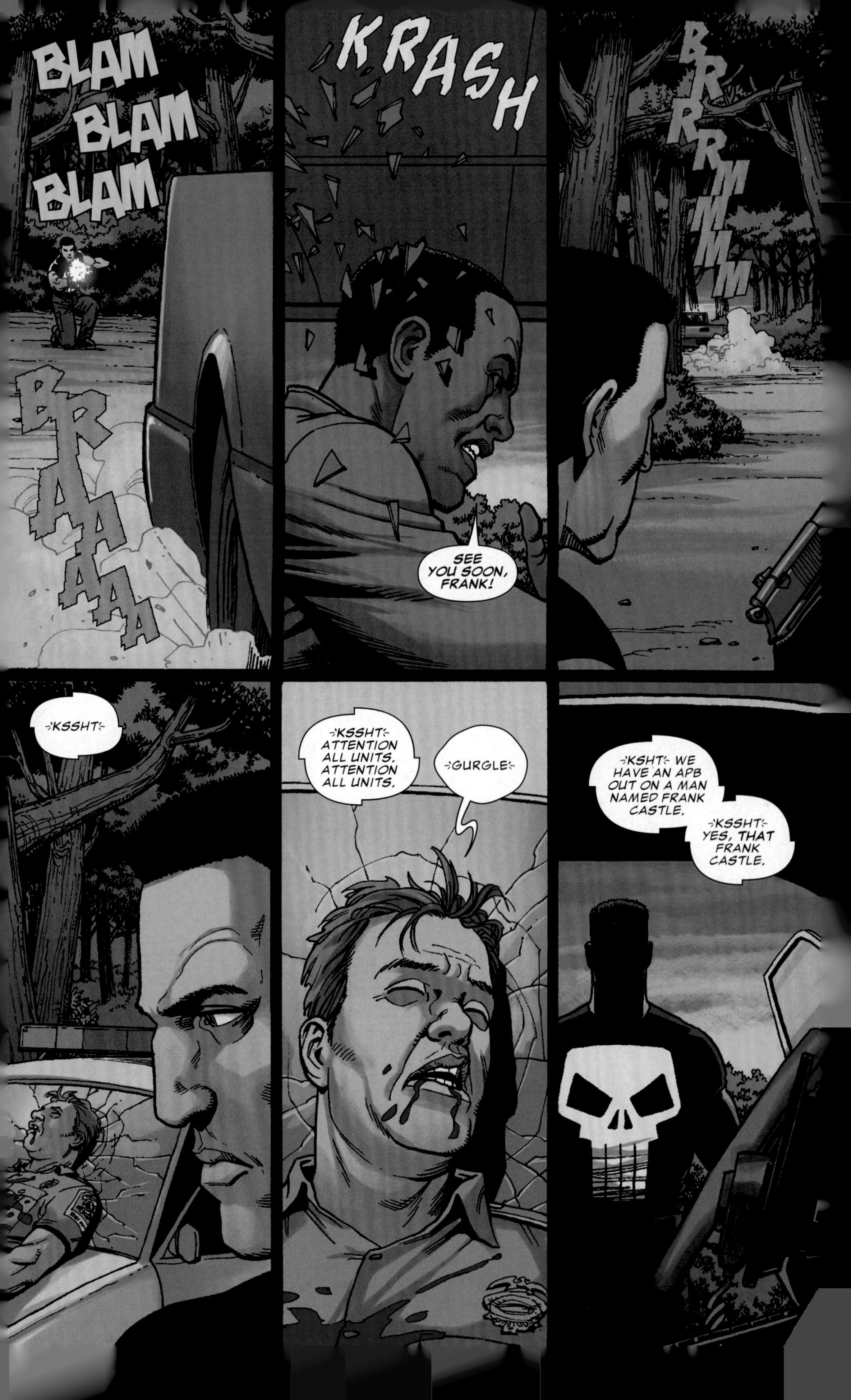
BLAM
BLAM
BLAM
BRAAAAAA
KRASH
SEE YOU SOON, FRANK!
BRRRMMMM
-KSSHT-
-KSSHT- ATTENTION ALL UNITS. ATTENTION ALL UNITS.
-GURGLE-
-KSHT- WE HAVE AN APB OUT ON A MAN NAMED FRANK CASTLE.
-KSSHT- YES, THAT FRANK CASTLE.

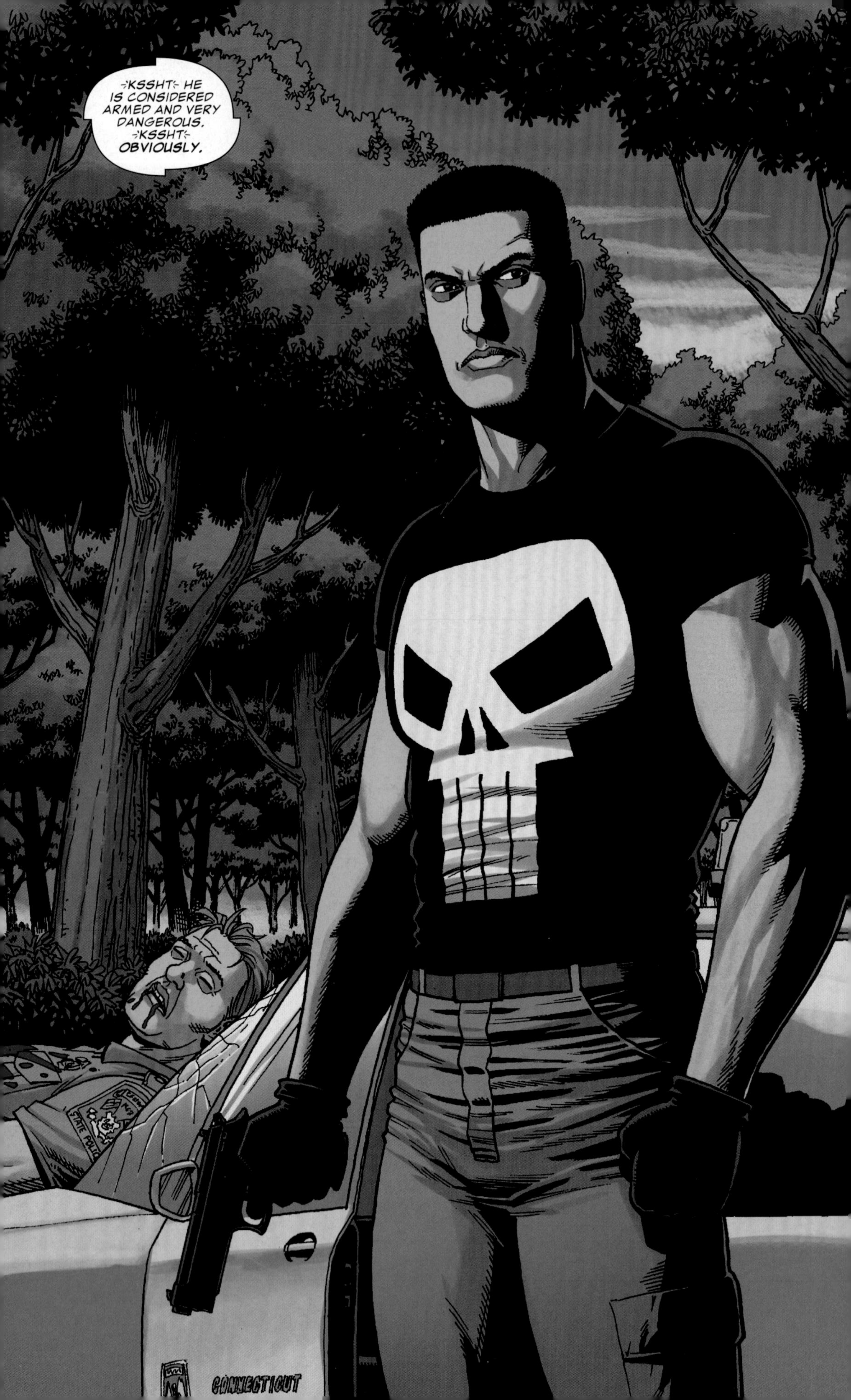

-KSSHT- HE IS CONSIDERED ARMED AND VERY DANGEROUS. -KSSHT- OBVIOUSLY.
CONNECTICUT

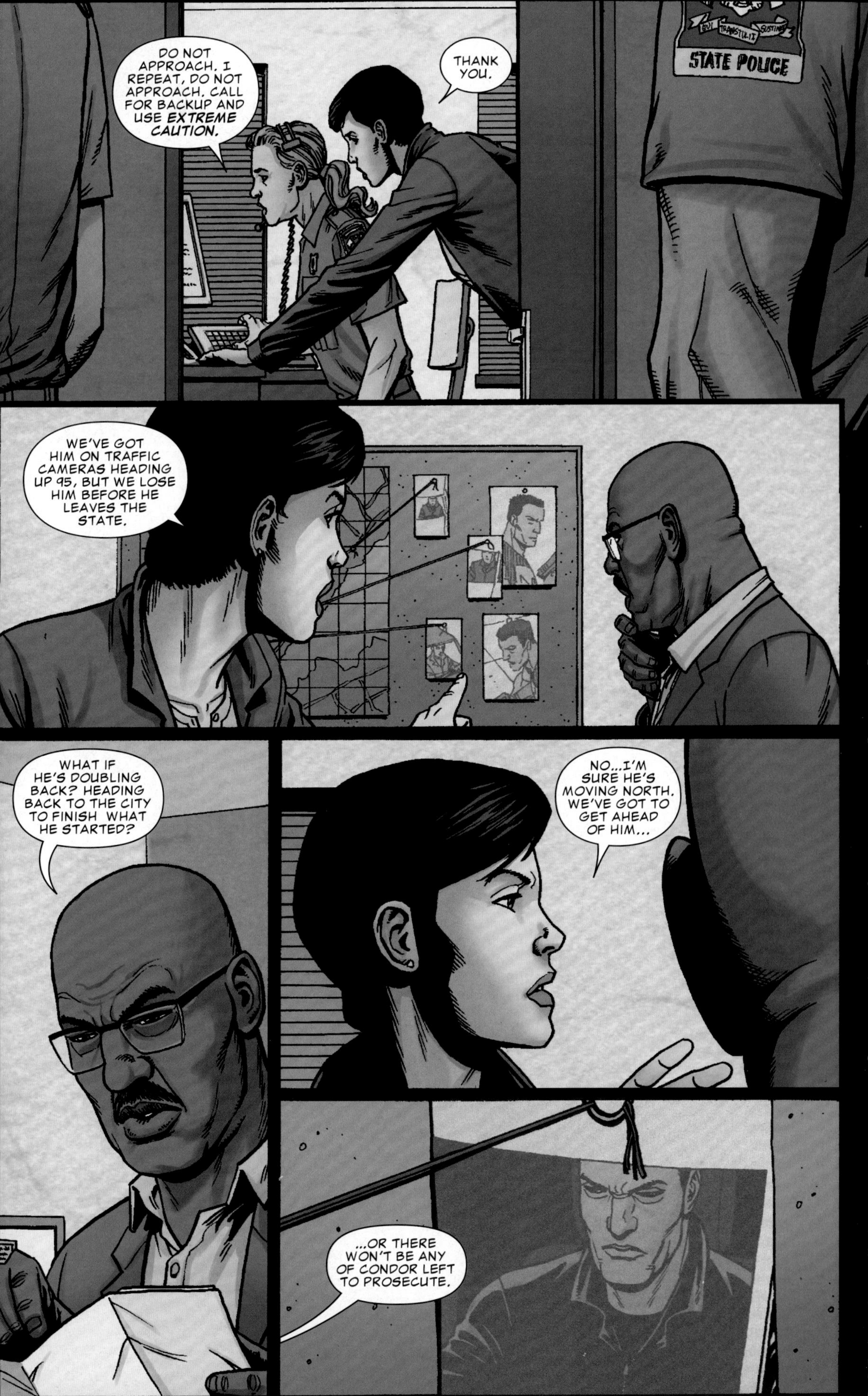
STATE POLICE
DO NOT APPROACH. I REPEAT, DO NOT APPROACH. CALL FOR BACKUP AND USE **EXTREME CAUTION.**
THANK YOU.
WE'VE GOT HIM ON TRAFFIC CAMERAS HEADING UP 95, BUT WE LOSE HIM BEFORE HE LEAVES THE STATE.
WHAT IF HE'S DOUBLING BACK? HEADING BACK TO THE CITY TO FINISH WHAT HE STARTED?
NO...I'M SURE HE'S MOVING NORTH. WE'VE GOT TO GET AHEAD OF HIM...
...OR THERE WON'T BE ANY OF CONDOR LEFT TO PROSECUTE.

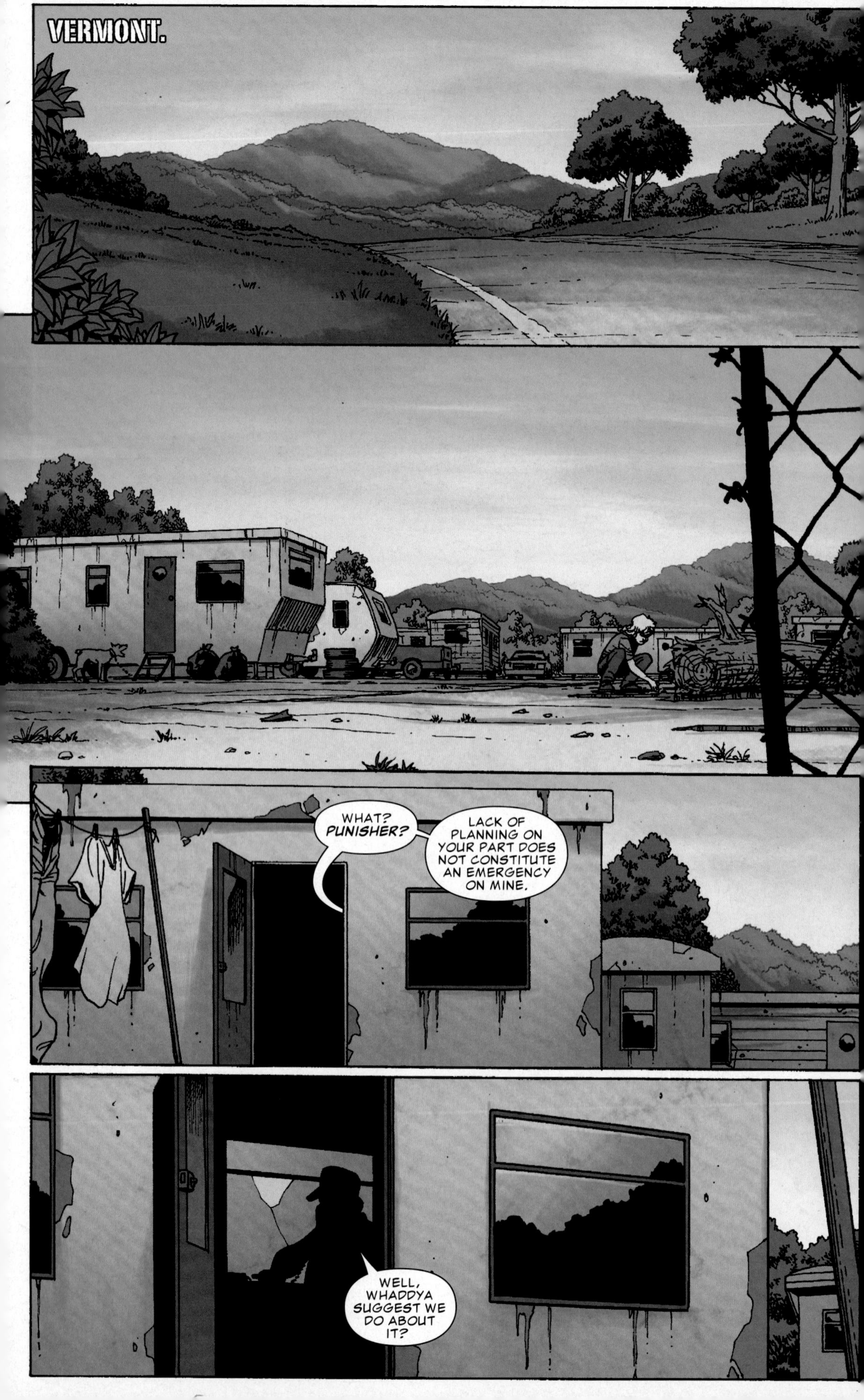
VERMONT.
WHAT? PUNISHER?
LACK OF PLANNING ON YOUR PART DOES NOT CONSTITUTE AN EMERGENCY ON MINE.
WELL, WHADDYA SUGGEST WE DO ABOUT IT?

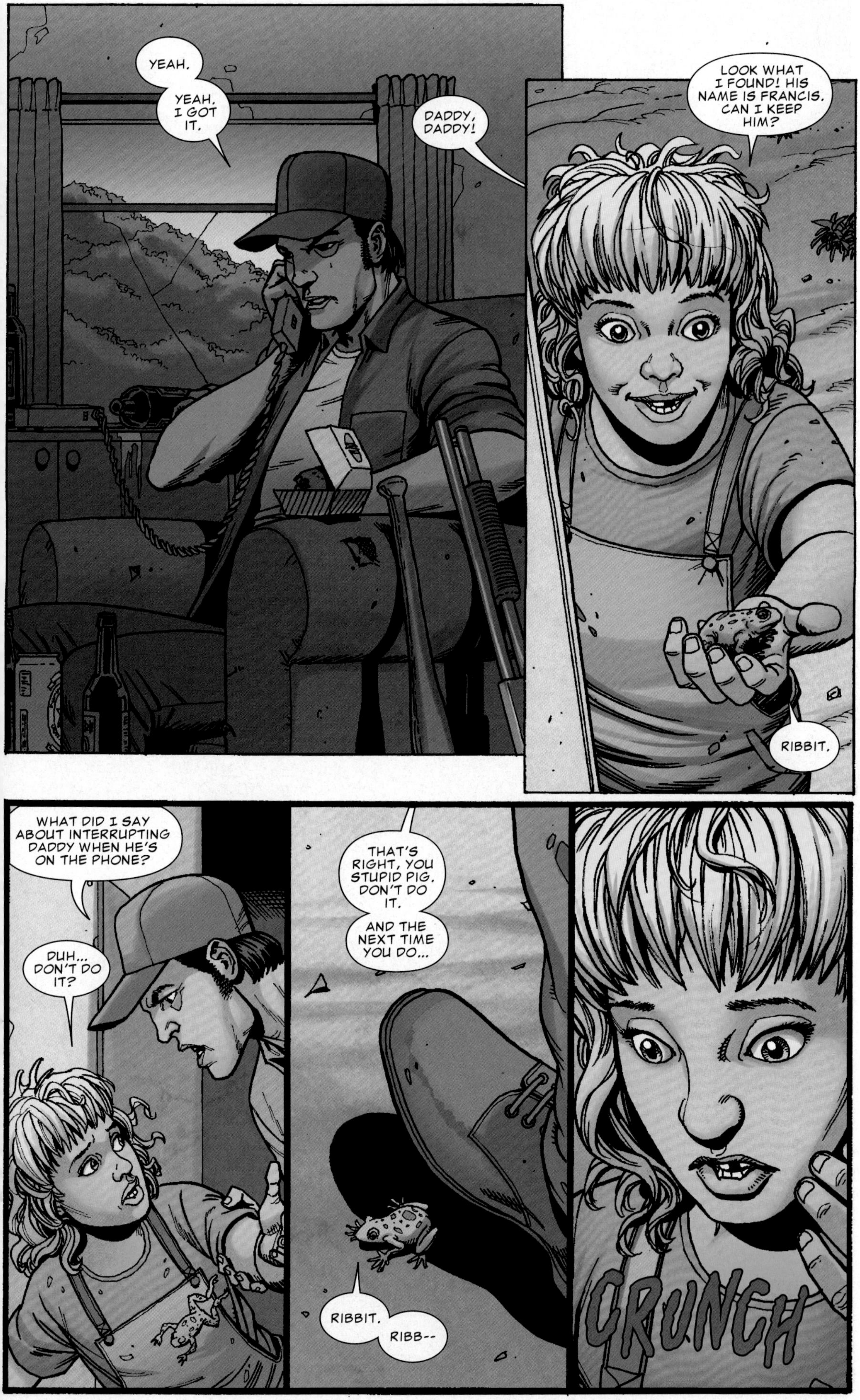
YEAH.
YEAH. I GOT IT.
DADDY, DADDY!
LOOK WHAT I FOUND! HIS NAME IS FRANCIS. CAN I KEEP HIM?
RIBBIT.
WHAT DID I SAY ABOUT INTERRUPTING DADDY WHEN HE'S ON THE PHONE?
DUH... DON'T DO IT?
THAT'S RIGHT, YOU STUPID PIG. DON'T DO IT.
AND THE NEXT TIME YOU DO...
RIBBIT.
RIBB--
CRUNCH

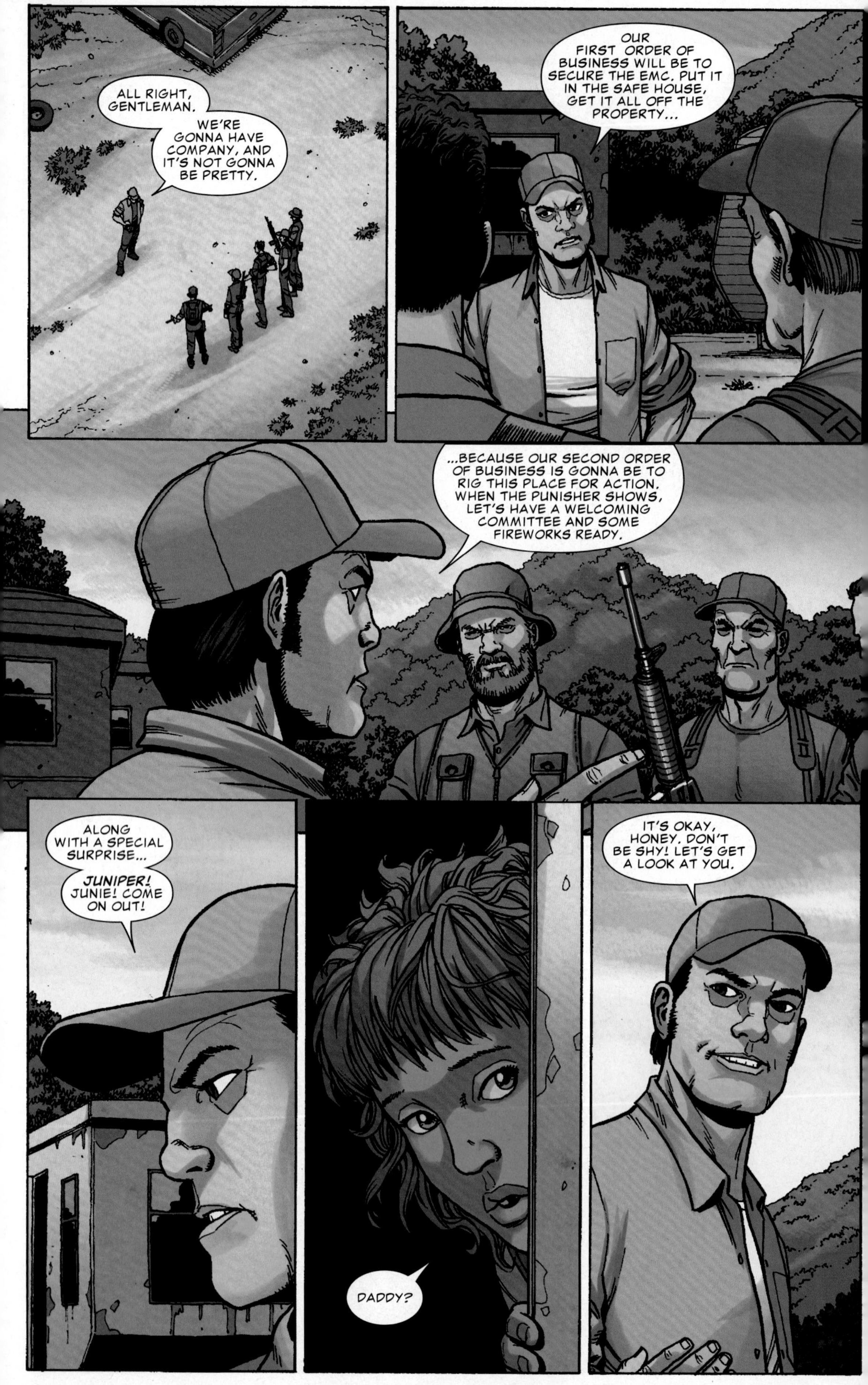
ALL RIGHT, GENTLEMAN.
WE'RE GONNA HAVE COMPANY, AND IT'S NOT GONNA BE PRETTY.
OUR FIRST ORDER OF BUSINESS WILL BE TO SECURE THE EMC. PUT IT IN THE SAFE HOUSE, GET IT ALL OFF THE PROPERTY...
...BECAUSE OUR SECOND ORDER OF BUSINESS IS GONNA BE TO RIG THIS PLACE FOR ACTION. WHEN THE PUNISHER SHOWS, LET'S HAVE A WELCOMING COMMITTEE AND SOME FIREWORKS READY.
ALONG WITH A SPECIAL SURPRISE...
JUNIPER! JUNIE! COME ON OUT!
DADDY?
IT'S OKAY, HONEY. DON'T BE SHY! LET'S GET A LOOK AT YOU.

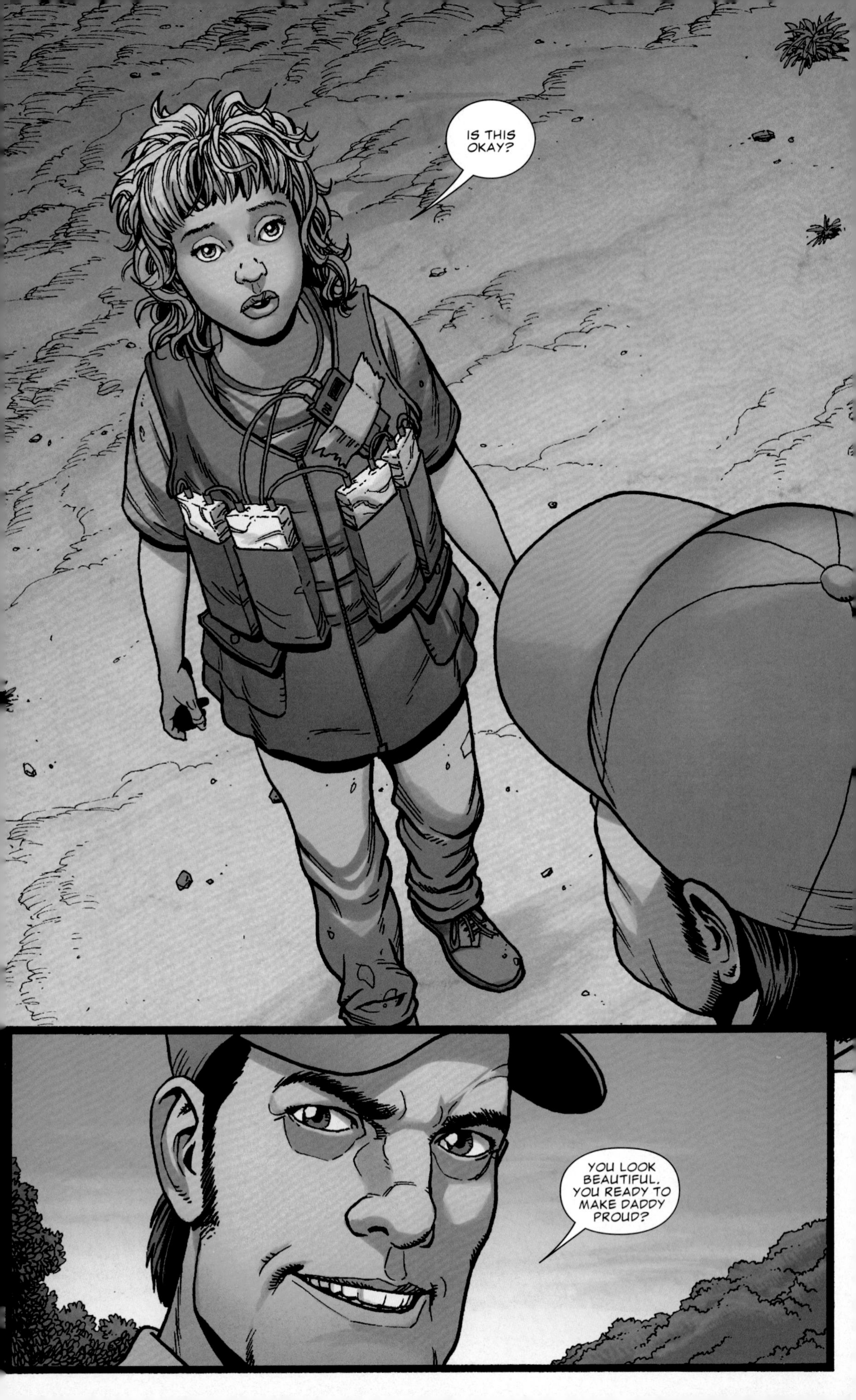
IS THIS OKAY?
YOU LOOK BEAUTIFUL. YOU READY TO MAKE DADDY PROUD?

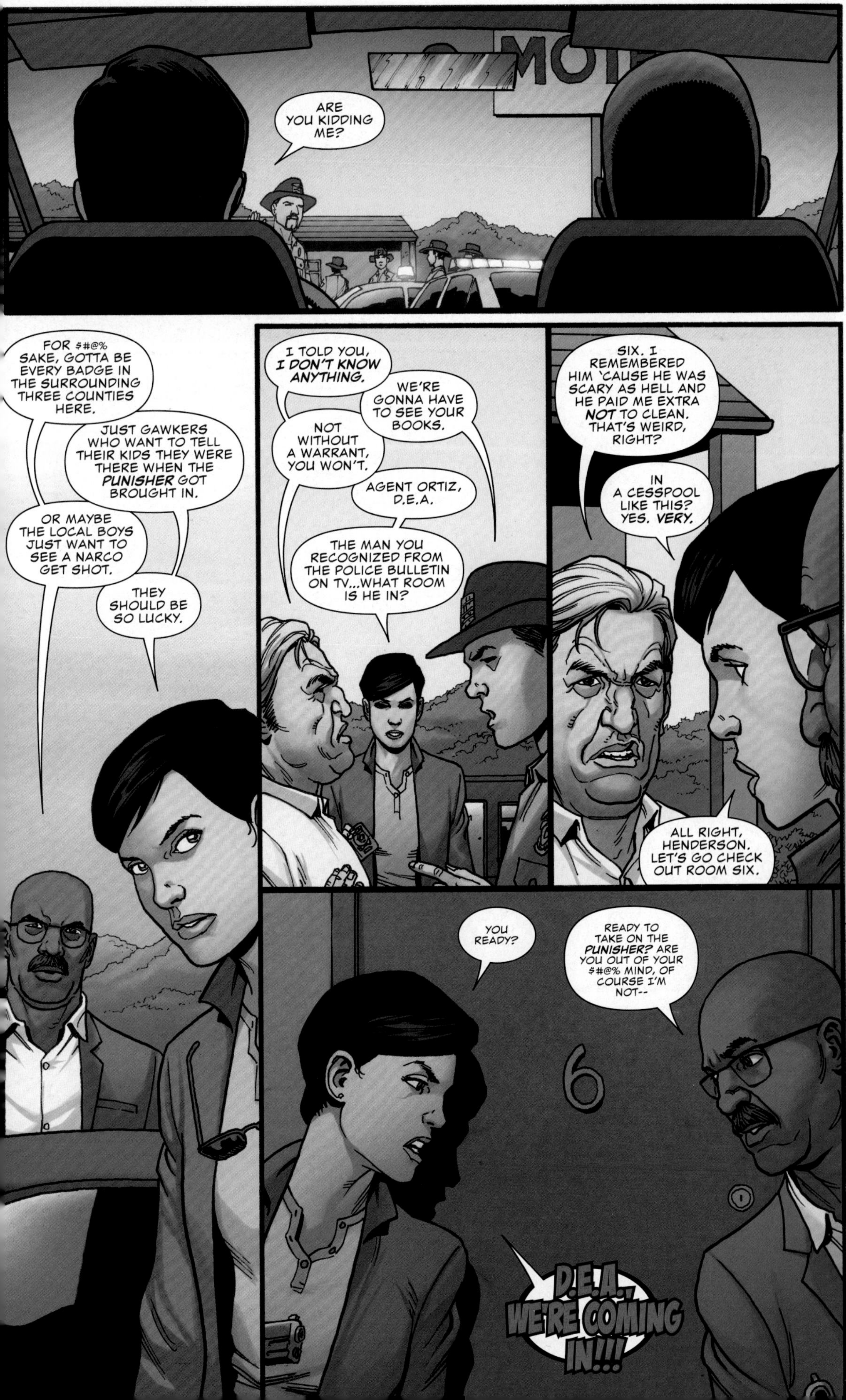
MOT
ARE YOU KIDDING ME?
FOR $#@% SAKE, GOTTA BE EVERY BADGE IN THE SURROUNDING THREE COUNTIES HERE.
JUST GAWKERS WHO WANT TO TELL THEIR KIDS THEY WERE THERE WHEN THE PUNISHER GOT BROUGHT IN.
OR MAYBE THE LOCAL BOYS JUST WANT TO SEE A NARCO GET SHOT.
THEY SHOULD BE SO LUCKY.
I TOLD YOU, I DON'T KNOW ANYTHING.
WE'RE GONNA HAVE TO SEE YOUR BOOKS.
NOT WITHOUT A WARRANT, YOU WON'T.
AGENT ORTIZ, D.E.A.
THE MAN YOU RECOGNIZED FROM THE POLICE BULLETIN ON TV...WHAT ROOM IS HE IN?
SIX. I REMEMBERED HIM 'CAUSE HE WAS SCARY AS HELL AND HE PAID ME EXTRA NOT TO CLEAN. THAT'S WEIRD, RIGHT?
IN A CESSPOOL LIKE THIS? YES. VERY.
ALL RIGHT, HENDERSON. LET'S GO CHECK OUT ROOM SIX.
YOU READY?
READY TO TAKE ON THE PUNISHER? ARE YOU OUT OF YOUR $#@% MIND, OF COURSE I'M NOT--
6
D.E.A., WE'RE COMING IN!!!

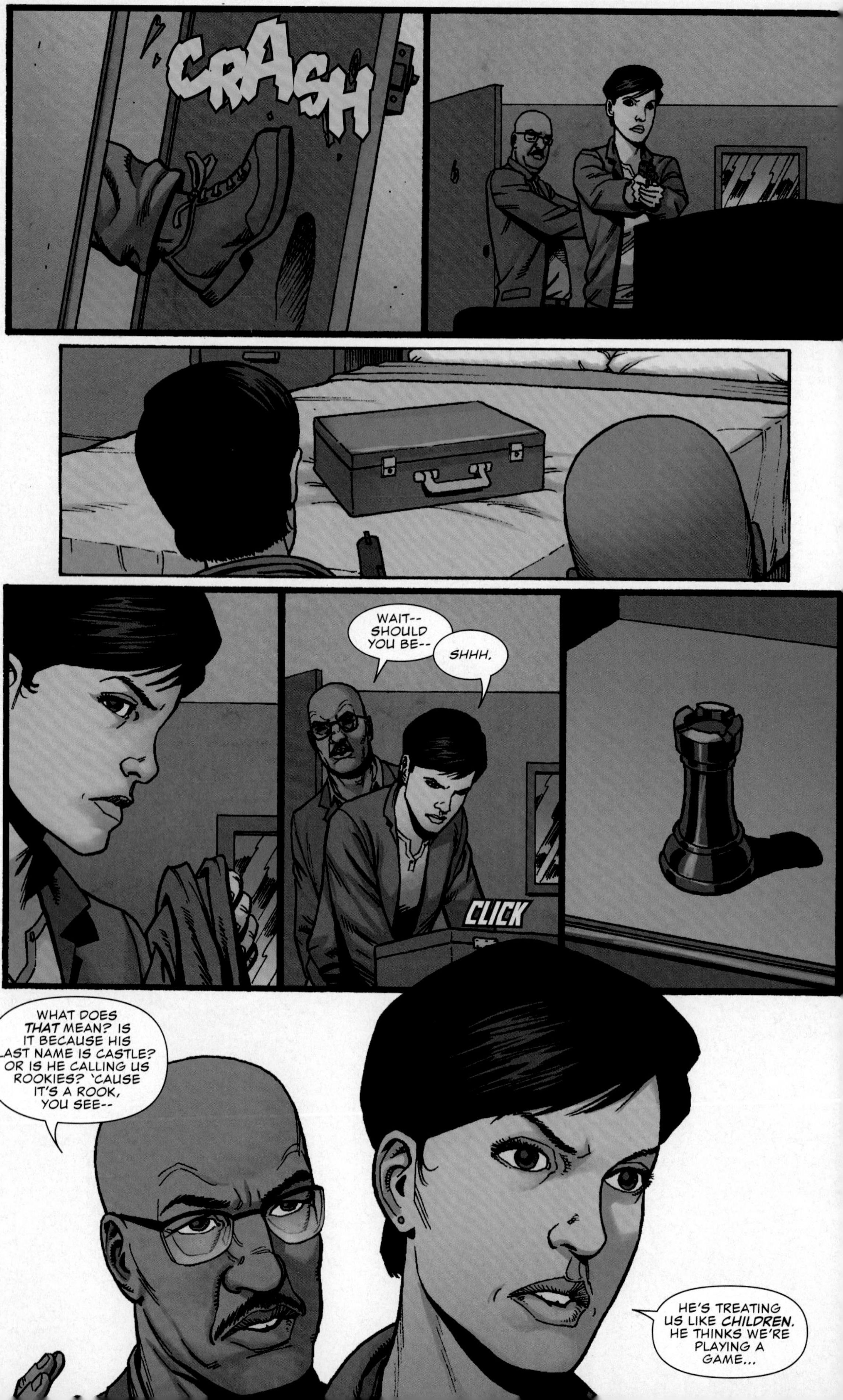
CRASH
WAIT-- SHOULD YOU BE--
SHHH.
CLICK
WHAT DOES THAT MEAN? IS IT BECAUSE HIS LAST NAME IS CASTLE? OR IS HE CALLING US ROOKIES? 'CAUSE IT'S A ROOK, YOU SEE--
HE'S TREATING US LIKE CHILDREN. HE THINKS WE'RE PLAYING A GAME...

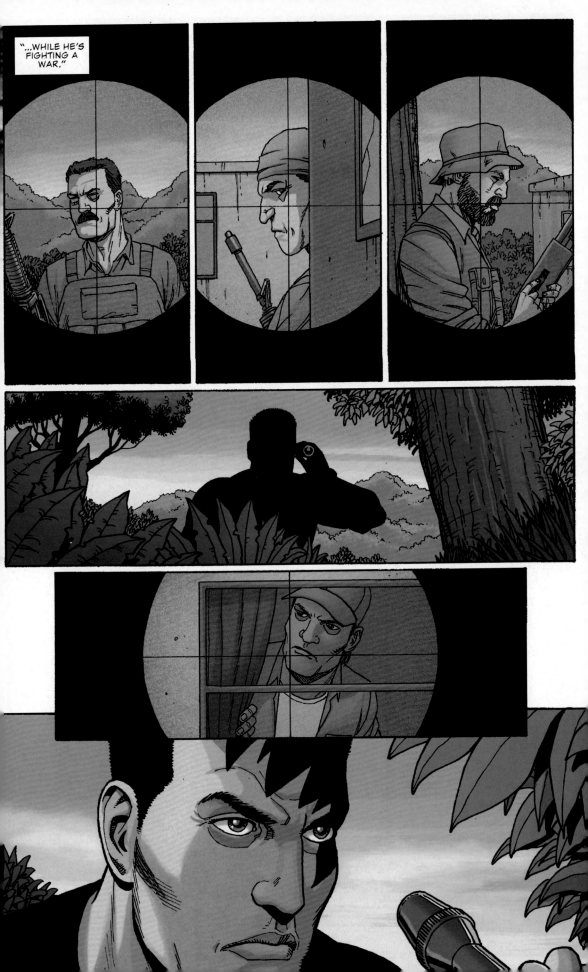

"...WHILE HE'S FIGHTING A WAR."

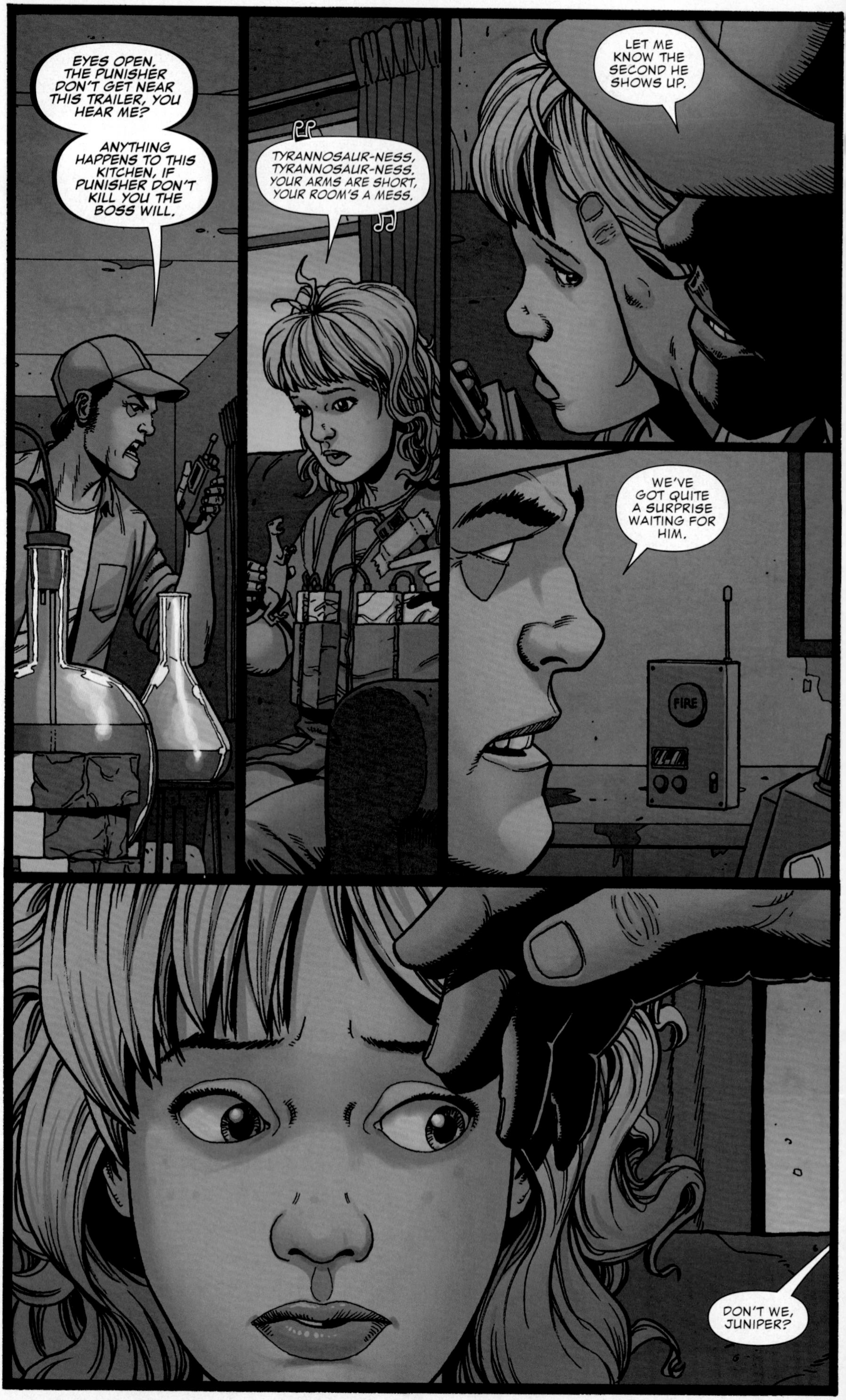
EYES OPEN. THE PUNISHER DON'T GET NEAR THIS TRAILER, YOU HEAR ME?
ANYTHING HAPPENS TO THIS KITCHEN, IF PUNISHER DON'T KILL YOU THE BOSS WILL.
TYRANNOSAUR-NESS, TYRANNOSAUR-NESS. YOUR ARMS ARE SHORT, YOUR ROOM'S A MESS.
LET ME KNOW THE SECOND HE SHOWS UP.
WE'VE GOT QUITE A SURPRISE WAITING FOR HIM.
FIRE
DON'T WE, JUNIPER?

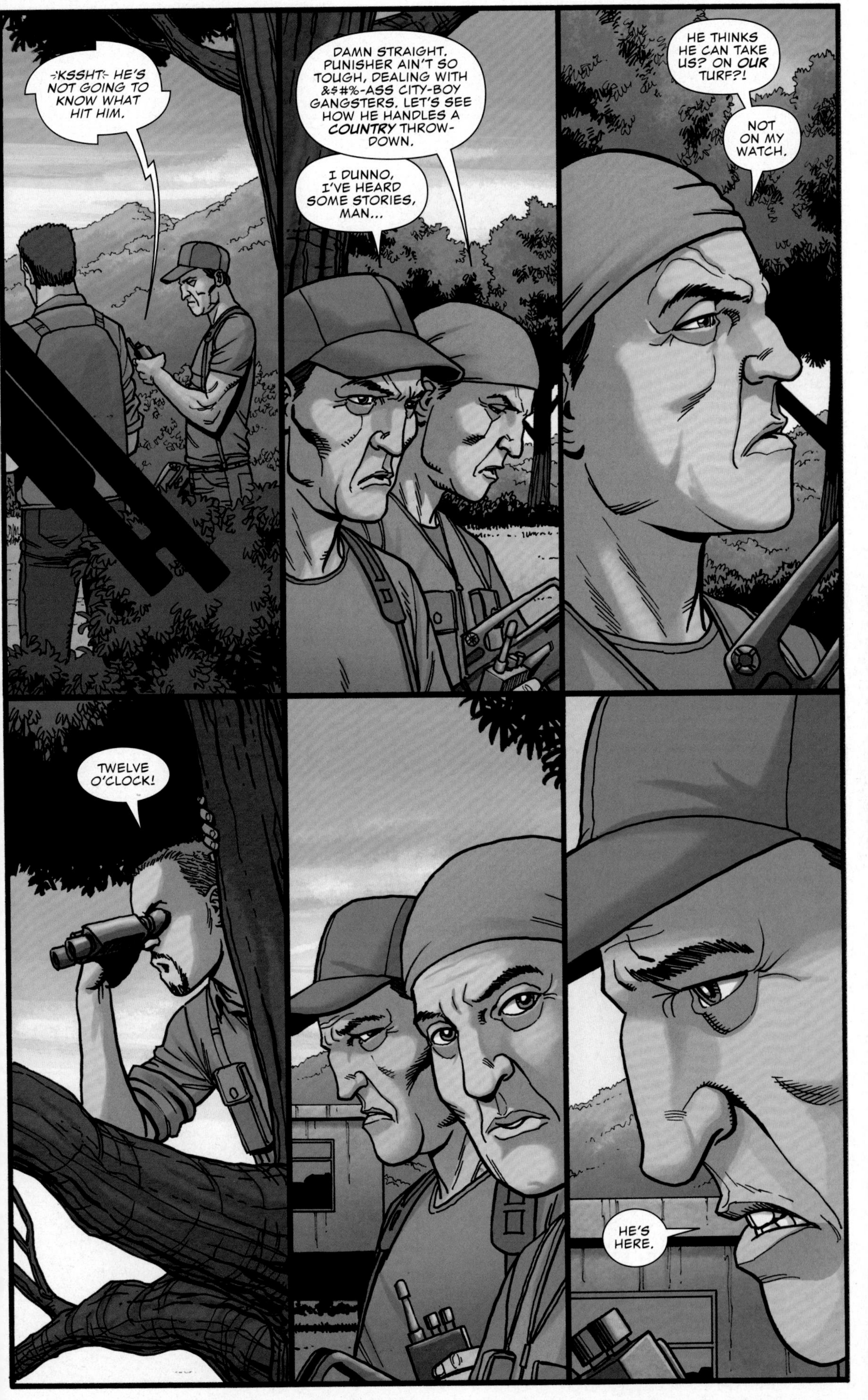
-KSSHT- HE'S NOT GOING TO KNOW WHAT HIT HIM.
DAMN STRAIGHT. PUNISHER AIN'T SO TOUGH, DEALING WITH &$#%-ASS CITY-BOY GANGSTERS. LET'S SEE HOW HE HANDLES A COUNTRY THROW-DOWN.
I DUNNO, I'VE HEARD SOME STORIES, MAN...
HE THINKS HE CAN TAKE US? ON OUR TURF?!
NOT ON MY WATCH.
TWELVE O'CLOCK!
HE'S HERE.

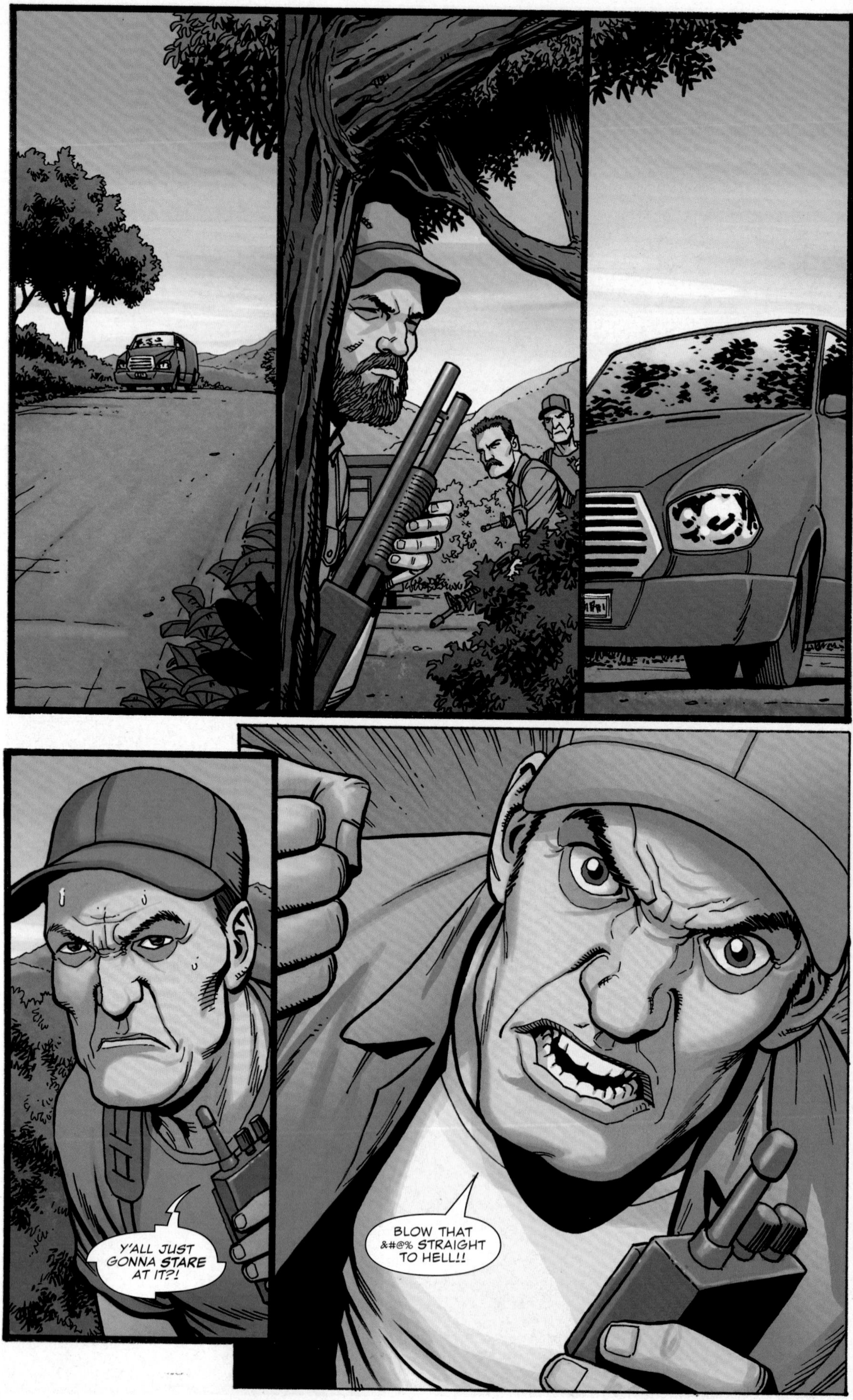
Y'ALL JUST GONNA STARE AT IT?!
BLOW THAT &#@% STRAIGHT TO HELL!!

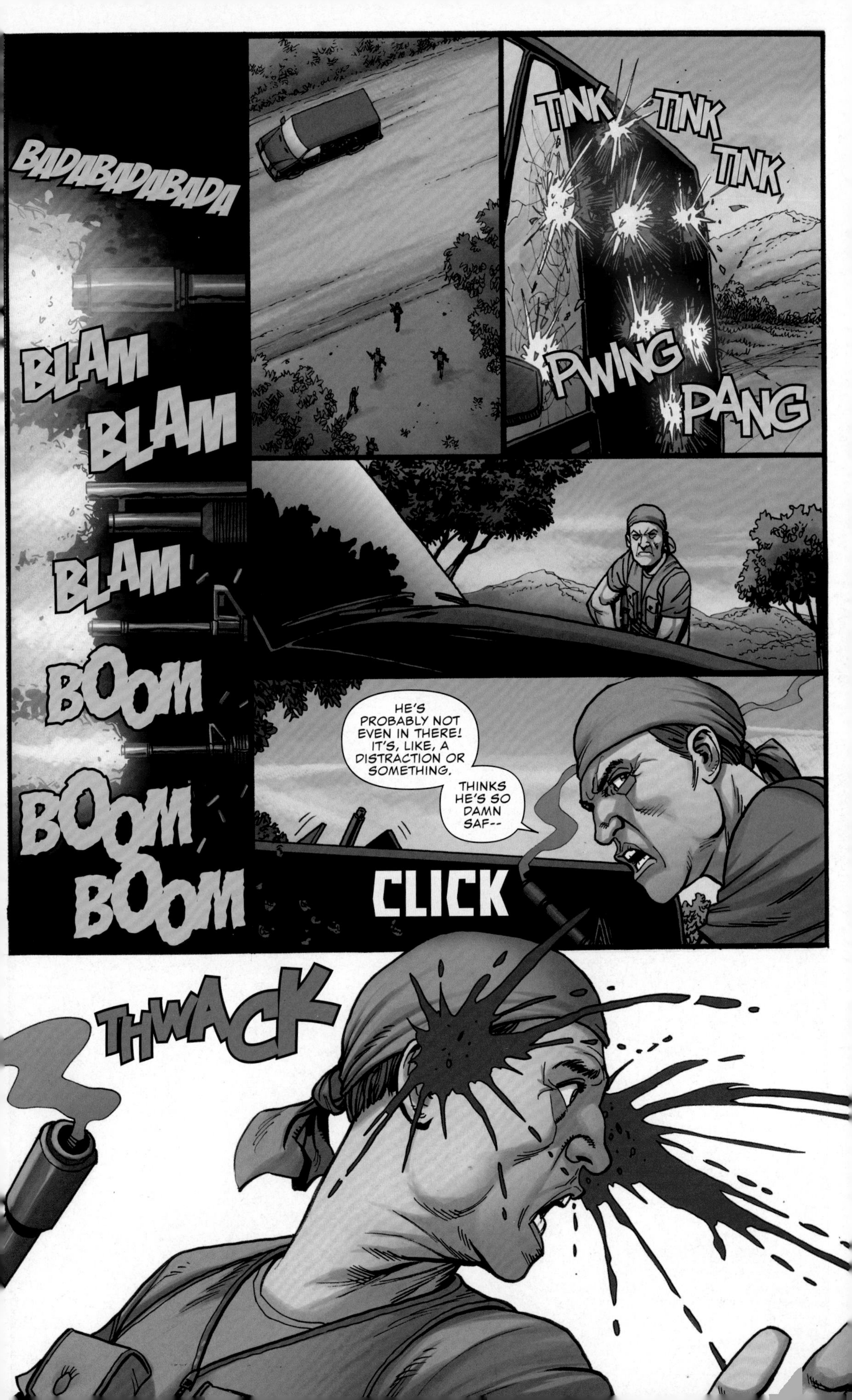
BADABADABADA
BLAM
BLAM
BLAM
BOOM
BOOM
BOOM
TINK
TINK
TINK
PWING
PANG
HE'S PROBABLY NOT EVEN IN THERE! IT'S, LIKE, A DISTRACTION OR SOMETHING.
THINKS HE'S SO DAMN SAF--
CLICK
THWACK

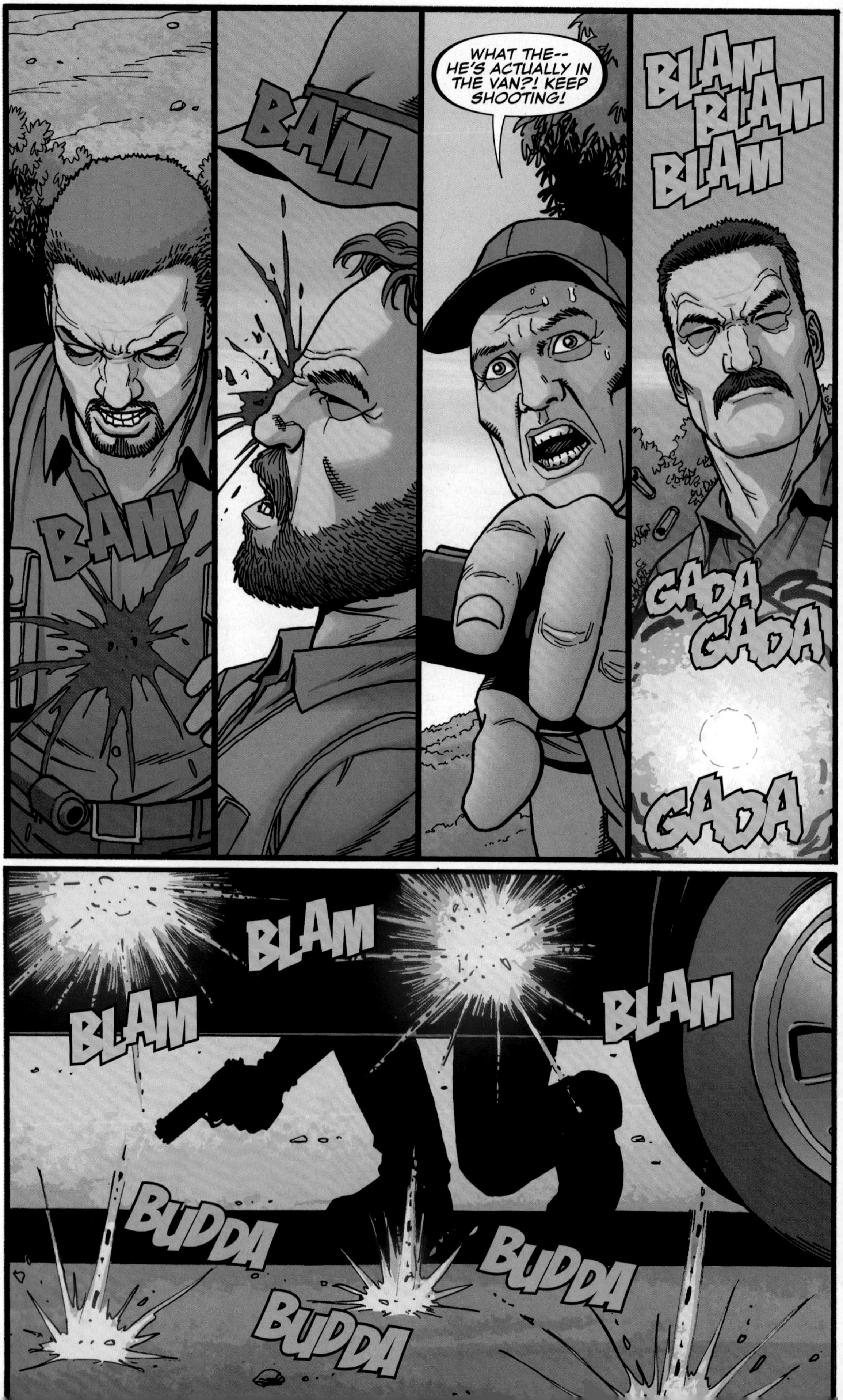
BAM
BAM
WHAT THE-- HE'S ACTUALLY IN THE VAN?! KEEP SHOOTING!
BLAM BLAM BLAM
GADA GADA
GADA
BLAM
BLAM
BLAM
BUDDA
BUDDA
BUDDA

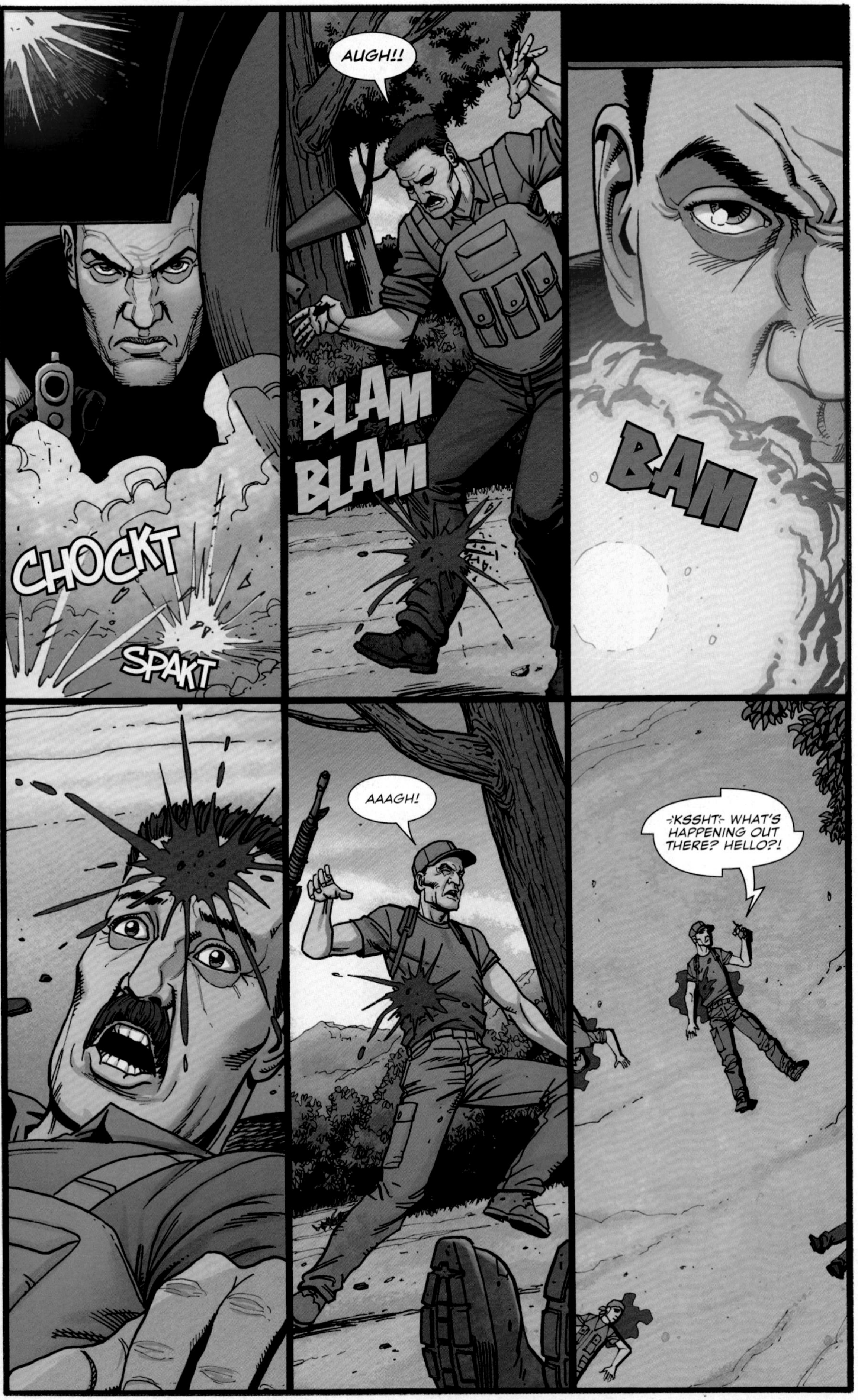
AUGH!!
CHOCKT
SPAKT
BLAM
BLAM
BAM
AAAGH!
-KSSHT- WHAT'S HAPPENING OUT THERE? HELLO?!

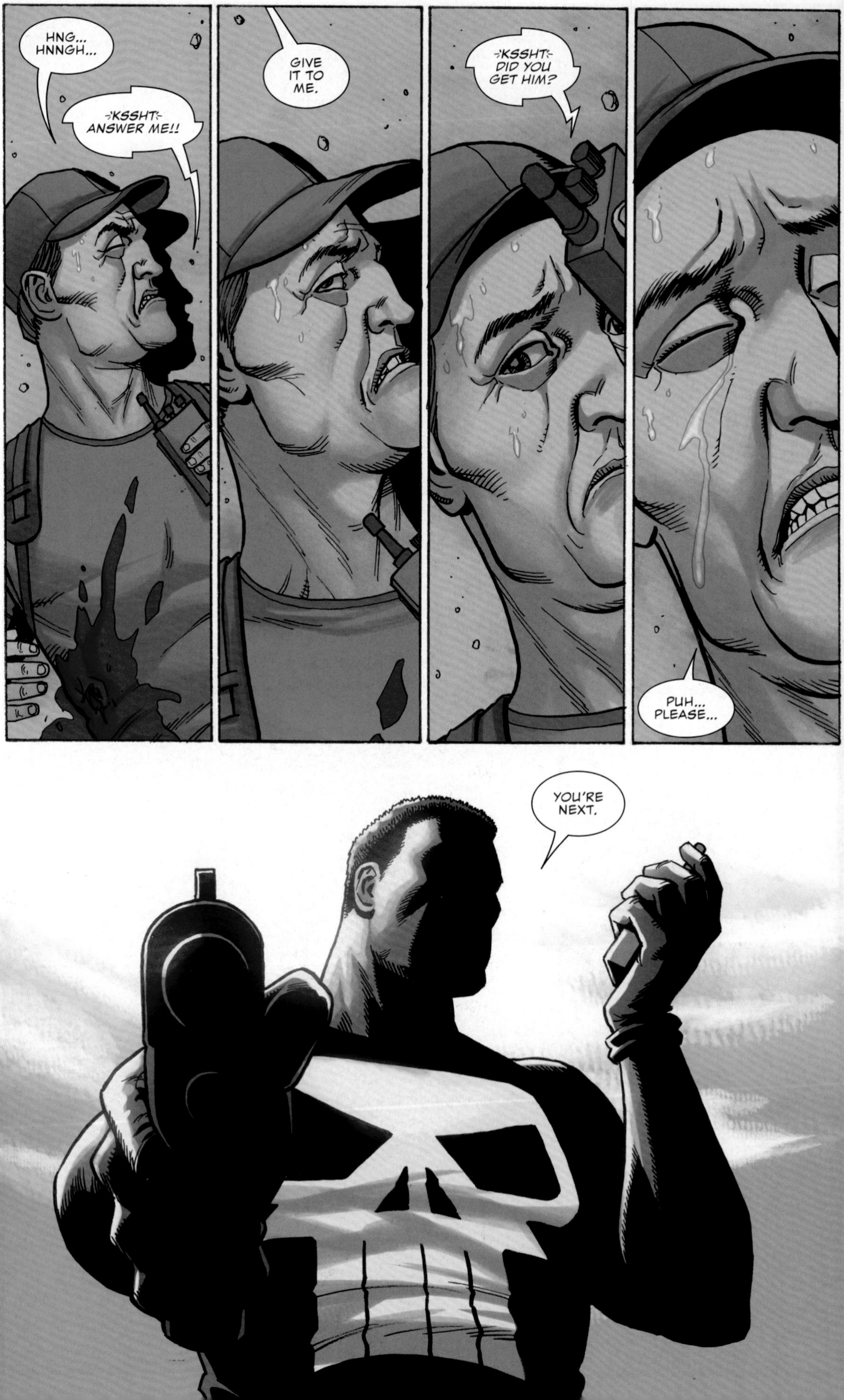
HNG... HNNGH...
-KSSHT- ANSWER ME!!
GIVE IT TO ME.
-KSSHT- DID YOU GET HIM?
PUH... PLEASE...
YOU'RE NEXT.

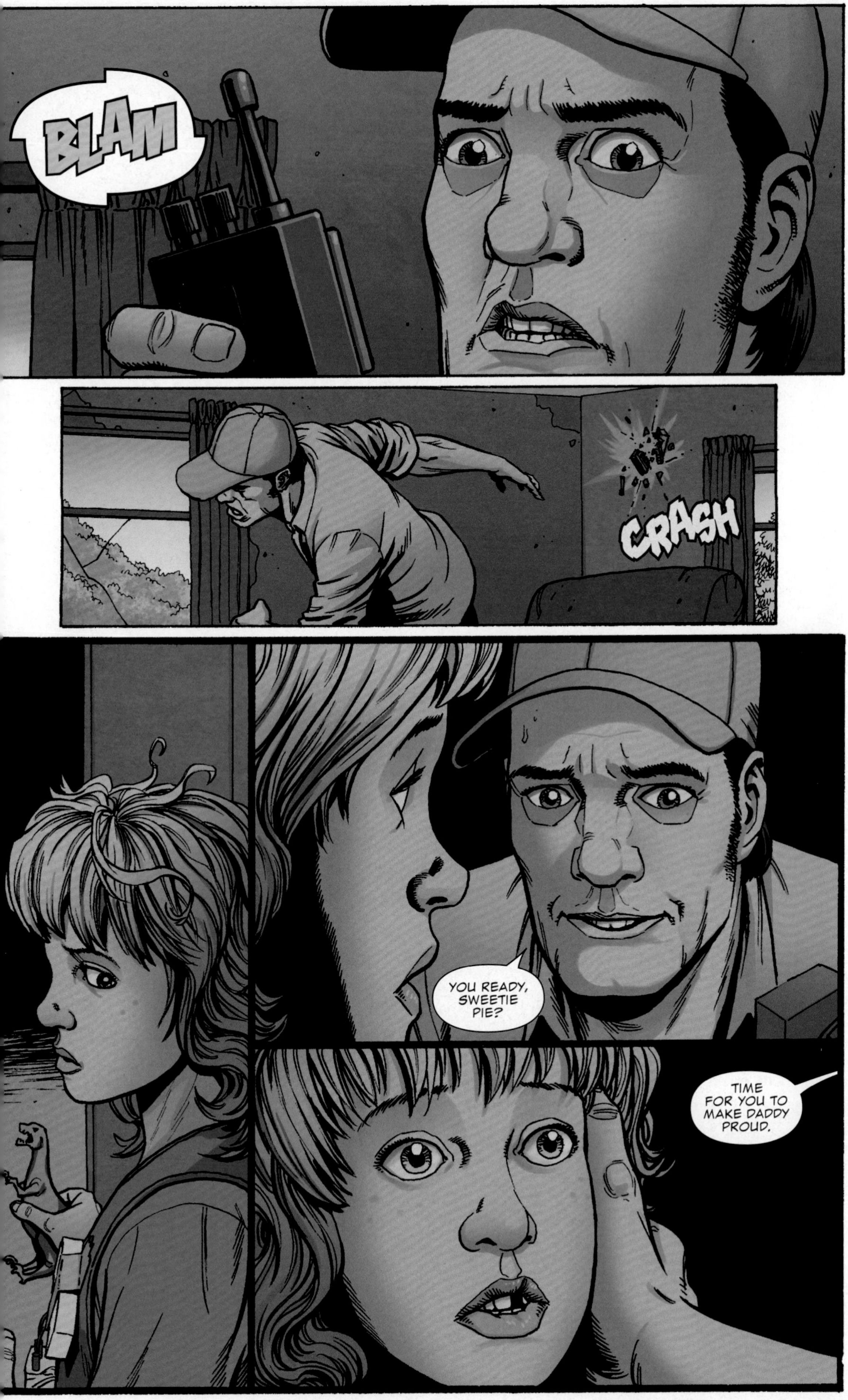
BLAM
CRASH
YOU READY, SWEETIE PIE?
TIME FOR YOU TO MAKE DADDY PROUD.

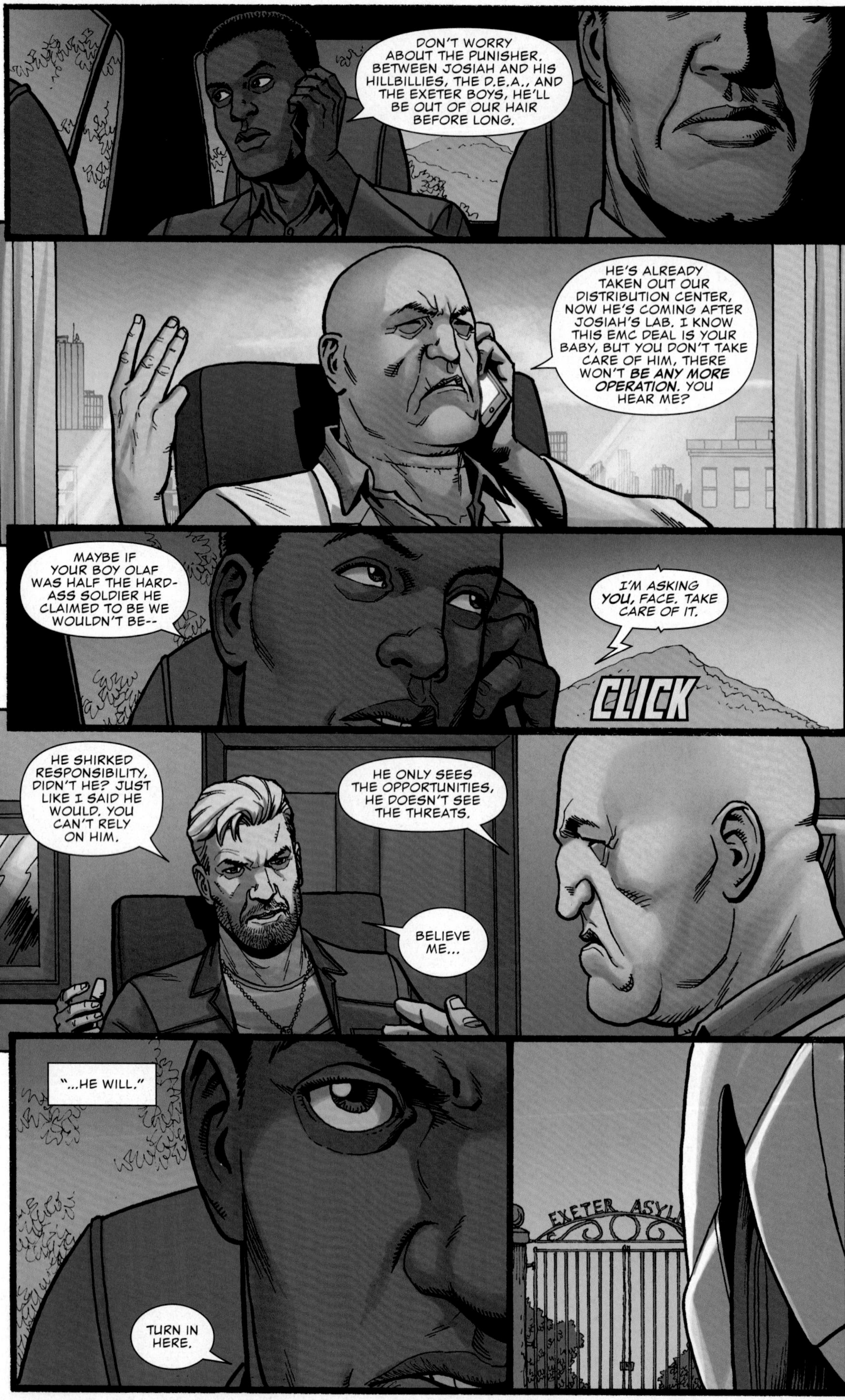
DON'T WORRY ABOUT THE PUNISHER. BETWEEN JOSIAH AND HIS HILLBILLIES, THE D.E.A., AND THE EXETER BOYS, HE'LL BE OUT OF OUR HAIR BEFORE LONG.
HE'S ALREADY TAKEN OUT OUR DISTRIBUTION CENTER, NOW HE'S COMING AFTER JOSIAH'S LAB. I KNOW THIS EMC DEAL IS YOUR BABY, BUT YOU DON'T TAKE CARE OF HIM, THERE WON'T BE ANY MORE OPERATION. YOU HEAR ME?
MAYBE IF YOUR BOY OLAF WAS HALF THE HARD-ASS SOLDIER HE CLAIMED TO BE WE WOULDN'T BE--
I'M ASKING YOU, FACE. TAKE CARE OF IT.
CLICK
HE SHIRKED RESPONSIBILITY, DIDN'T HE? JUST LIKE I SAID HE WOULD. YOU CAN'T RELY ON HIM.
HE ONLY SEES THE OPPORTUNITIES, HE DOESN'T SEE THE THREATS.
BELIEVE ME...
"...HE WILL."
EXETER ASYL
TURN IN HERE.

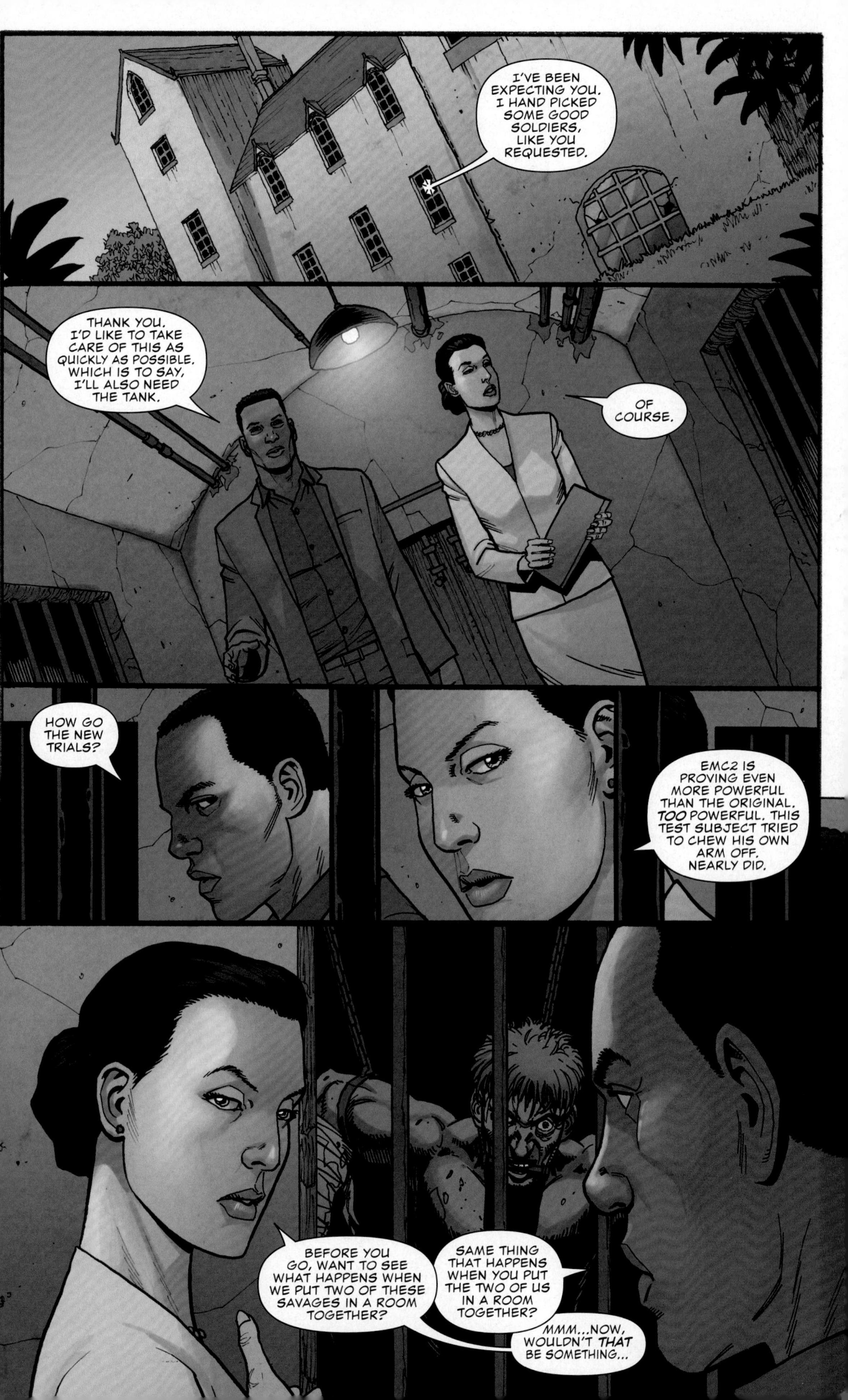
I'VE BEEN EXPECTING YOU. I HAND PICKED SOME GOOD SOLDIERS, LIKE YOU REQUESTED.
THANK YOU. I'D LIKE TO TAKE CARE OF THIS AS QUICKLY AS POSSIBLE. WHICH IS TO SAY, I'LL ALSO NEED THE TANK.
OF COURSE.
HOW GO THE NEW TRIALS?
EMC2 IS PROVING EVEN MORE POWERFUL THAN THE ORIGINAL. TOO POWERFUL. THIS TEST SUBJECT TRIED TO CHEW HIS OWN ARM OFF. NEARLY DID.
BEFORE YOU GO, WANT TO SEE WHAT HAPPENS WHEN WE PUT TWO OF THESE SAVAGES IN A ROOM TOGETHER?
SAME THING THAT HAPPENS WHEN YOU PUT THE TWO OF US IN A ROOM TOGETHER?
MMM...NOW, WOULDN'T THAT BE SOMETHING...

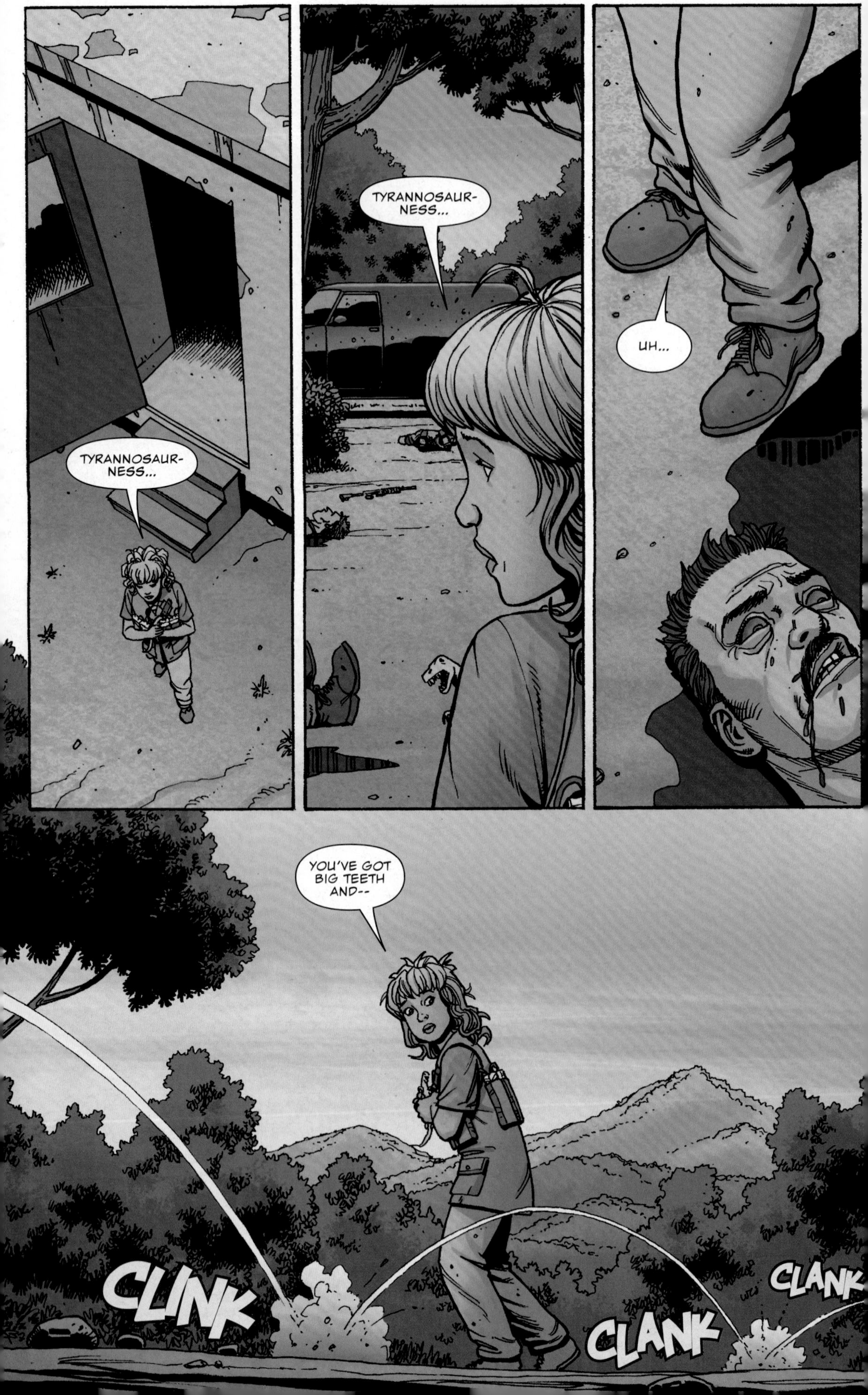
TYRANNOSAUR-NESS...
TYRANNOSAUR-NESS...
UH...
YOU'VE GOT BIG TEETH AND--
CLINK
CLANK
CLANK

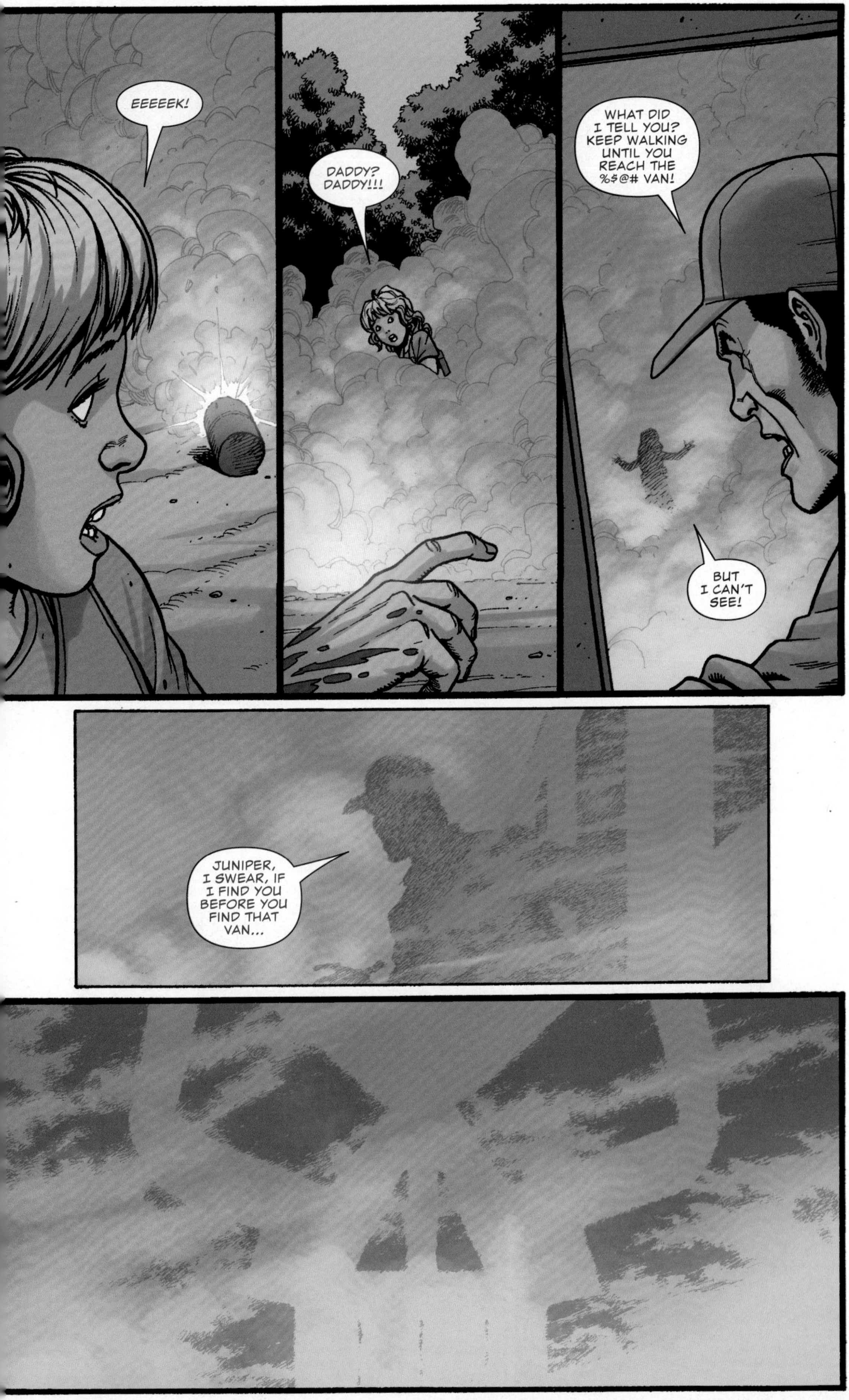
EEEEEK!
DADDY? DADDY!!!
WHAT DID I TELL YOU? KEEP WALKING UNTIL YOU REACH THE %$@# VAN!
BUT I CAN'T SEE!
JUNIPER, I SWEAR, IF I FIND YOU BEFORE YOU FIND THAT VAN...

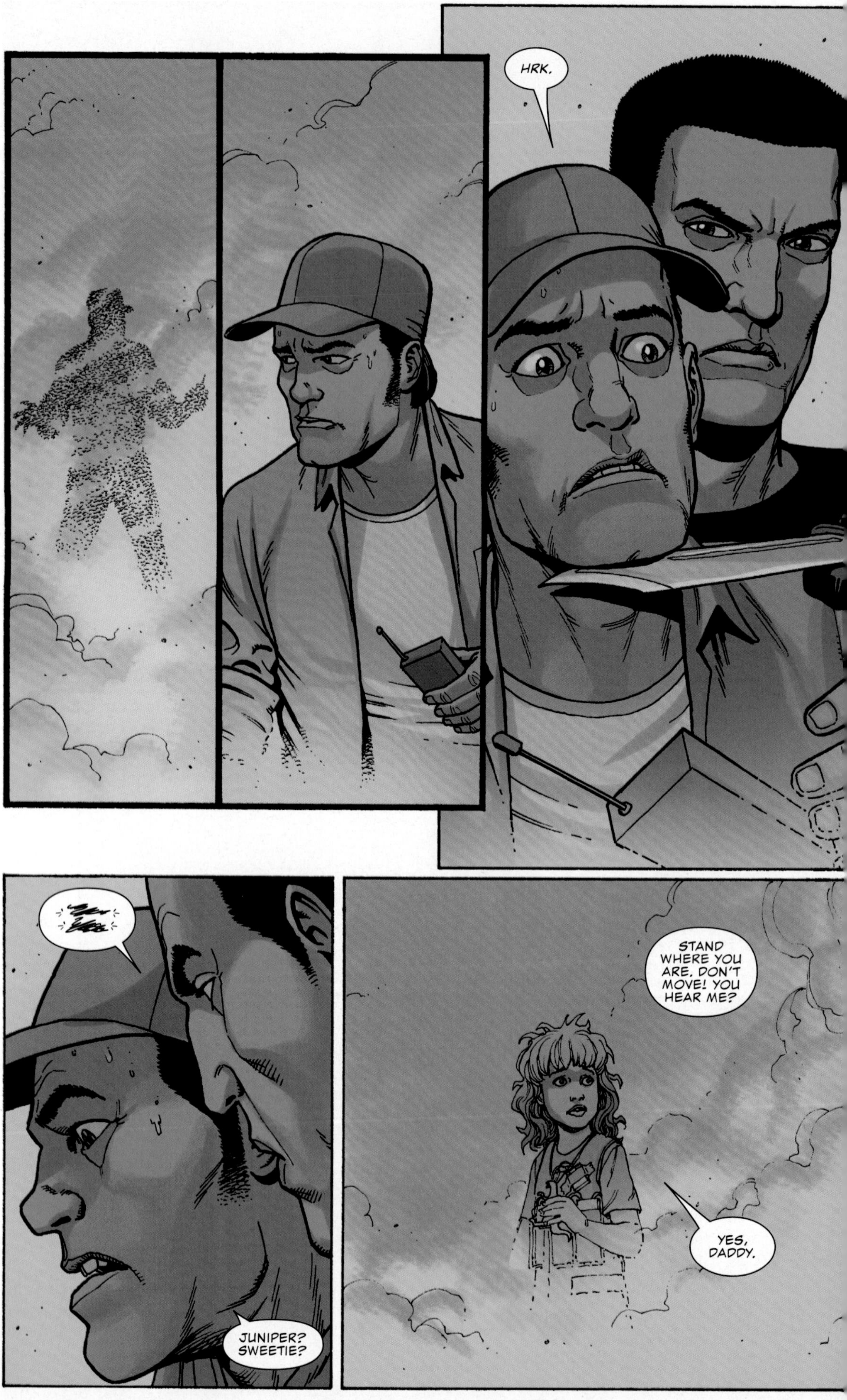
HRK.
JUNIPER? SWEETIE?
STAND WHERE YOU ARE. DON'T MOVE! YOU HEAR ME?
YES, DADDY.

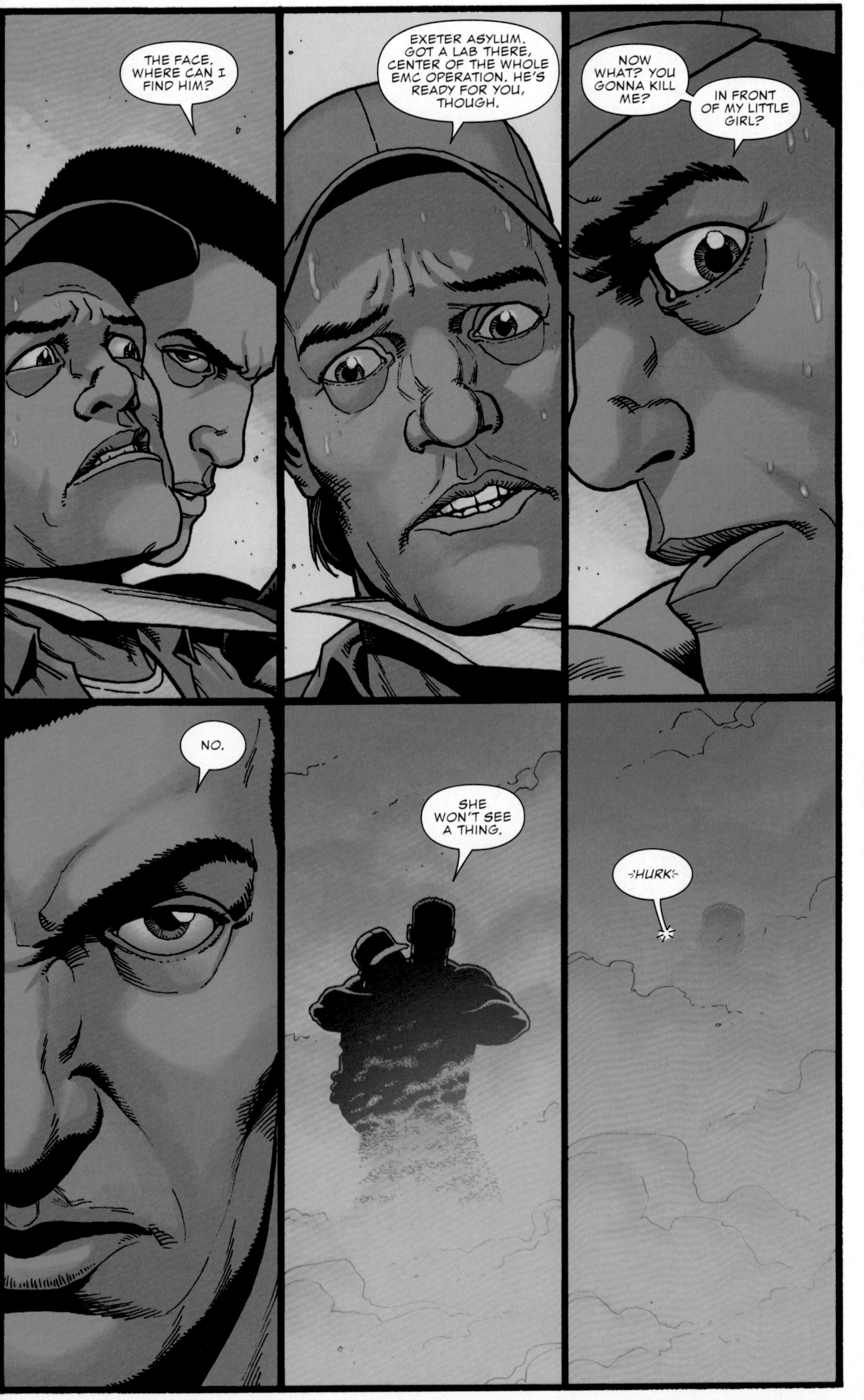
THE FACE. WHERE CAN I FIND HIM?
EXETER ASYLUM. GOT A LAB THERE, CENTER OF THE WHOLE EMC OPERATION. HE'S READY FOR YOU, THOUGH.
NOW WHAT? YOU GONNA KILL ME?
IN FRONT OF MY LITTLE GIRL?
NO.
SHE WON'T SEE A THING.
HURK

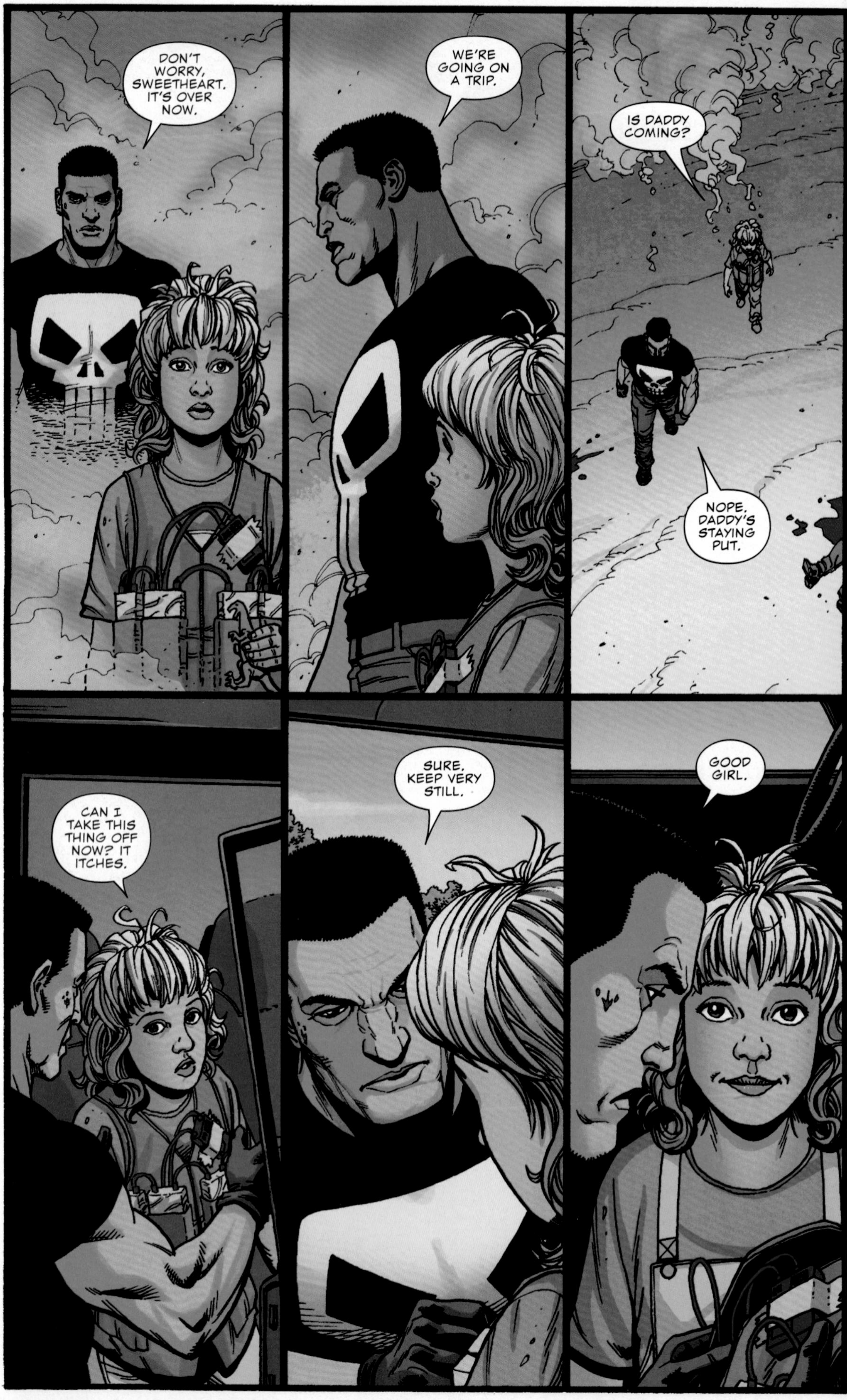
DON'T WORRY, SWEETHEART. IT'S OVER NOW.
WE'RE GOING ON A TRIP.
IS DADDY COMING?
NOPE. DADDY'S STAYING PUT.
CAN I TAKE THIS THING OFF NOW? IT ITCHES.
SURE. KEEP VERY STILL.
GOOD GIRL.

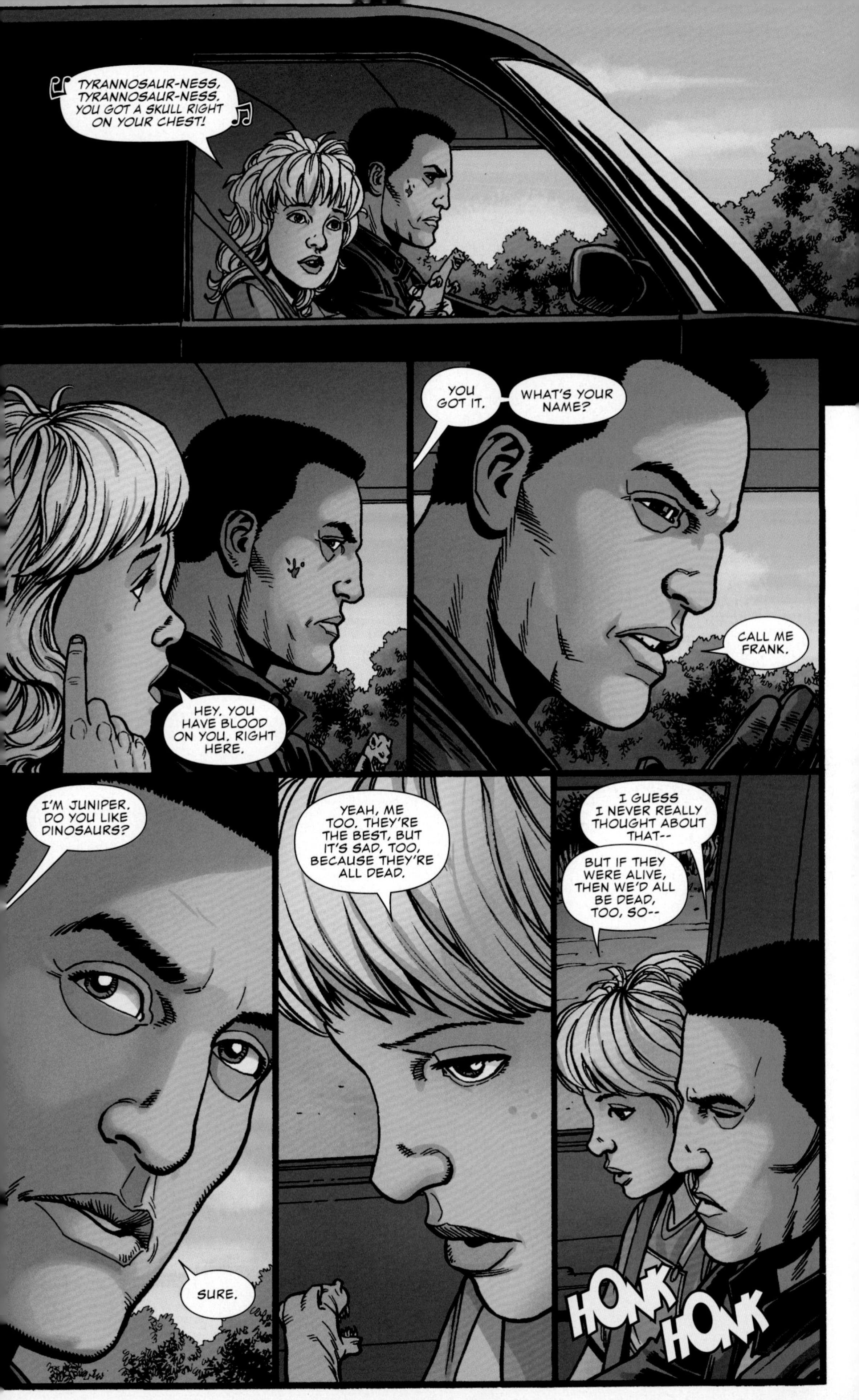
TYRANNOSAUR-NESS, TYRANNOSAUR-NESS. YOU GOT A SKULL RIGHT ON YOUR CHEST!
HEY. YOU HAVE BLOOD ON YOU. RIGHT HERE.
YOU GOT IT.
WHAT'S YOUR NAME?
CALL ME FRANK.
I'M JUNIPER. DO YOU LIKE DINOSAURS?
SURE.
YEAH, ME TOO. THEY'RE THE BEST, BUT IT'S SAD, TOO, BECAUSE THEY'RE ALL DEAD.
I GUESS I NEVER REALLY THOUGHT ABOUT THAT--
BUT IF THEY WERE ALIVE, THEN WE'D ALL BE DEAD, TOO, SO--
HONK HONK

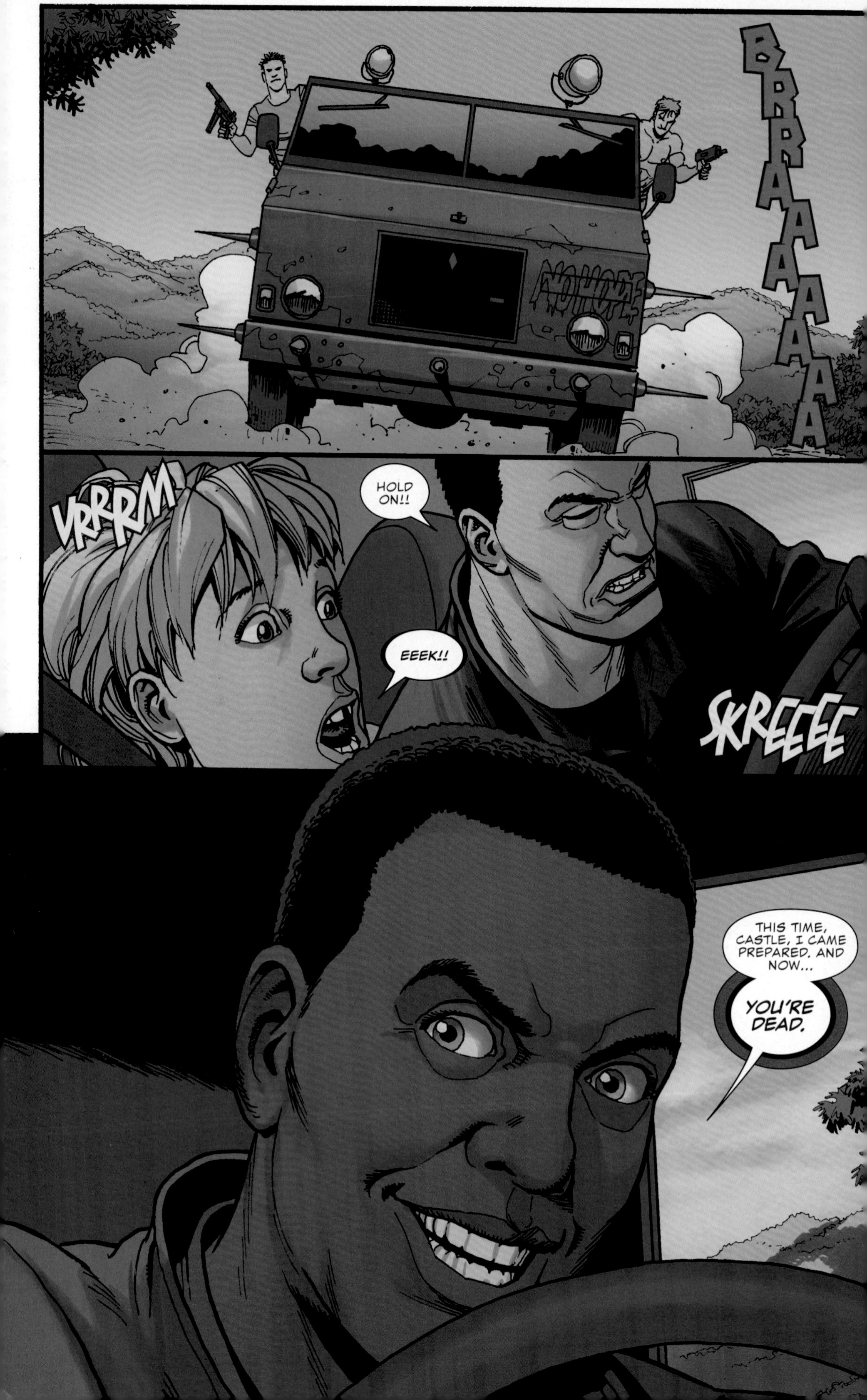
BRRAAAAAAA
NO HOPE
VRRRM
HOLD ON!!
EEEK!!
SKREEEE
THIS TIME, CASTLE, I CAME PREPARED. AND NOW...
YOU'RE DEAD.

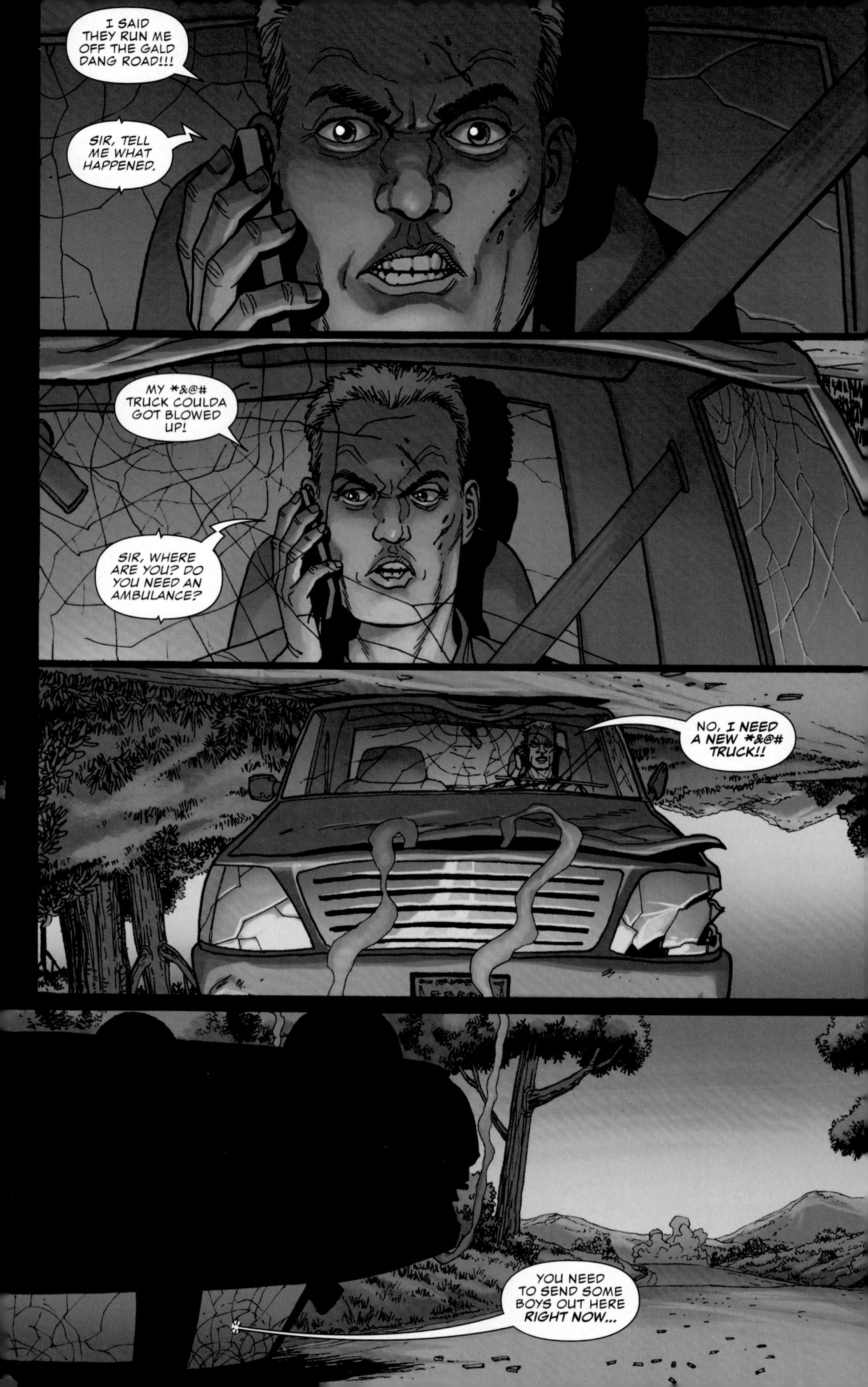
I SAID THEY RUN ME OFF THE GALD DANG ROAD!!!
SIR, TELL ME WHAT HAPPENED.
MY *&@# TRUCK COULDA GOT BLOWED UP!
SIR, WHERE ARE YOU? DO YOU NEED AN AMBULANCE?
NO, I NEED A NEW *&@# TRUCK!!
YOU NEED TO SEND SOME BOYS OUT HERE RIGHT NOW...

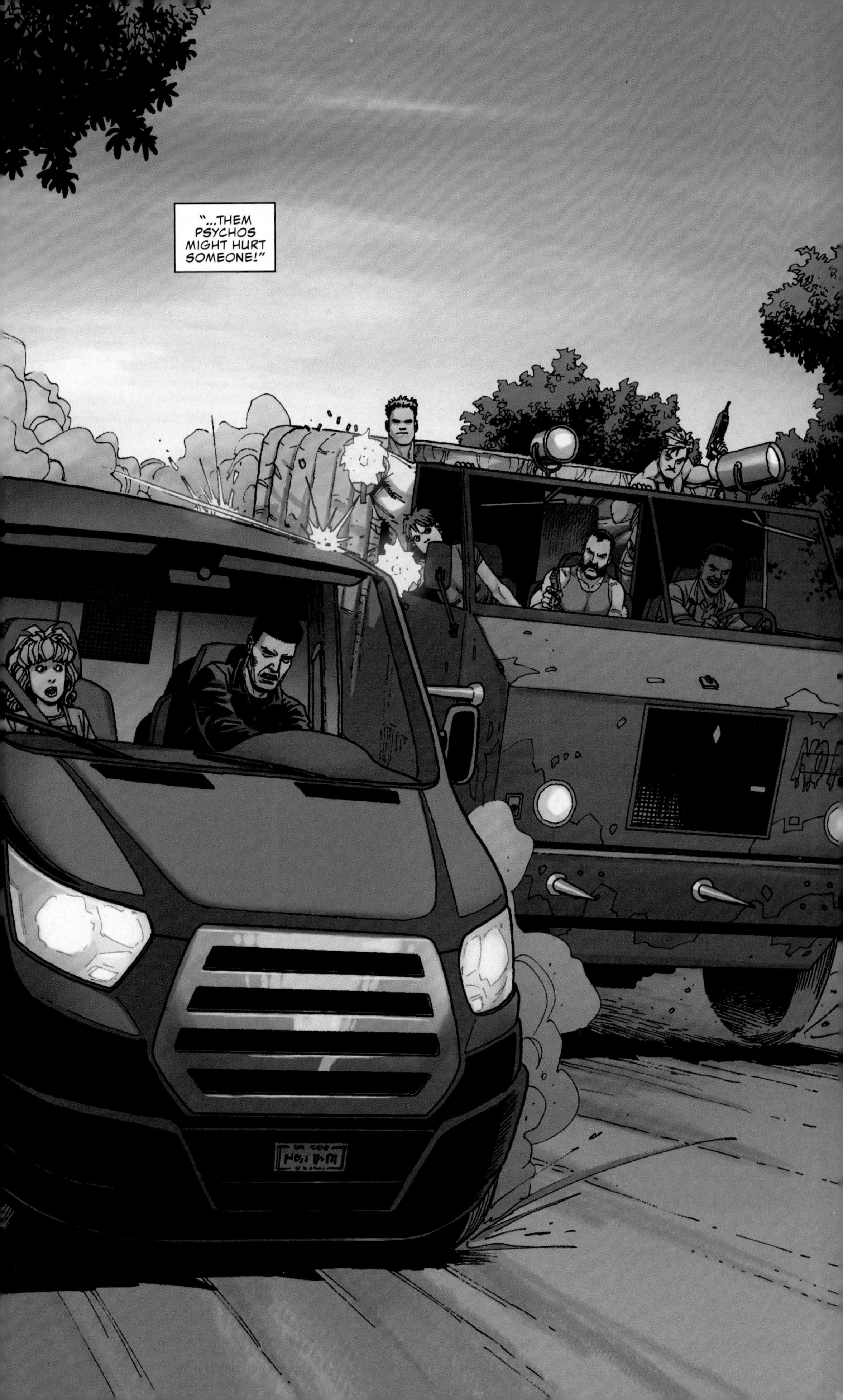
"...THEM PSYCHOS MIGHT HURT SOMEONE!"

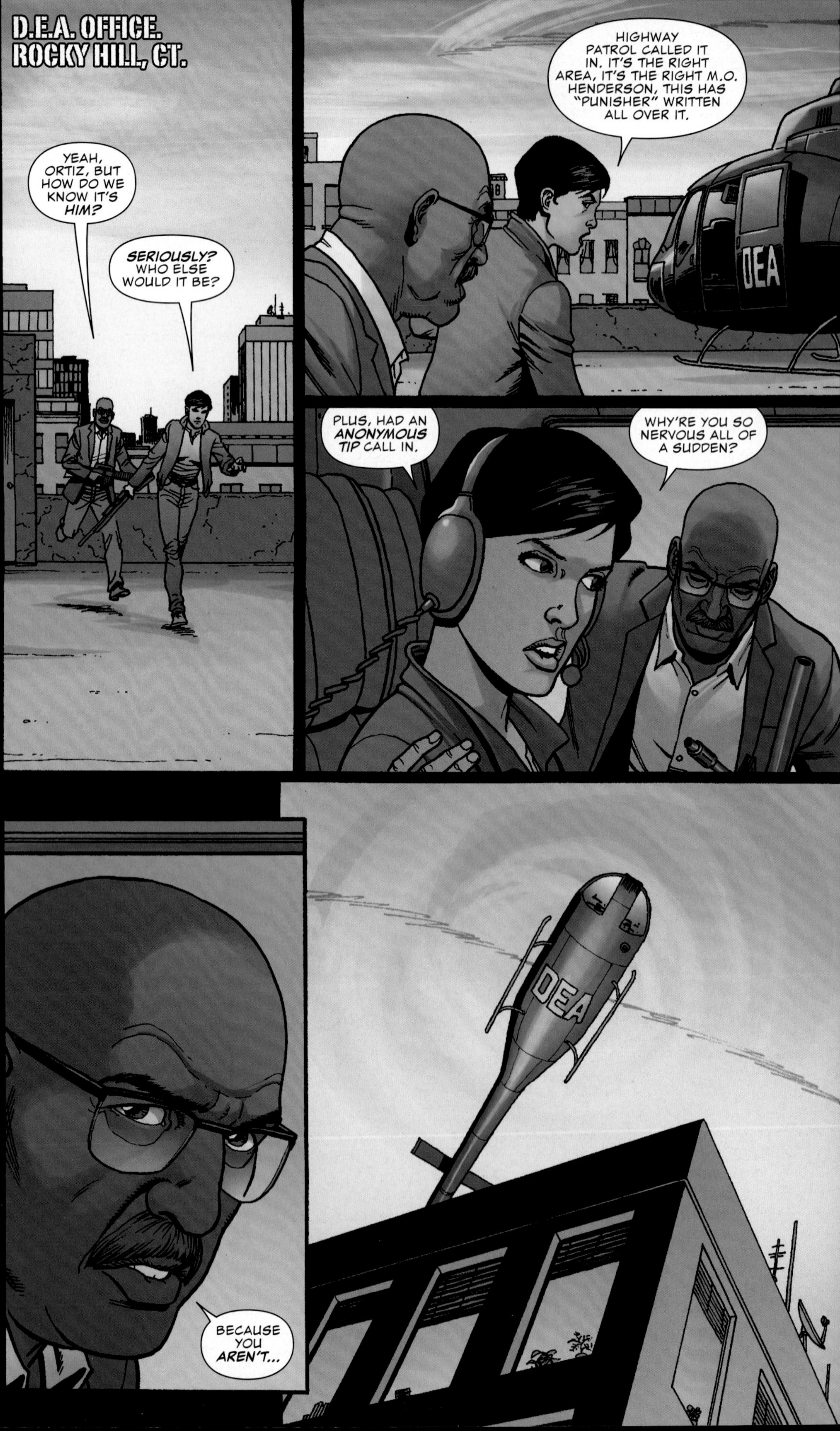
D.E.A. OFFICE. ROCKY HILL, CT.
YEAH, ORTIZ, BUT HOW DO WE KNOW IT'S HIM?
SERIOUSLY? WHO ELSE WOULD IT BE?
HIGHWAY PATROL CALLED IT IN. IT'S THE RIGHT AREA, IT'S THE RIGHT M.O. HENDERSON, THIS HAS "PUNISHER" WRITTEN ALL OVER IT.
DEA
PLUS, HAD AN ANONYMOUS TIP CALL IN.
WHY'RE YOU SO NERVOUS ALL OF A SUDDEN?
BECAUSE YOU AREN'T...
DEA

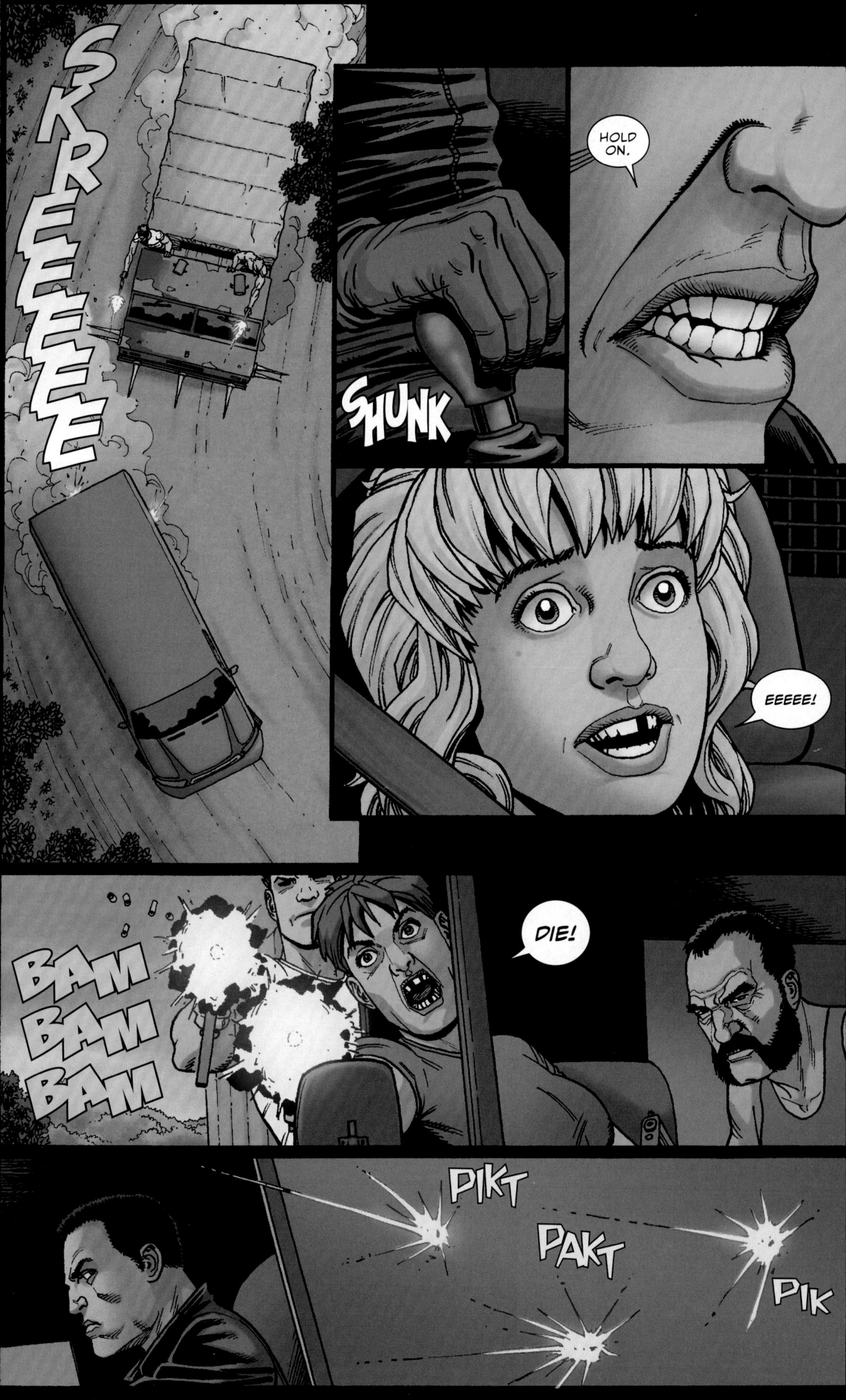
SKREEEEEEE
SHUNK
HOLD ON.
EEEEE!
BAM BAM BAM
DIE!
PIKT
PAKT
PIK

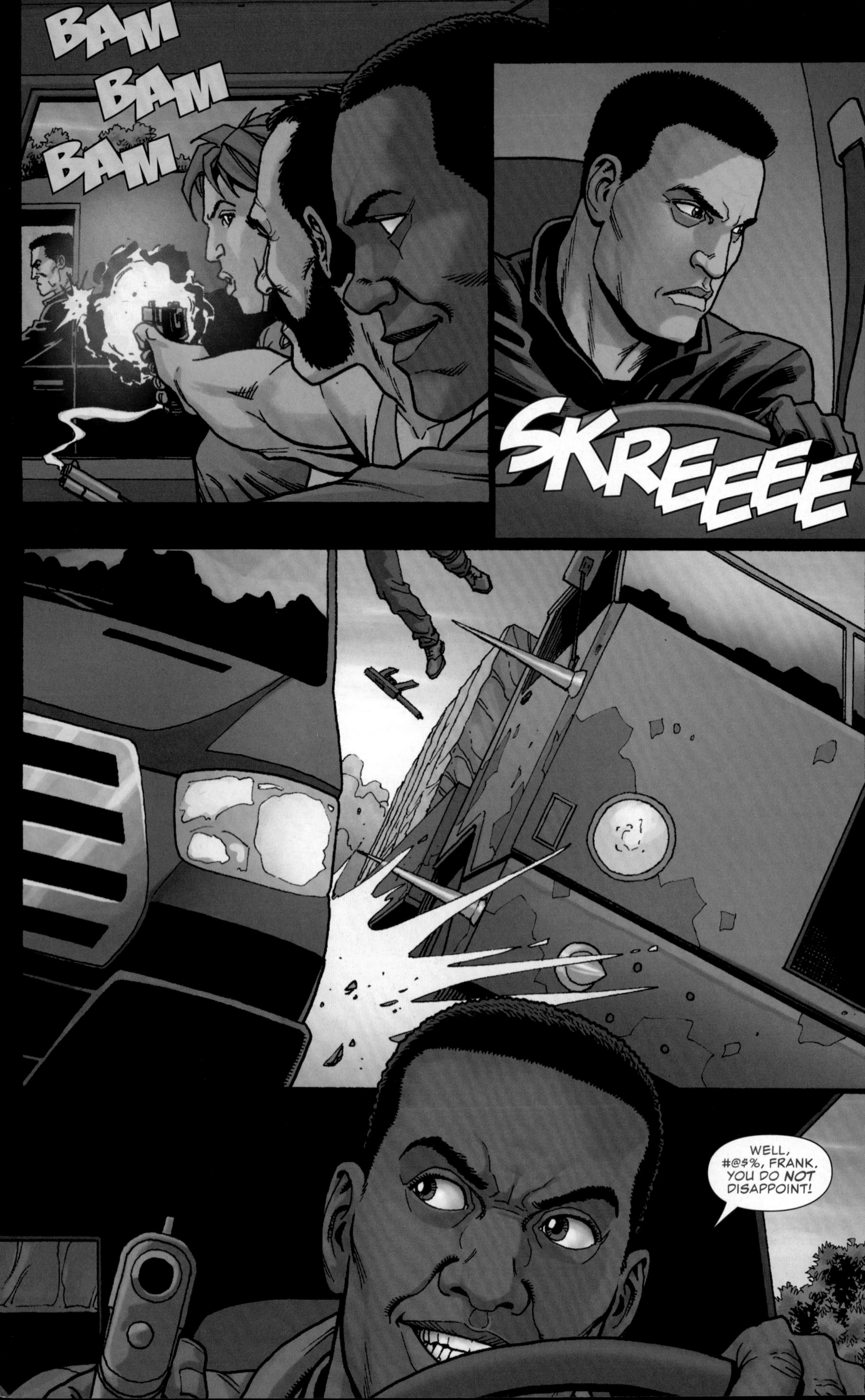
BAM
BAM
BAM
SKREEEE
WELL, #@$%, FRANK. YOU DO NOT DISAPPOINT!

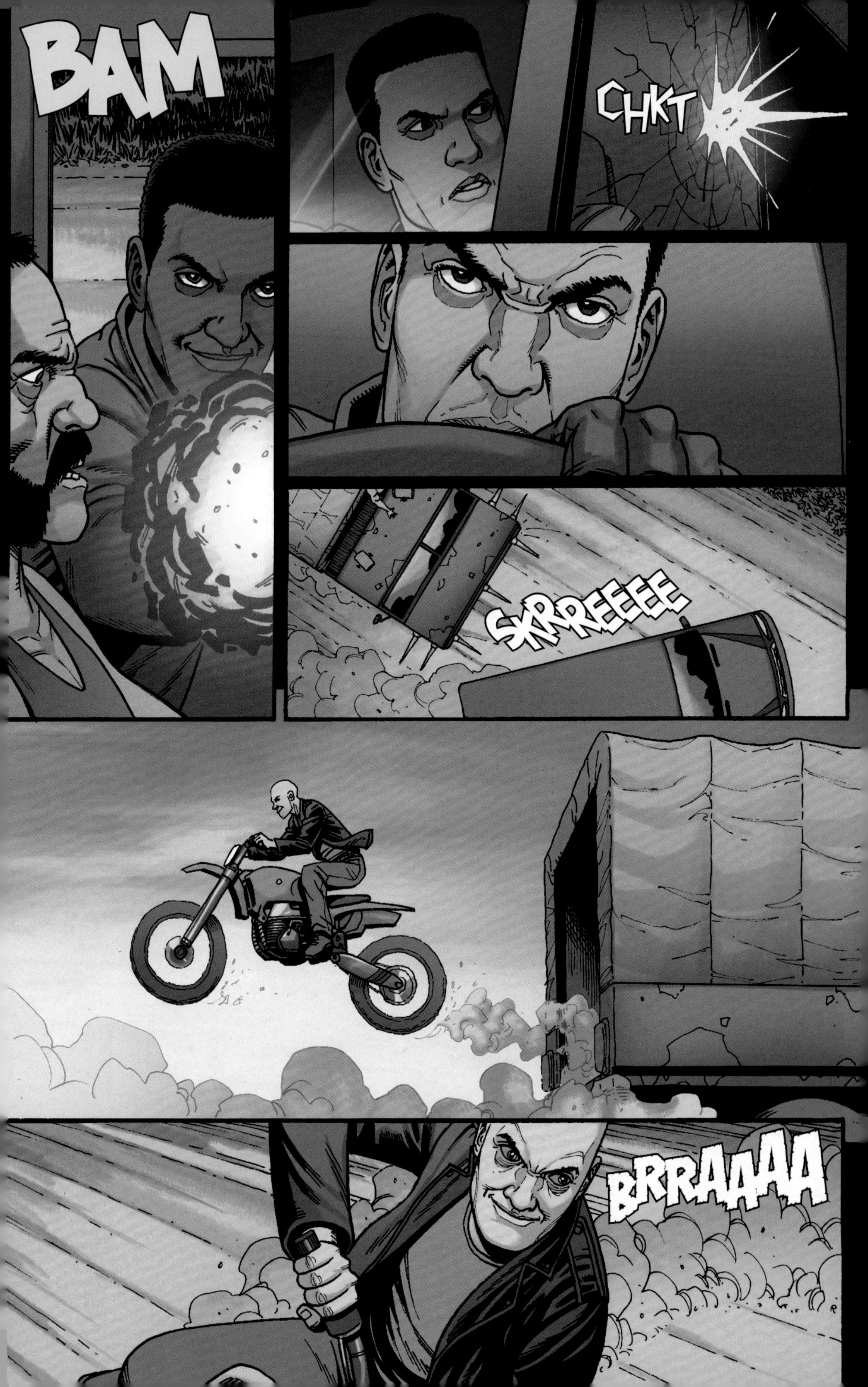
BAM
CHKT
SKRREEEE
BRRAAAA

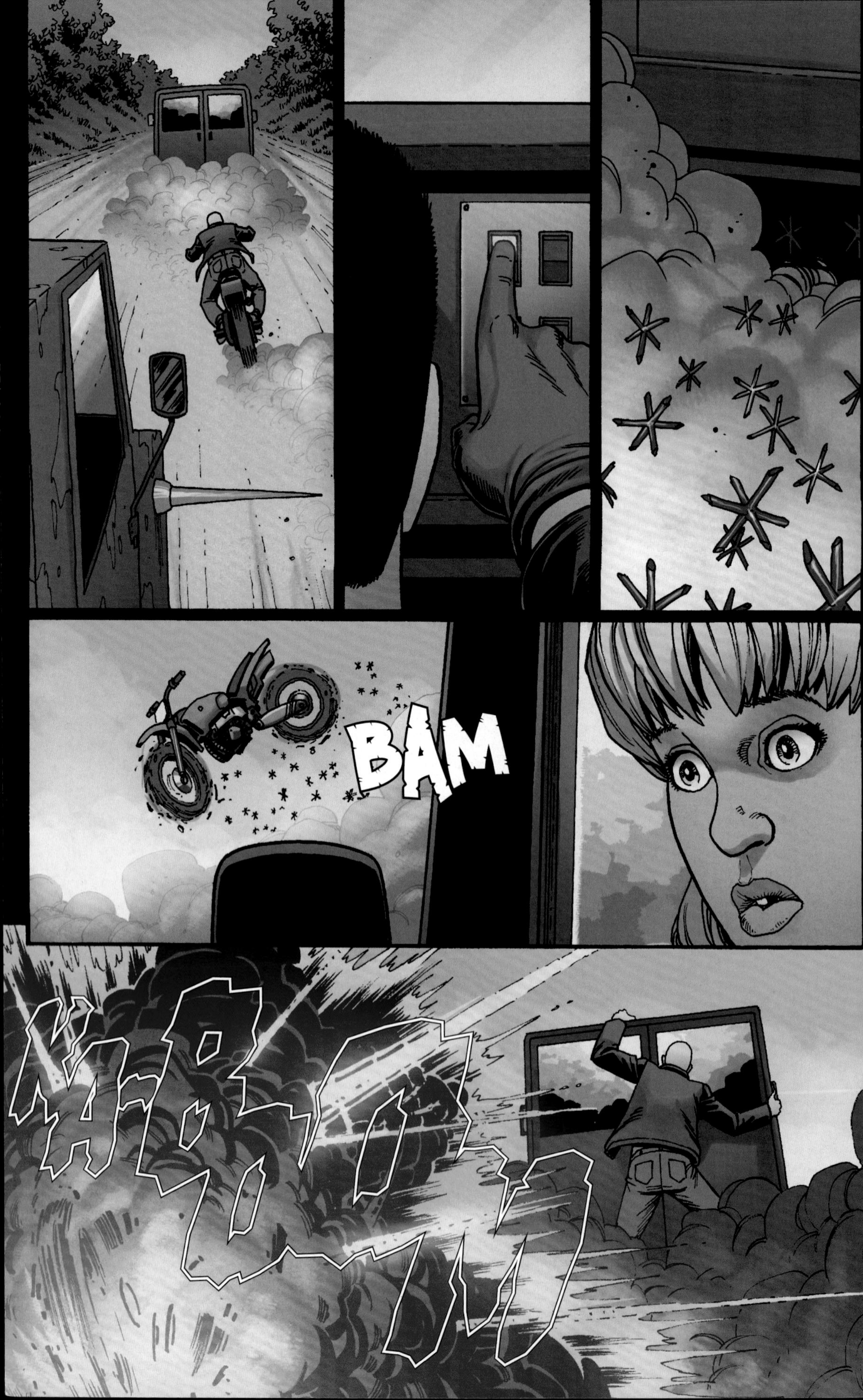
BAM

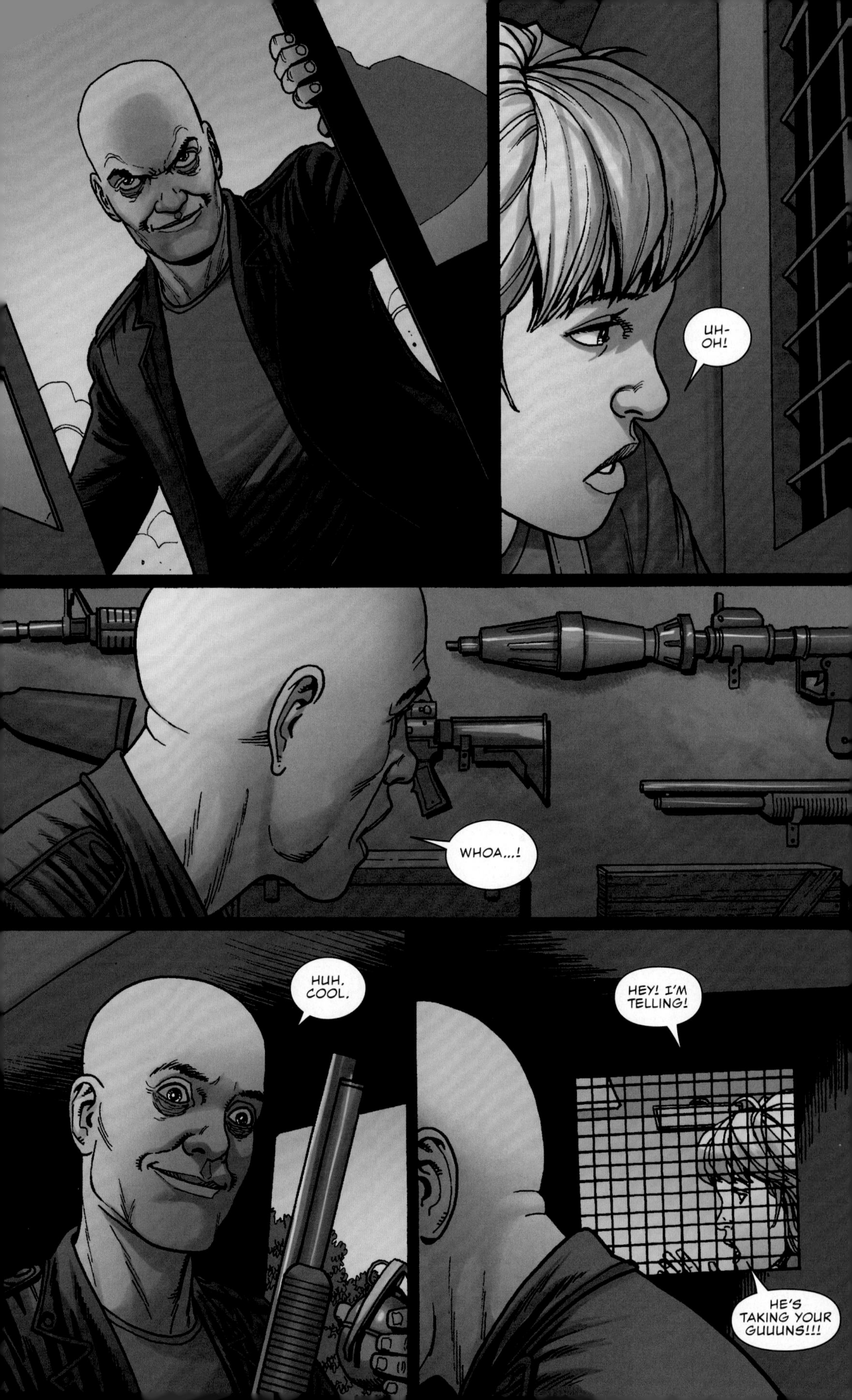
UH-OH!
WHOA...!
HUH. COOL.
HEY! I'M TELLING!
HE'S TAKING YOUR GUUUNS!!!

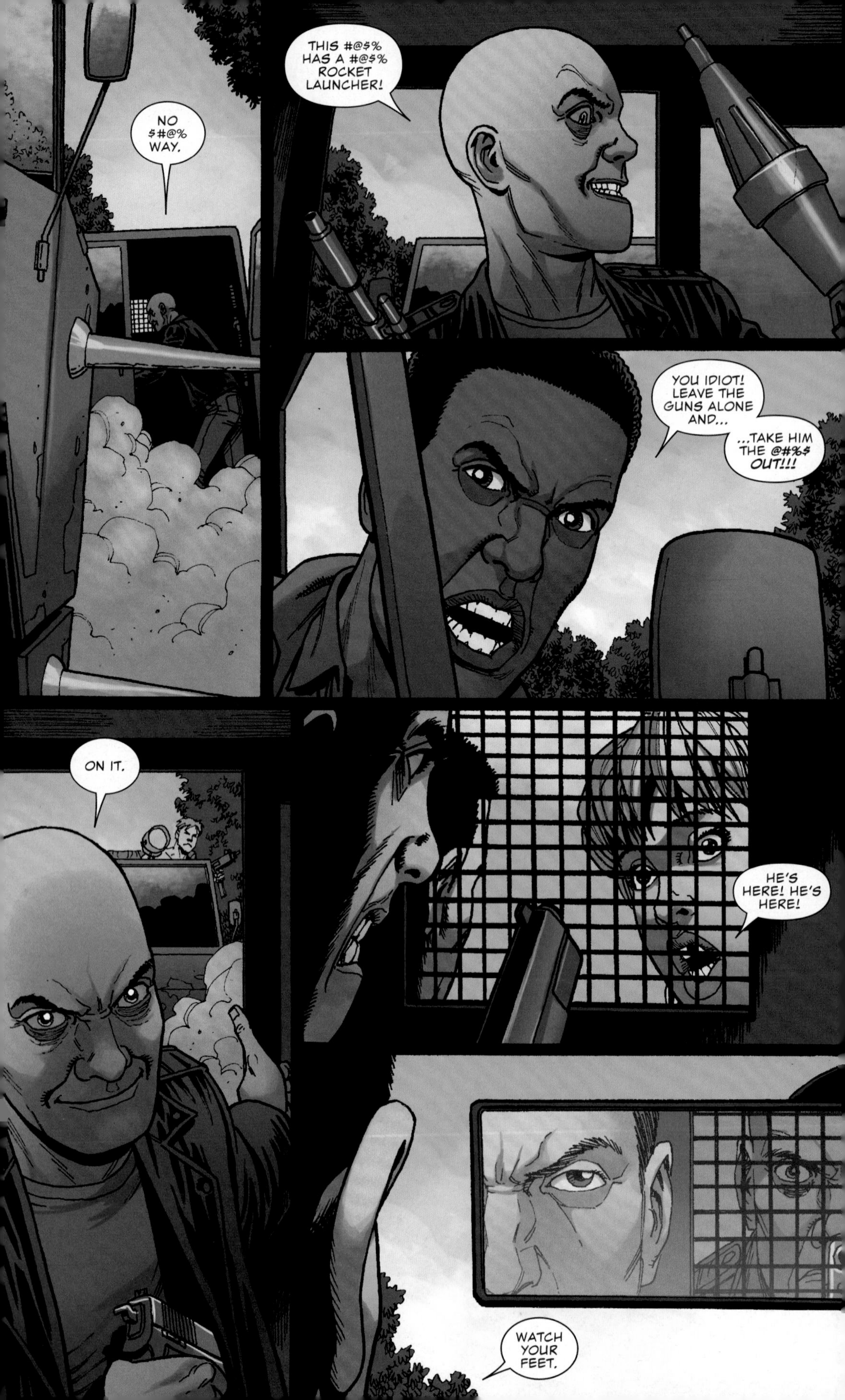
NO $#@% WAY.
THIS #@$% HAS A #@$% ROCKET LAUNCHER!
YOU IDIOT! LEAVE THE GUNS ALONE AND...
...TAKE HIM THE @#%$ OUT!!!
ON IT.
HE'S HERE! HE'S HERE!
WATCH YOUR FEET.

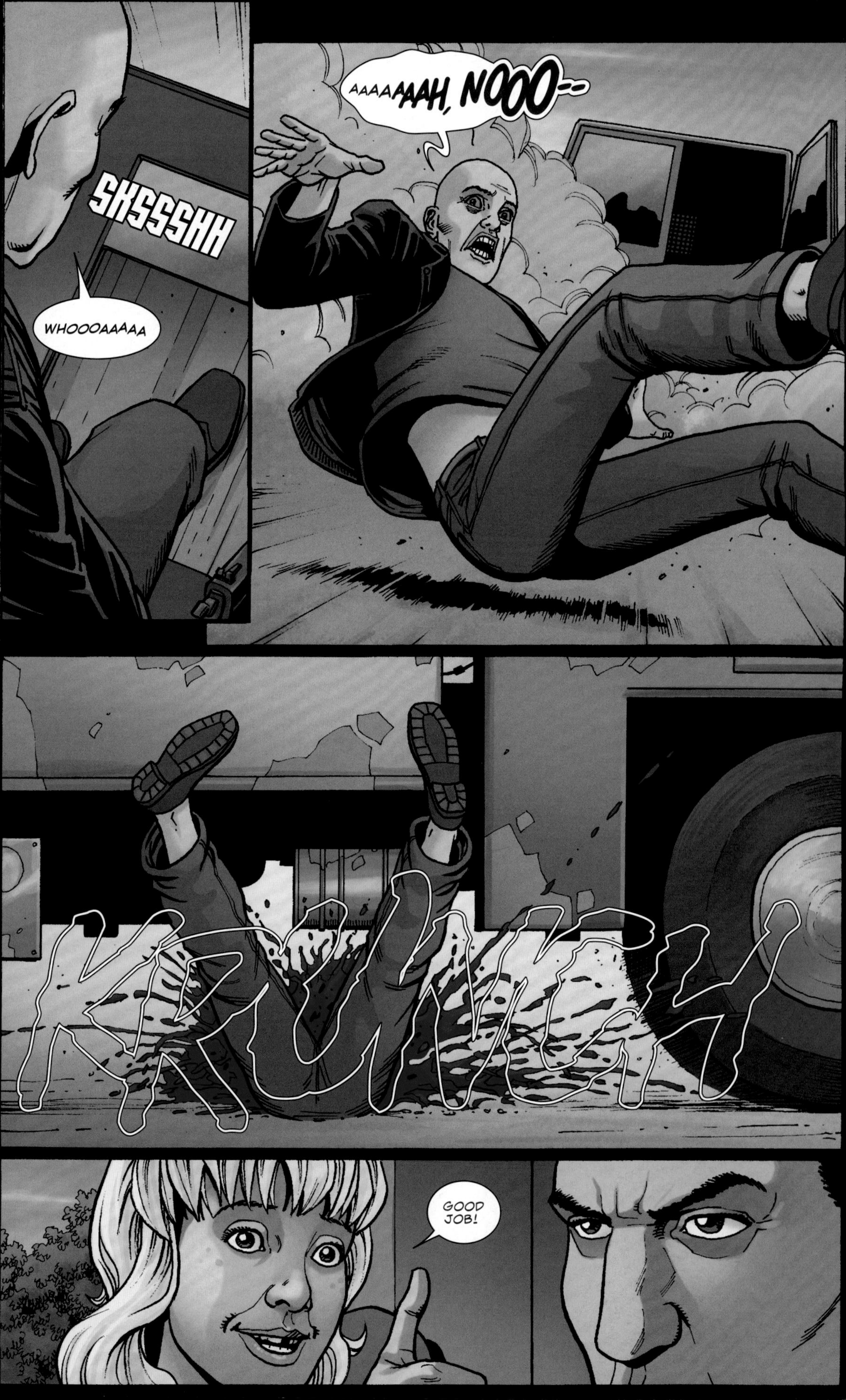
SKSSSHH
WHOOOAAAAA
AAAAAAAH, NOOO--
KRUNCH
GOOD JOB!

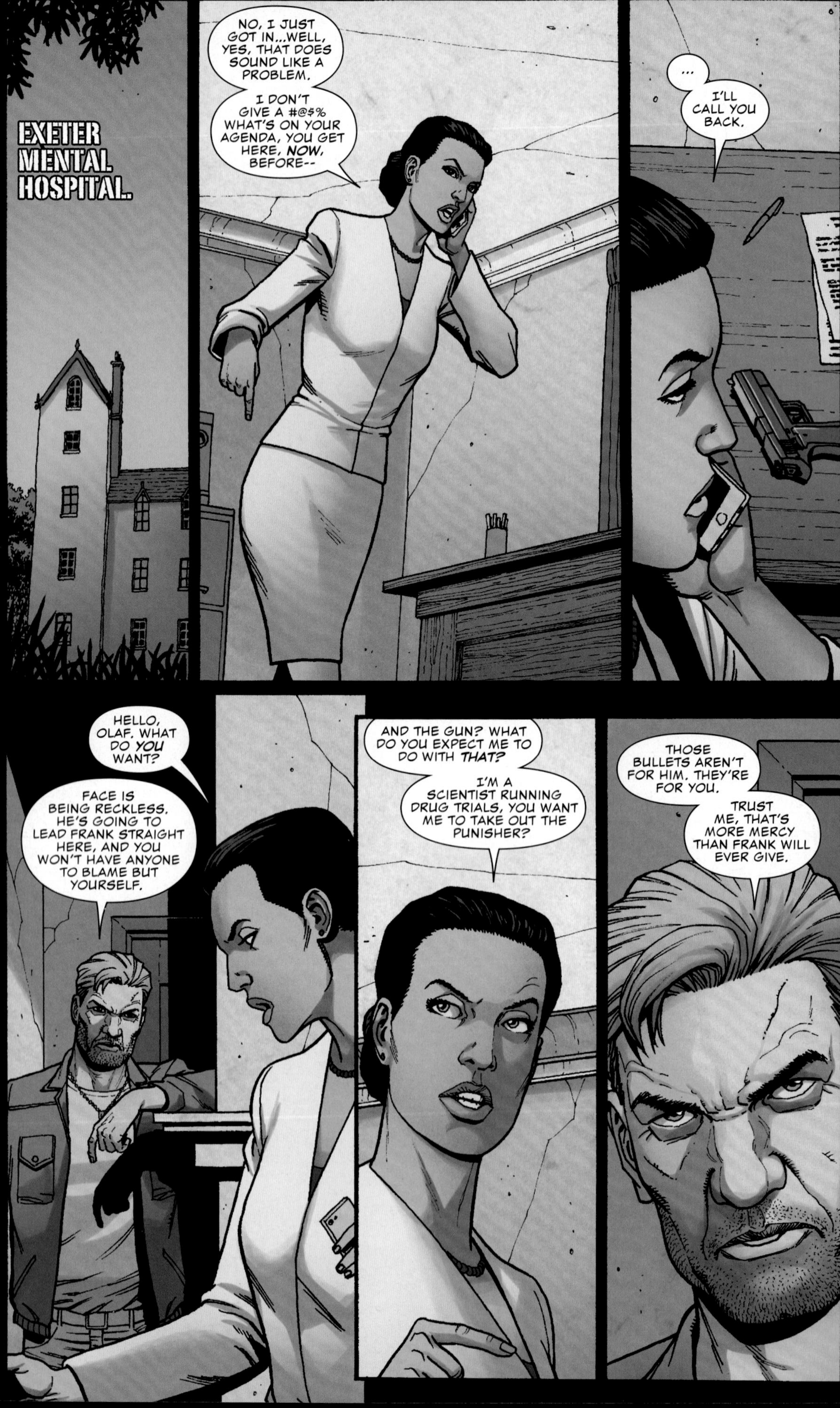
EXETER MENTAL HOSPITAL.
NO, I JUST GOT IN...WELL, YES, THAT DOES SOUND LIKE A PROBLEM.
I DON'T GIVE A #@$% WHAT'S ON YOUR AGENDA, YOU GET HERE, NOW, BEFORE--
...
I'LL CALL YOU BACK.
HELLO, OLAF. WHAT DO YOU WANT?
FACE IS BEING RECKLESS. HE'S GOING TO LEAD FRANK STRAIGHT HERE, AND YOU WON'T HAVE ANYONE TO BLAME BUT YOURSELF.
AND THE GUN? WHAT DO YOU EXPECT ME TO DO WITH THAT?
I'M A SCIENTIST RUNNING DRUG TRIALS, YOU WANT ME TO TAKE OUT THE PUNISHER?
THOSE BULLETS AREN'T FOR HIM. THEY'RE FOR YOU.
TRUST ME, THAT'S MORE MERCY THAN FRANK WILL EVER GIVE.

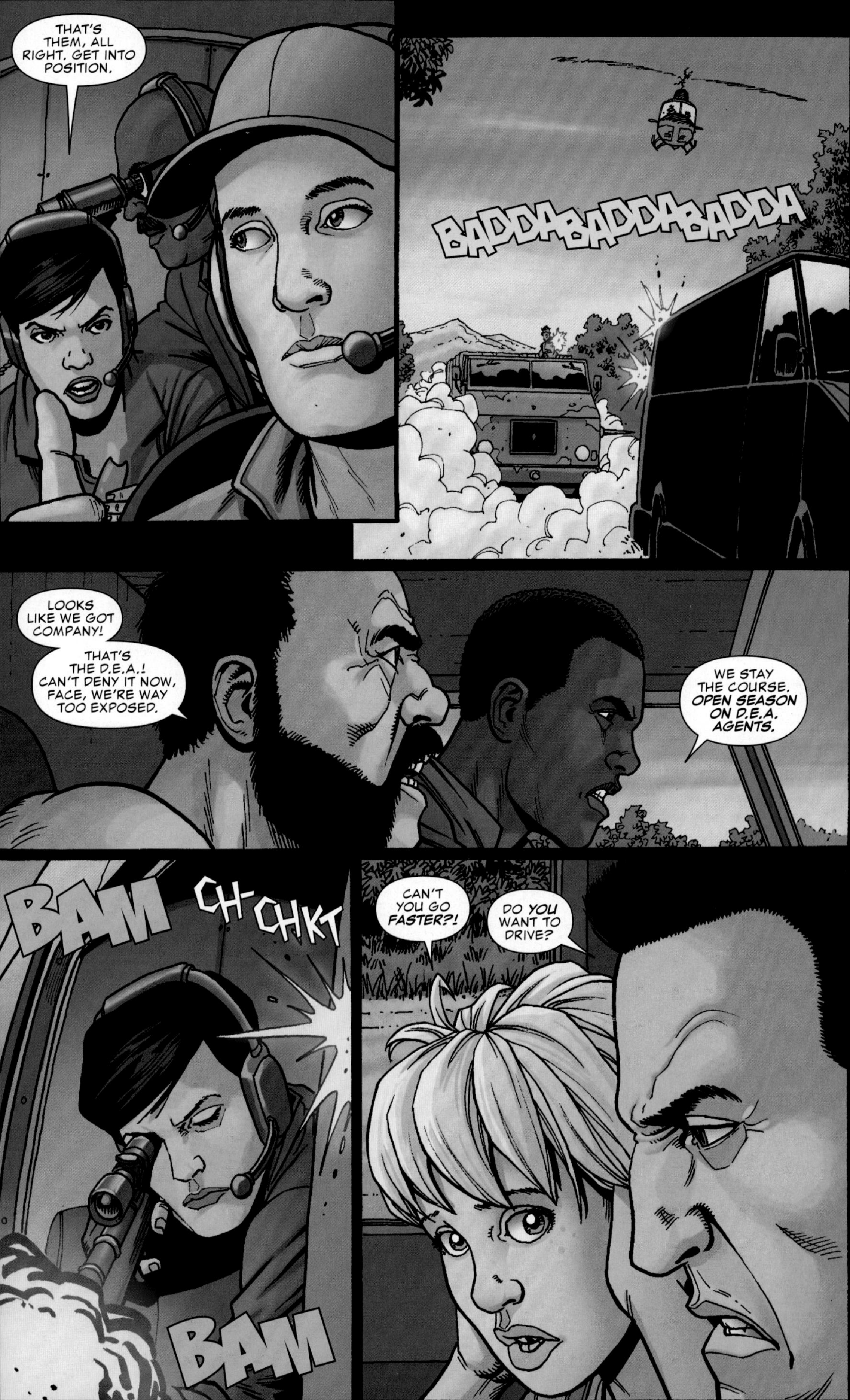
THAT'S THEM, ALL RIGHT. GET INTO POSITION.
BADDABADDABADDA
LOOKS LIKE WE GOT COMPANY!
THAT'S THE D.E.A.! CAN'T DENY IT NOW, FACE, WE'RE WAY TOO EXPOSED.
WE STAY THE COURSE. OPEN SEASON ON D.E.A. AGENTS.
BAM
CH-CHKT
BAM
CAN'T YOU GO FASTER?!
DO YOU WANT TO DRIVE?

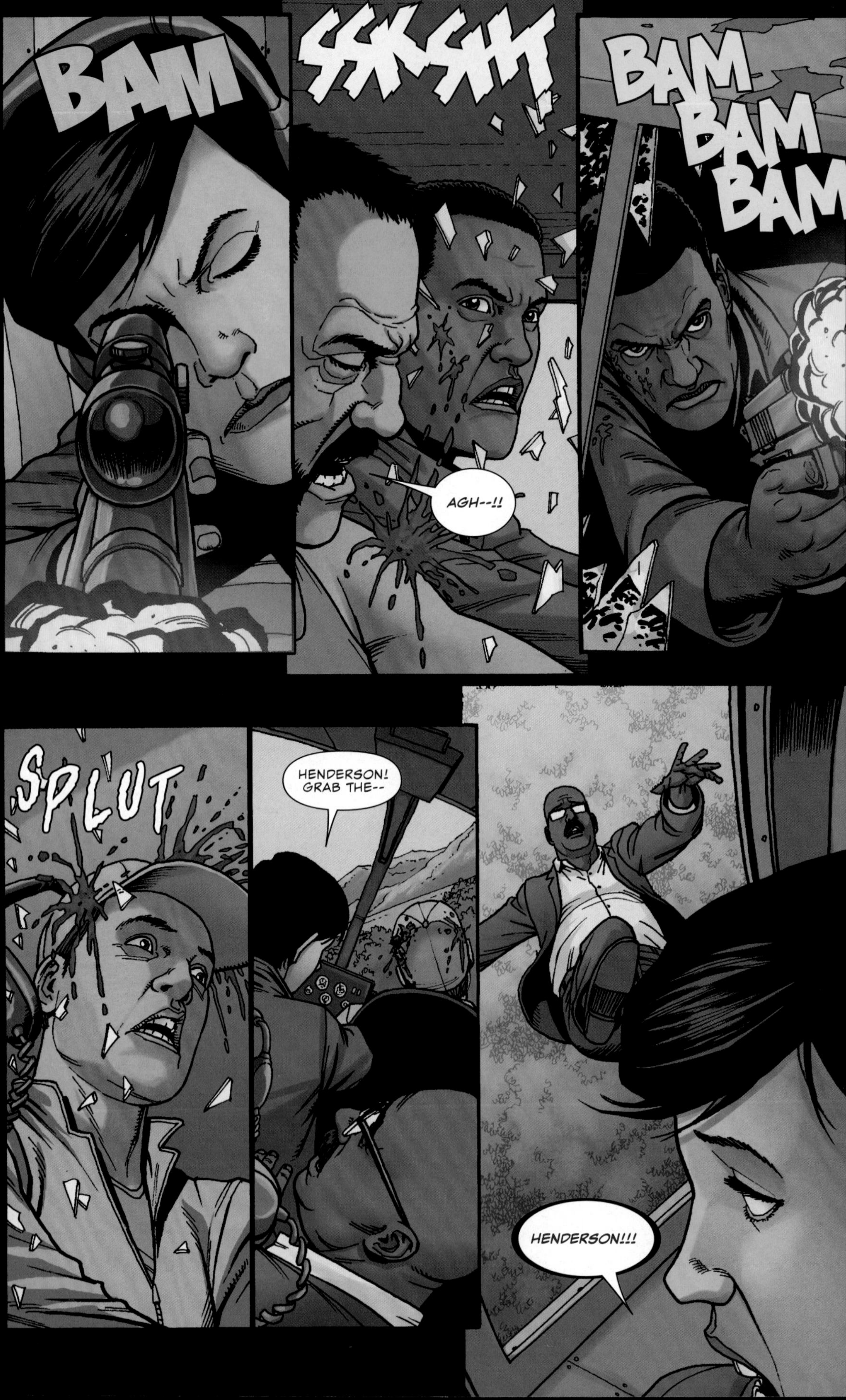
BAM
SSKSHT
AGH--!!
BAM
BAM
BAM
SPLUT
HENDERSON! GRAB THE--
HENDERSON!!!

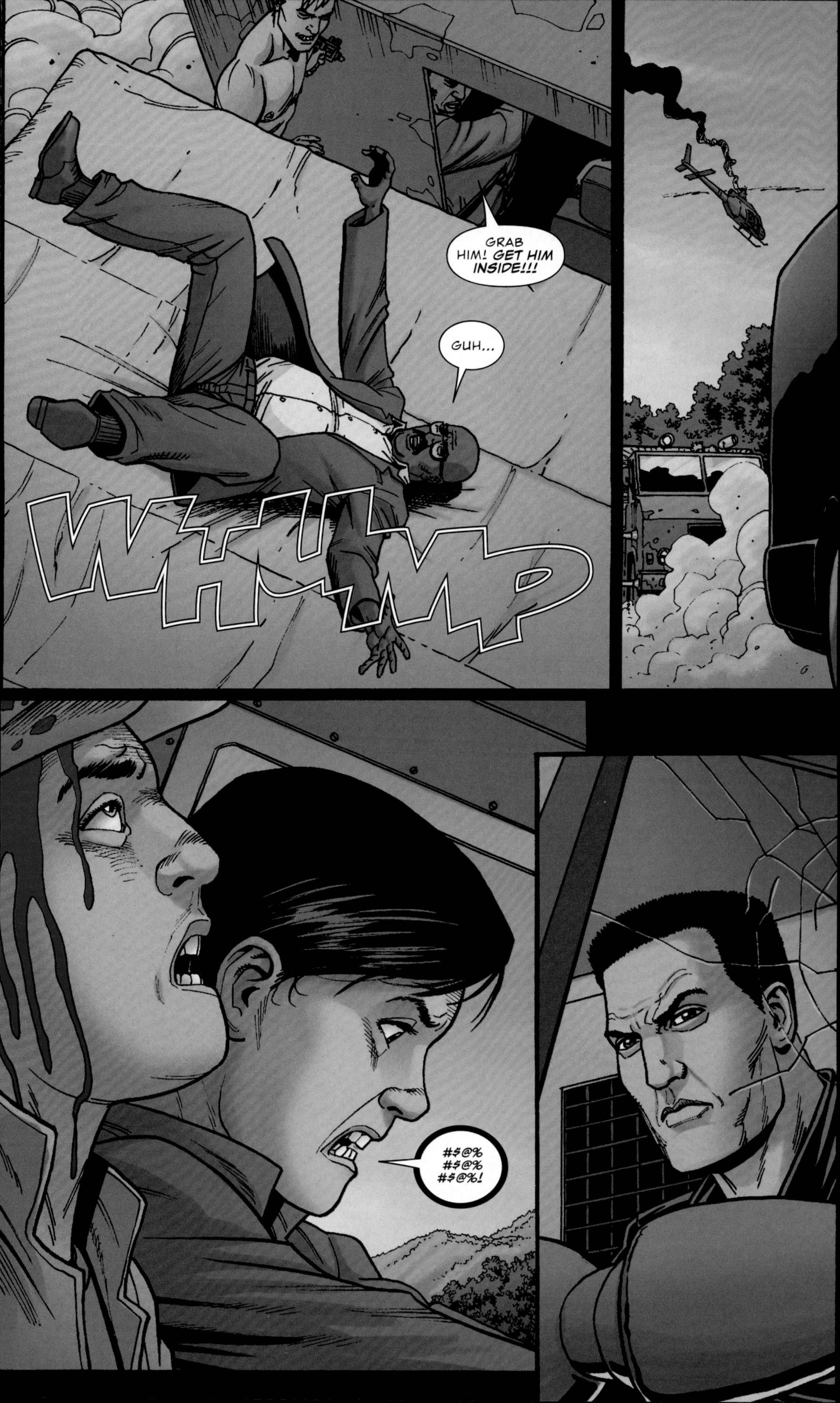
GRAB HIM! GET HIM INSIDE!!!
GUH...
WHUMP
#$@% #$@% #$@%!

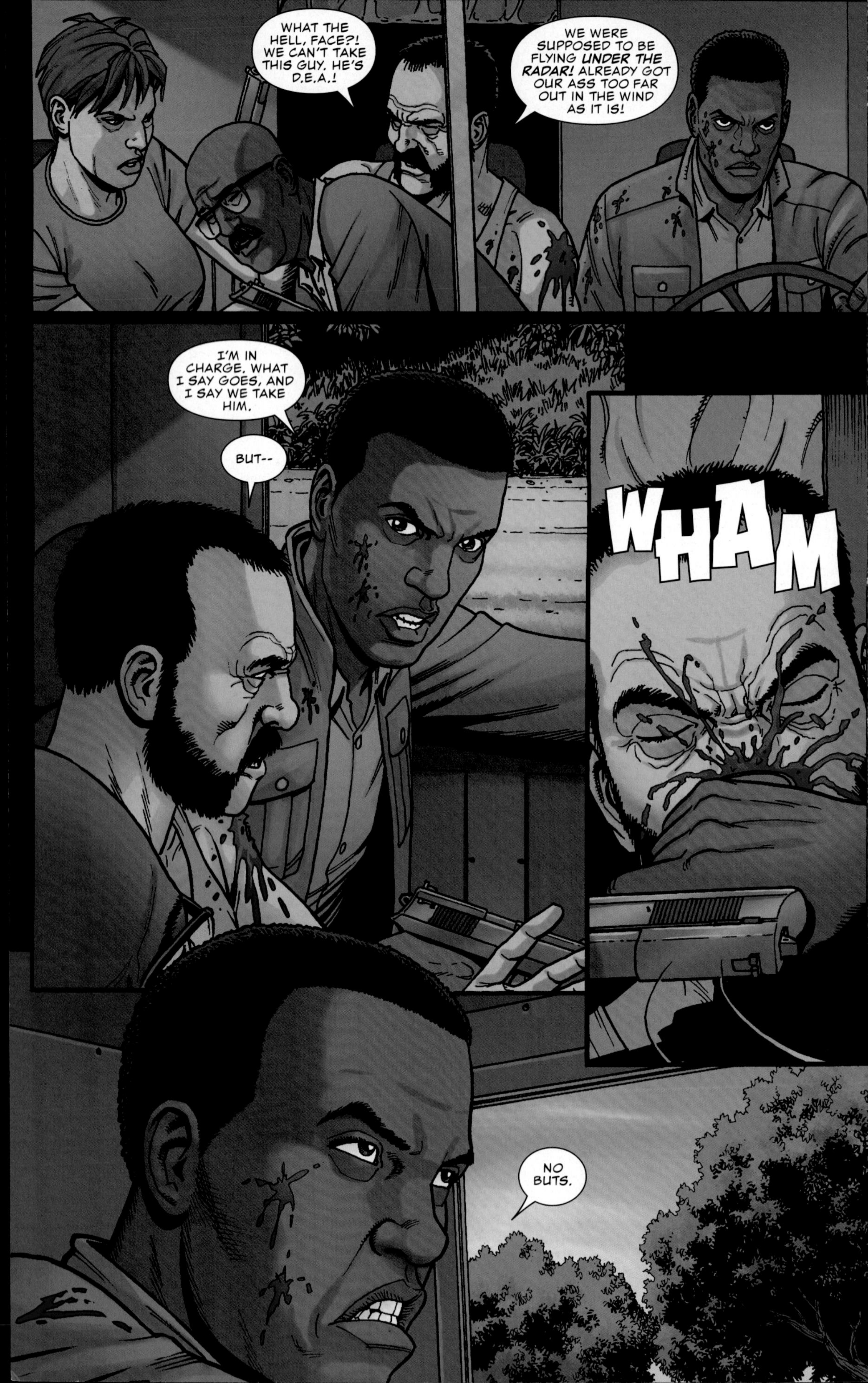
WHAT THE HELL, FACE?! WE CAN'T TAKE THIS GUY. HE'S D.E.A.!
WE WERE SUPPOSED TO BE FLYING UNDER THE RADAR! ALREADY GOT OUR ASS TOO FAR OUT IN THE WIND AS IT IS!
I'M IN CHARGE. WHAT I SAY GOES, AND I SAY WE TAKE HIM.
BUT--
WHAM
NO BUTS.

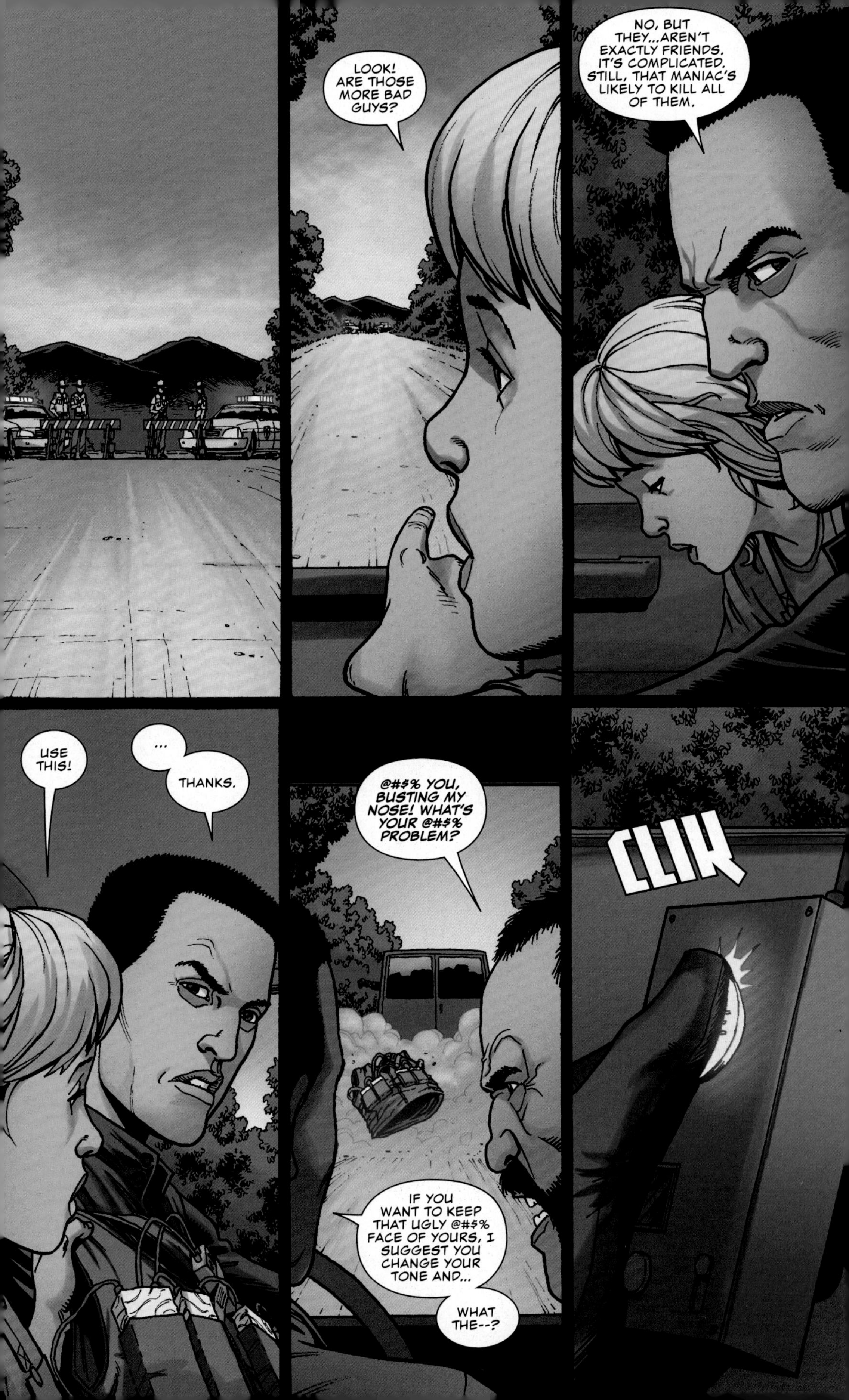
LOOK! ARE THOSE MORE BAD GUYS?
NO, BUT THEY...AREN'T EXACTLY FRIENDS. IT'S COMPLICATED. STILL, THAT MANIAC'S LIKELY TO KILL ALL OF THEM.
USE THIS!
...
THANKS.
@#$% YOU, BUSTING MY NOSE! WHAT'S YOUR @#$% PROBLEM?
IF YOU WANT TO KEEP THAT UGLY @#$% FACE OF YOURS, I SUGGEST YOU CHANGE YOUR TONE AND...
WHAT THE--?
CLIK

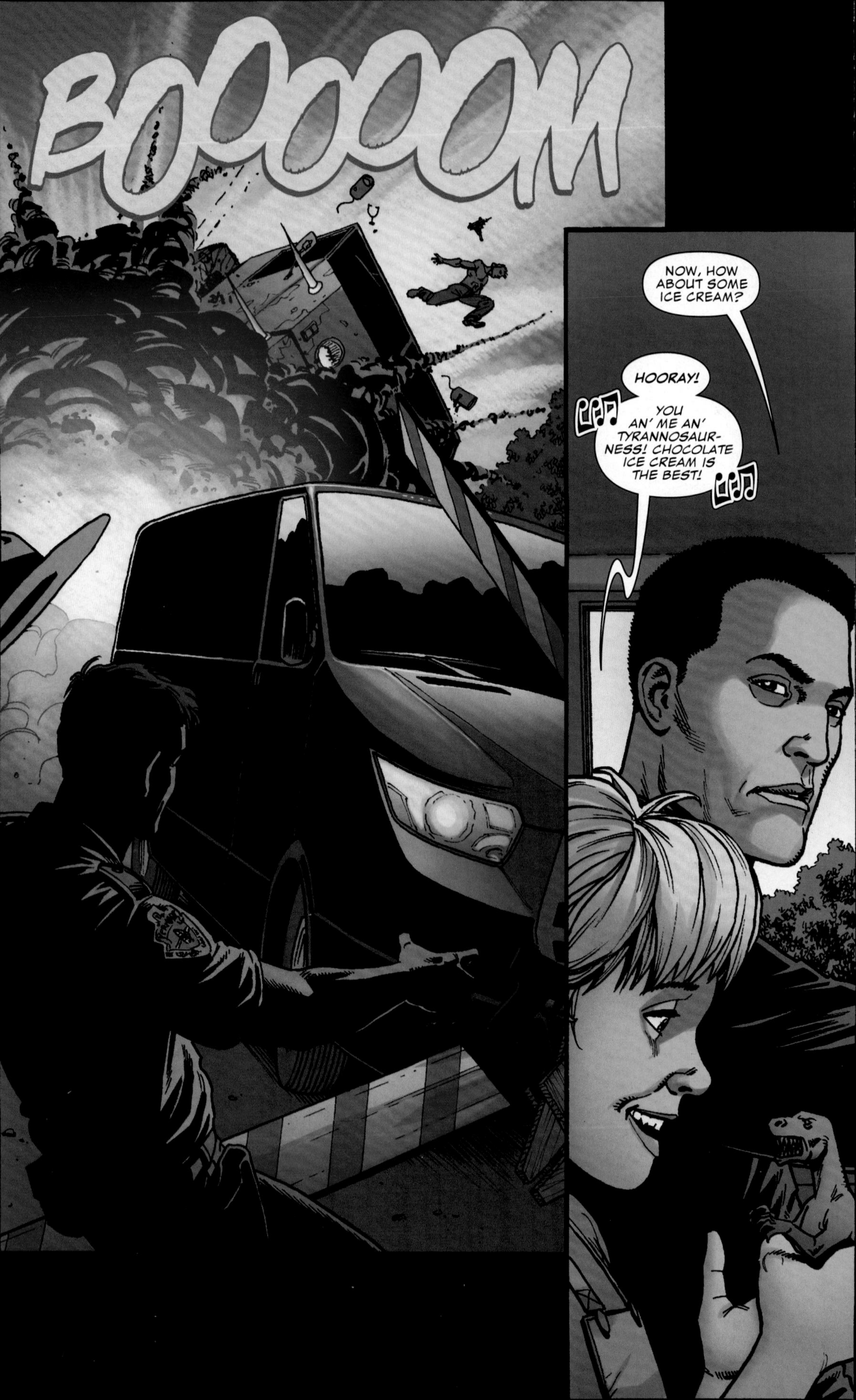
BOOOOOM
NOW, HOW ABOUT SOME ICE CREAM?
HOORAY!
YOU AN' ME AN' TYRANNOSAUR-NESS! CHOCOLATE ICE CREAM IS THE BEST!

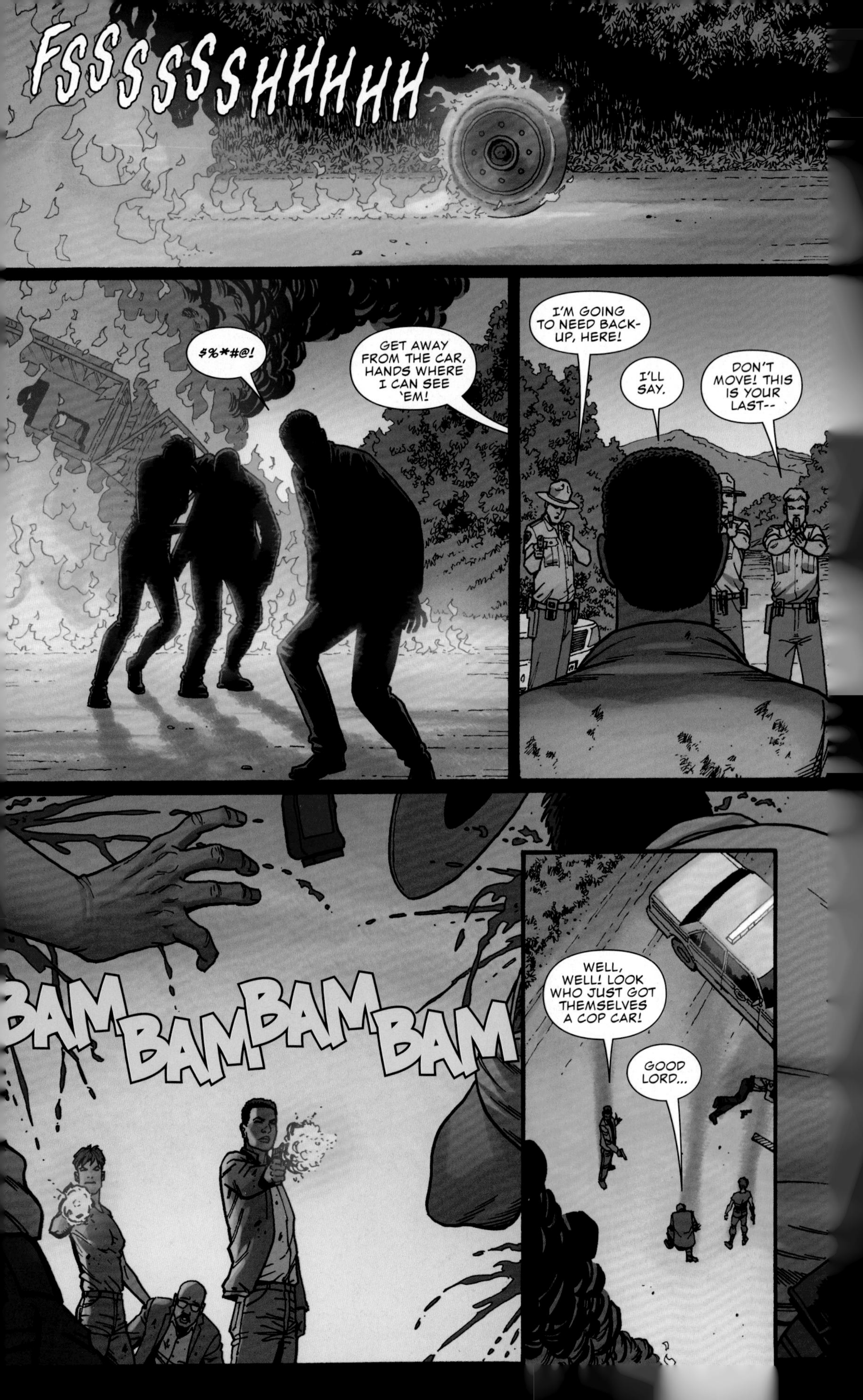
FSSSSSSHHHHH
$%*#@!
GET AWAY FROM THE CAR, HANDS WHERE I CAN SEE 'EM!
I'M GOING TO NEED BACK-UP, HERE!
I'LL SAY.
DON'T MOVE! THIS IS YOUR LAST--
BAM BAM BAM BAM
WELL, WELL! LOOK WHO JUST GOT THEMSELVES A COP CAR!
GOOD LORD...

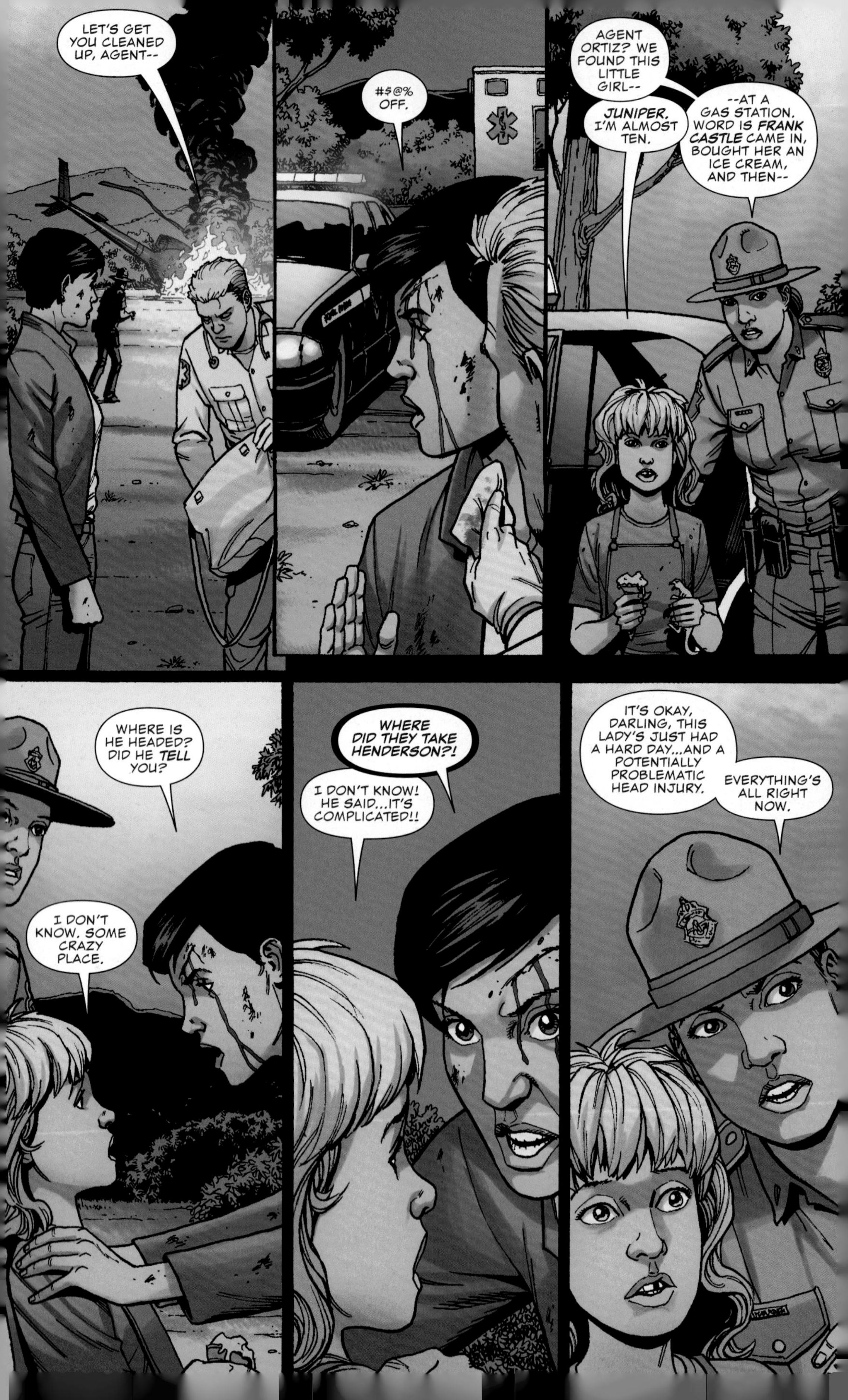
LET'S GET YOU CLEANED UP, AGENT--
#$@% OFF.
AGENT ORTIZ? WE FOUND THIS LITTLE GIRL--
JUNIPER. I'M ALMOST TEN.
--AT A GAS STATION. WORD IS FRANK CASTLE CAME IN, BOUGHT HER AN ICE CREAM, AND THEN--
WHERE IS HE HEADED? DID HE TELL YOU?
I DON'T KNOW. SOME CRAZY PLACE.
WHERE DID THEY TAKE HENDERSON?!
I DON'T KNOW! HE SAID...IT'S COMPLICATED!!
IT'S OKAY, DARLING, THIS LADY'S JUST HAD A HARD DAY...AND A POTENTIALLY PROBLEMATIC HEAD INJURY.
EVERYTHING'S ALL RIGHT NOW.

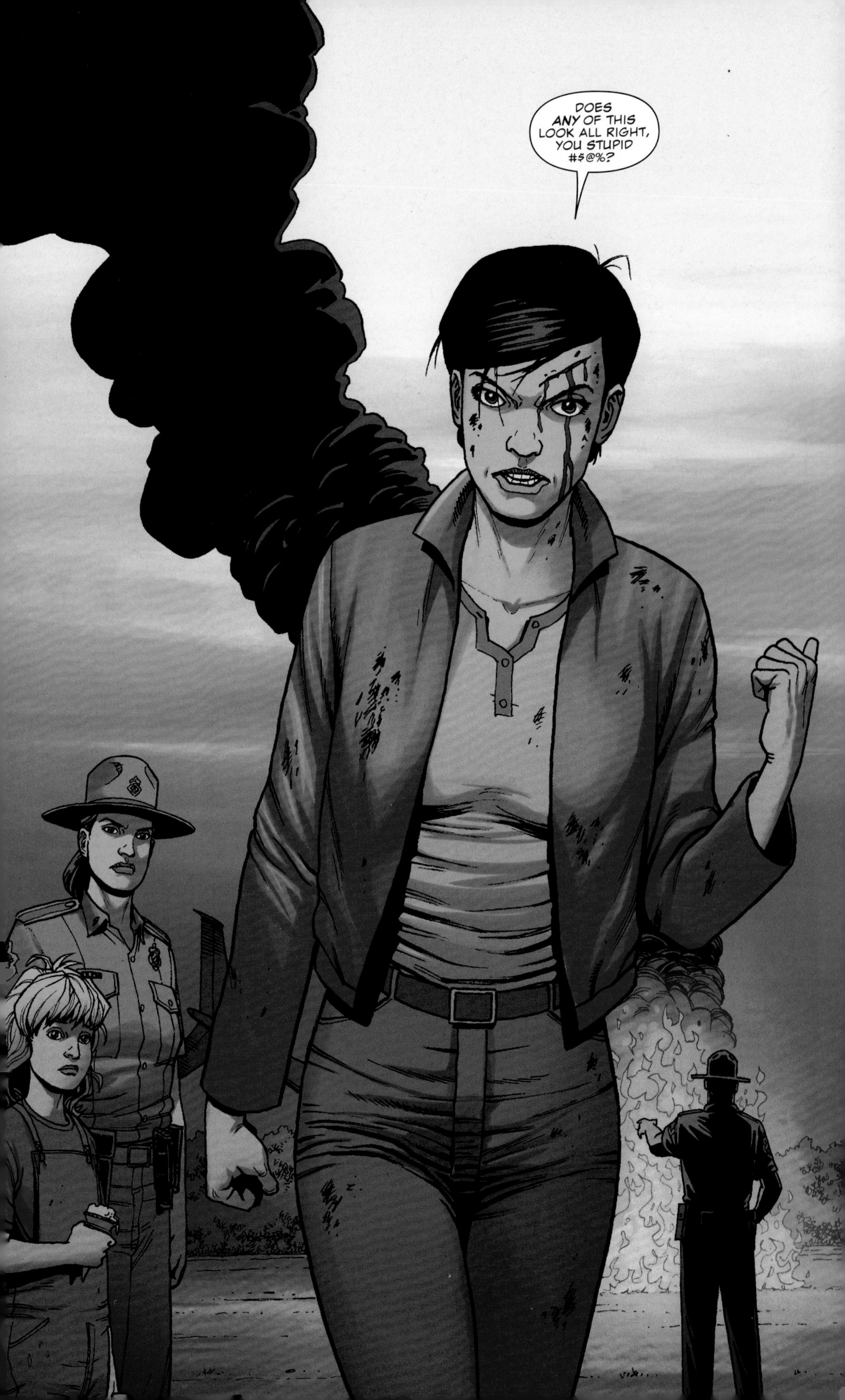
DOES ANY OF THIS LOOK ALL RIGHT, YOU STUPID #$@%?

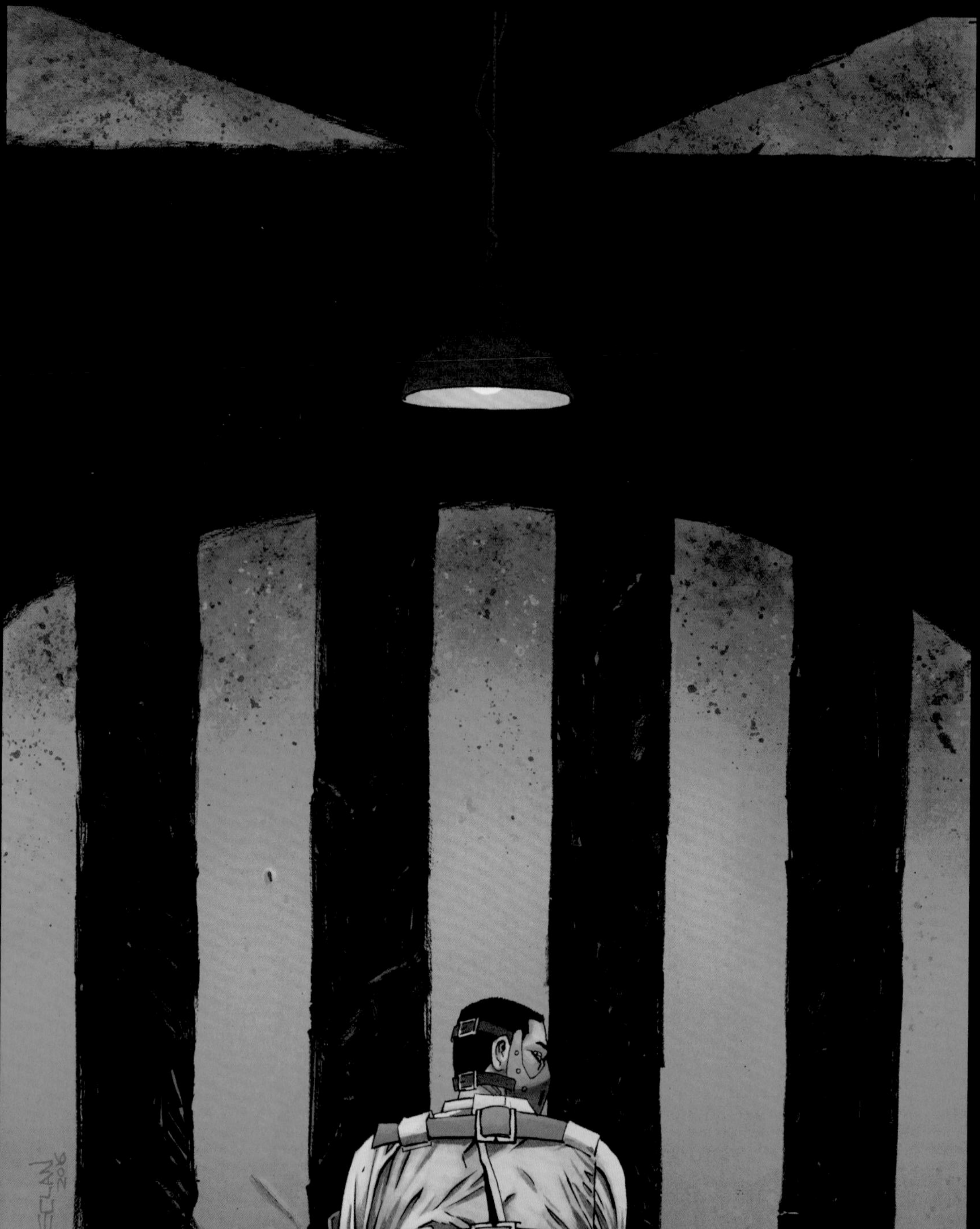

5

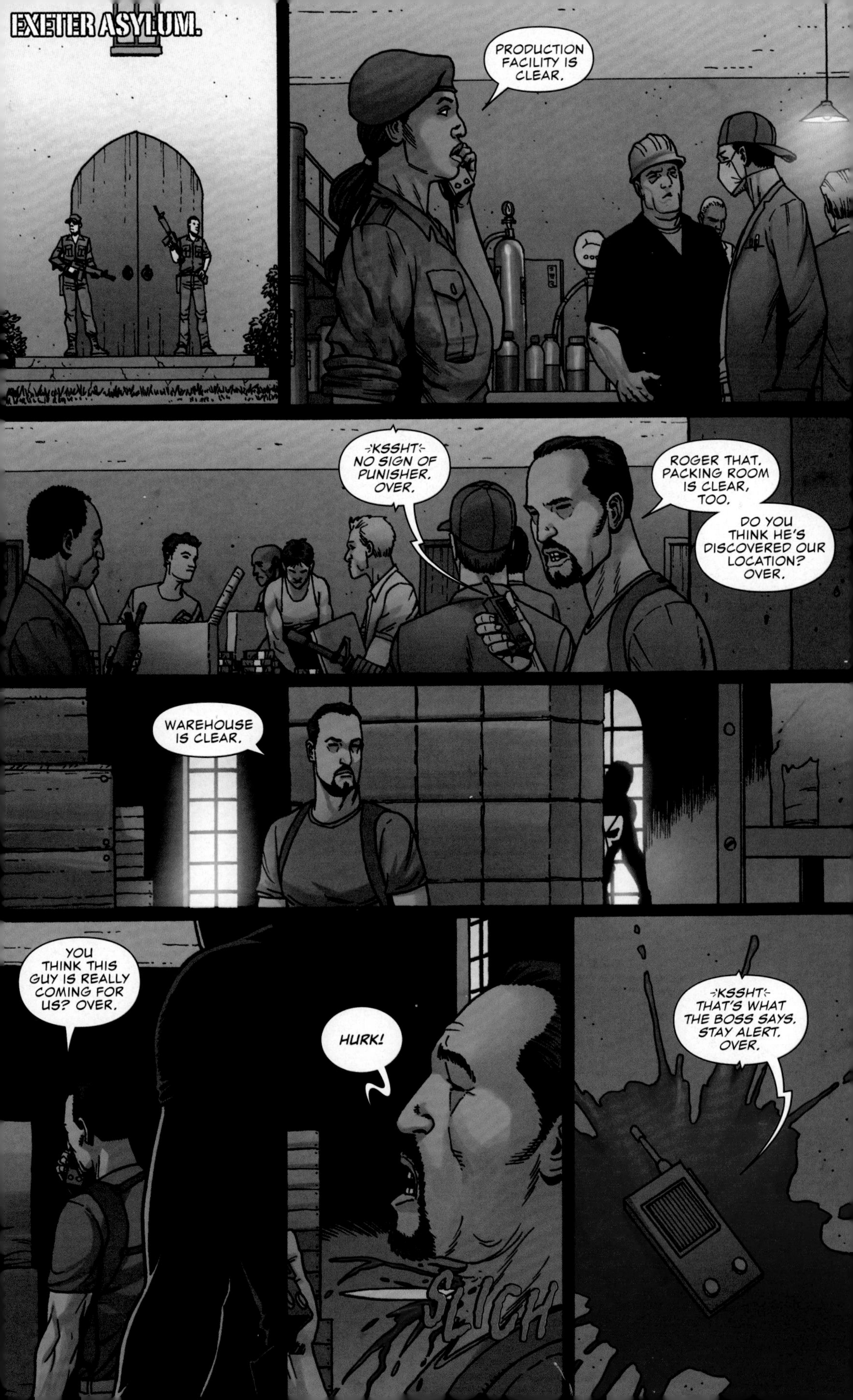
EXETER ASYLUM.
PRODUCTION FACILITY IS CLEAR.
-KSSHT- NO SIGN OF PUNISHER. OVER.
ROGER THAT. PACKING ROOM IS CLEAR, TOO.
DO YOU THINK HE'S DISCOVERED OUR LOCATION? OVER.
WAREHOUSE IS CLEAR.
YOU THINK THIS GUY IS REALLY COMING FOR US? OVER.
HURK!
SLICH
-KSSHT- THAT'S WHAT THE BOSS SAYS. STAY ALERT. OVER.

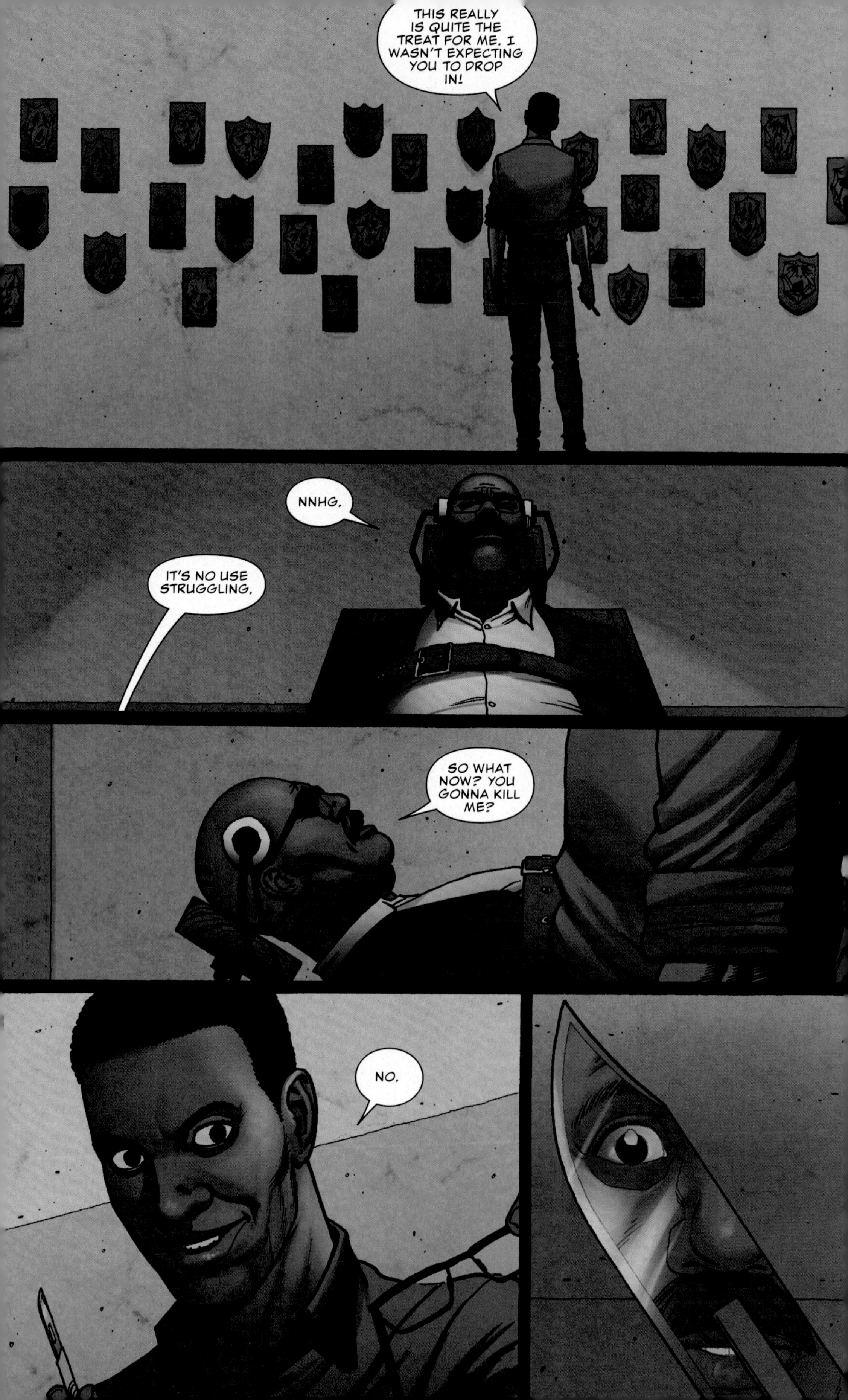
THIS REALLY IS QUITE THE TREAT FOR ME. I WASN'T EXPECTING YOU TO DROP IN!
NNHG.
IT'S NO USE STRUGGLING.
SO WHAT NOW? YOU GONNA KILL ME?
NO.

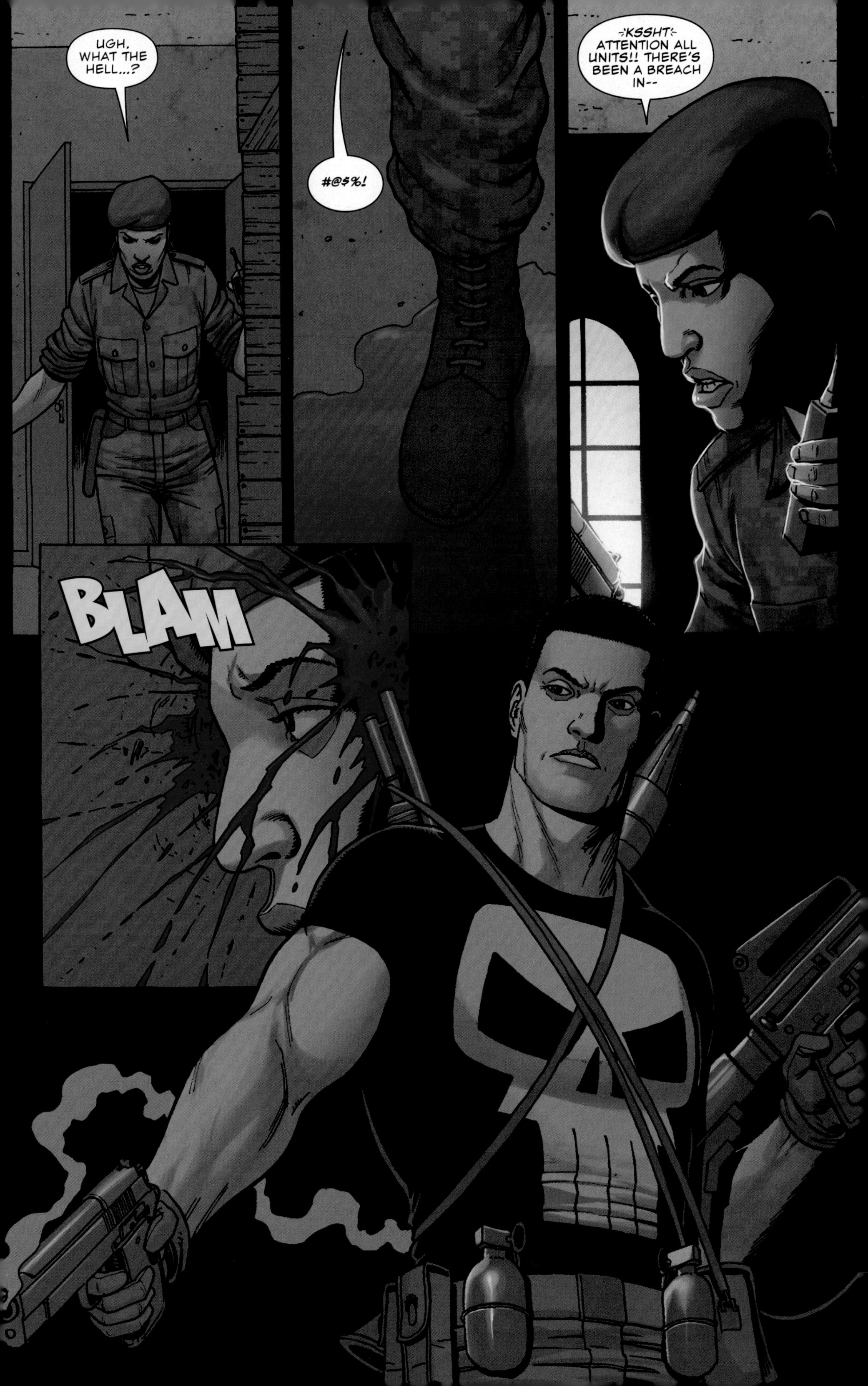
UGH. WHAT THE HELL...?
#@$%!
-KSSHT- ATTENTION ALL UNITS!! THERE'S BEEN A BREACH IN--
BLAM

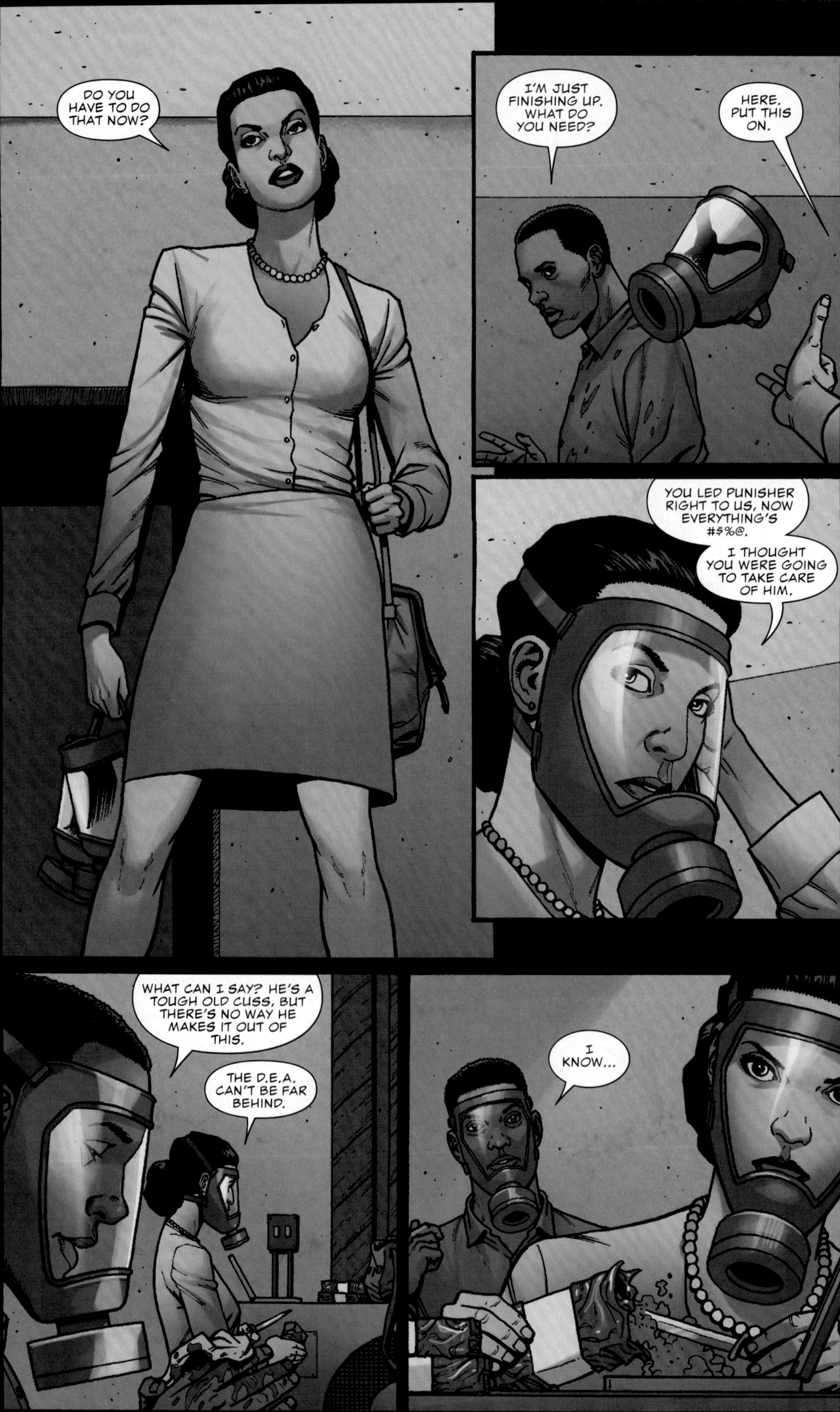
DO YOU HAVE TO DO THAT NOW?
I'M JUST FINISHING UP. WHAT DO YOU NEED?
HERE. PUT THIS ON.
YOU LED PUNISHER RIGHT TO US, NOW EVERYTHING'S #$%@.
I THOUGHT YOU WERE GOING TO TAKE CARE OF HIM.
WHAT CAN I SAY? HE'S A TOUGH OLD CUSS, BUT THERE'S NO WAY HE MAKES IT OUT OF THIS.
THE D.E.A. CAN'T BE FAR BEHIND.
I KNOW...

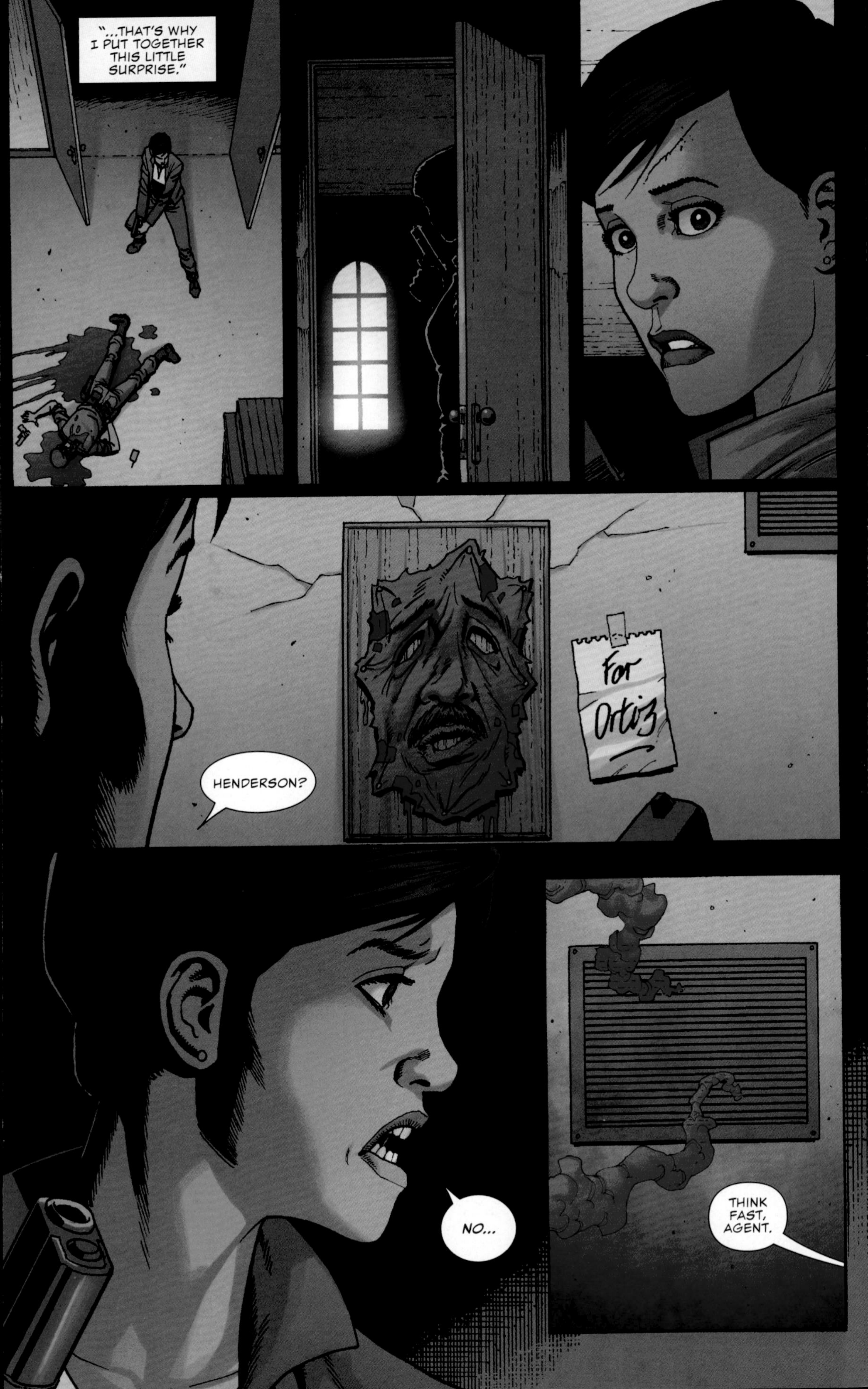
"...THAT'S WHY I PUT TOGETHER THIS LITTLE SURPRISE."
For Ortiz
HENDERSON?
NO...
THINK FAST, AGENT.

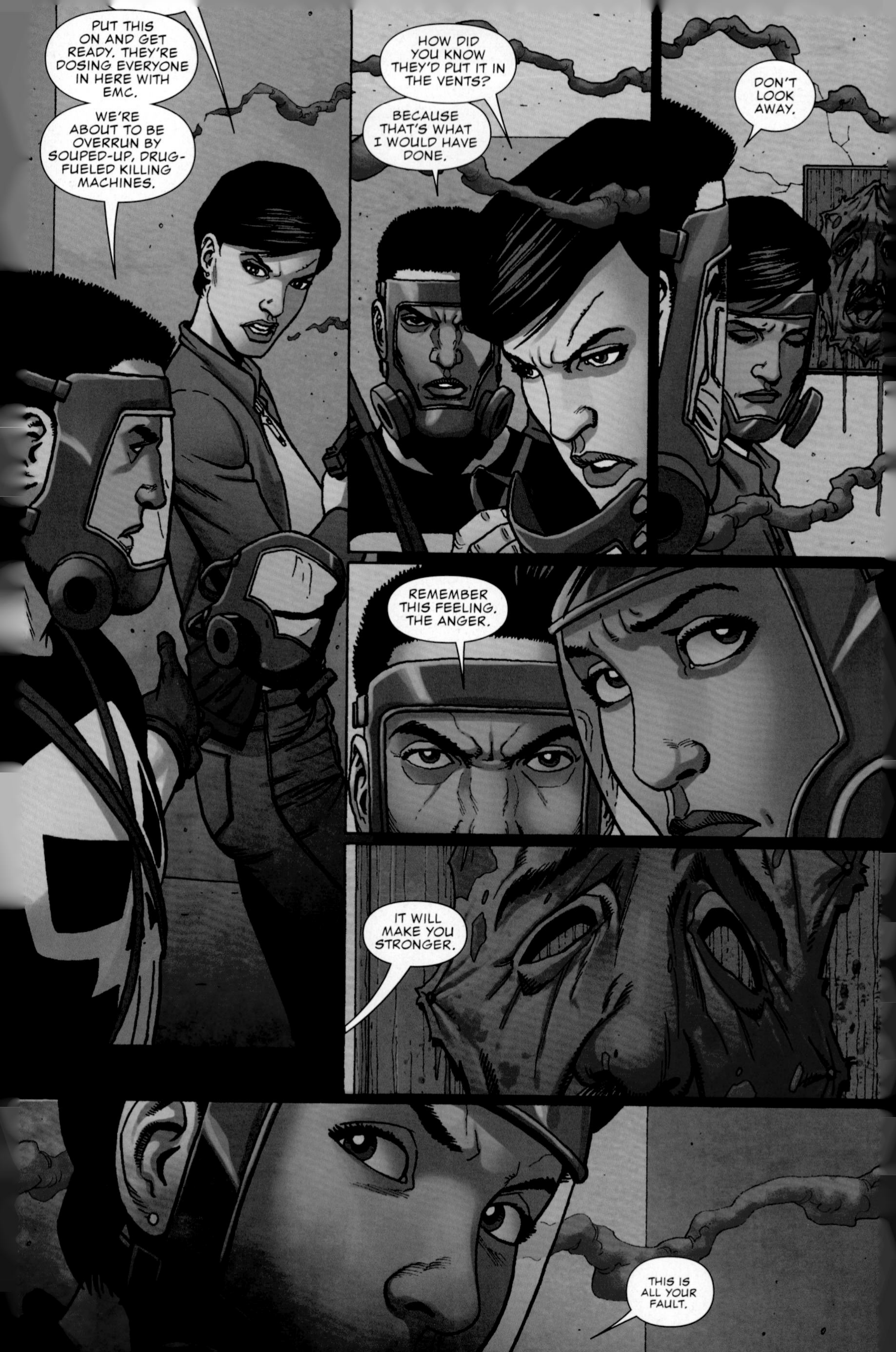
PUT THIS ON AND GET READY. THEY'RE DOSING EVERYONE IN HERE WITH EMC.
WE'RE ABOUT TO BE OVERRUN BY SOUPED-UP, DRUG-FUELED KILLING MACHINES.
HOW DID YOU KNOW THEY'D PUT IT IN THE VENTS?
BECAUSE THAT'S WHAT I WOULD HAVE DONE.
DON'T LOOK AWAY.
REMEMBER THIS FEELING. THE ANGER.
IT WILL MAKE YOU STRONGER.
THIS IS ALL YOUR FAULT.

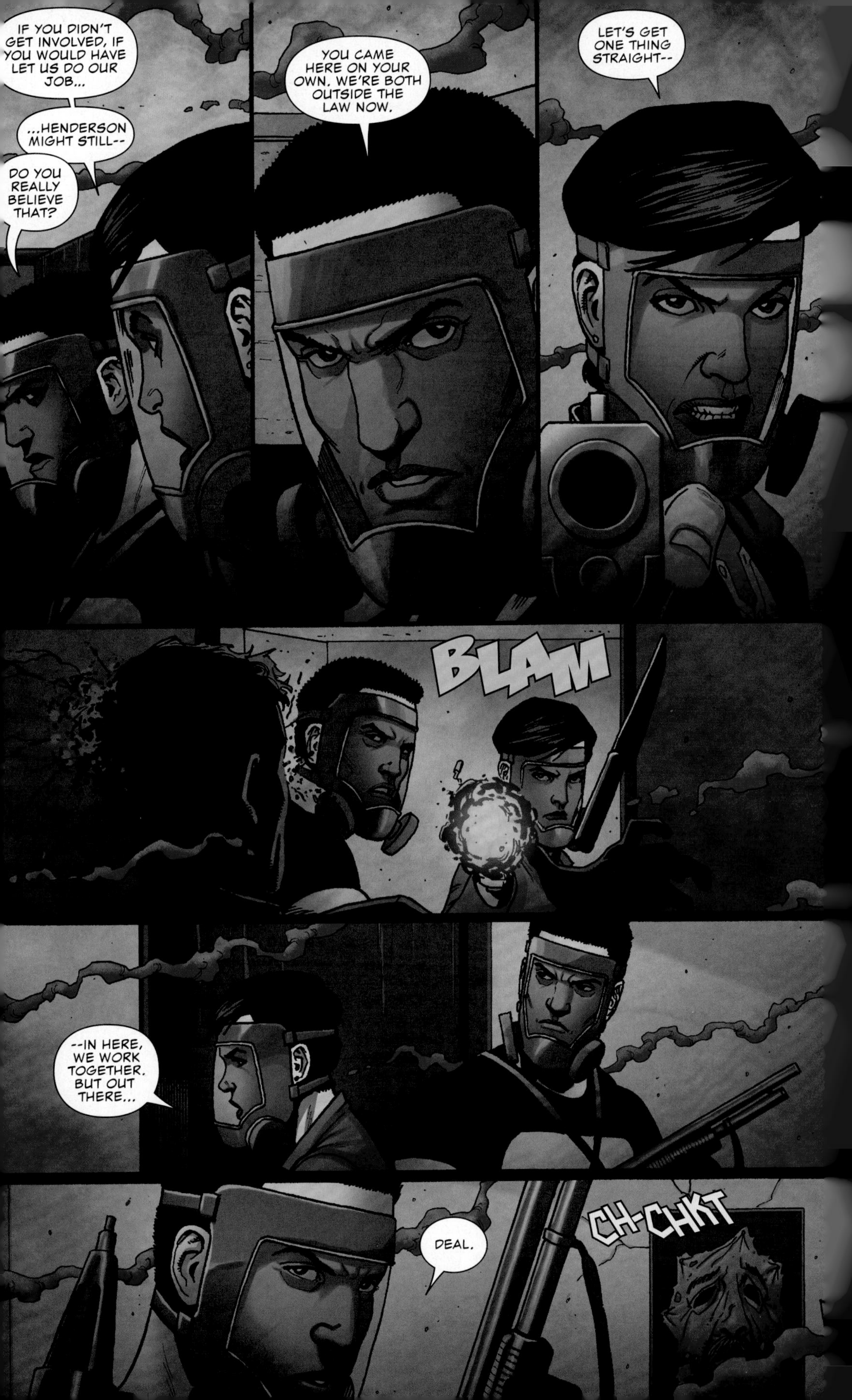

IF YOU DIDN'T GET INVOLVED, IF YOU WOULD HAVE LET US DO OUR JOB...
...HENDERSON MIGHT STILL--
DO YOU REALLY BELIEVE THAT?
YOU CAME HERE ON YOUR OWN. WE'RE BOTH OUTSIDE THE LAW NOW.
LET'S GET ONE THING STRAIGHT--
BLAM
--IN HERE, WE WORK TOGETHER. BUT OUT THERE...
DEAL.
CH-CHKT

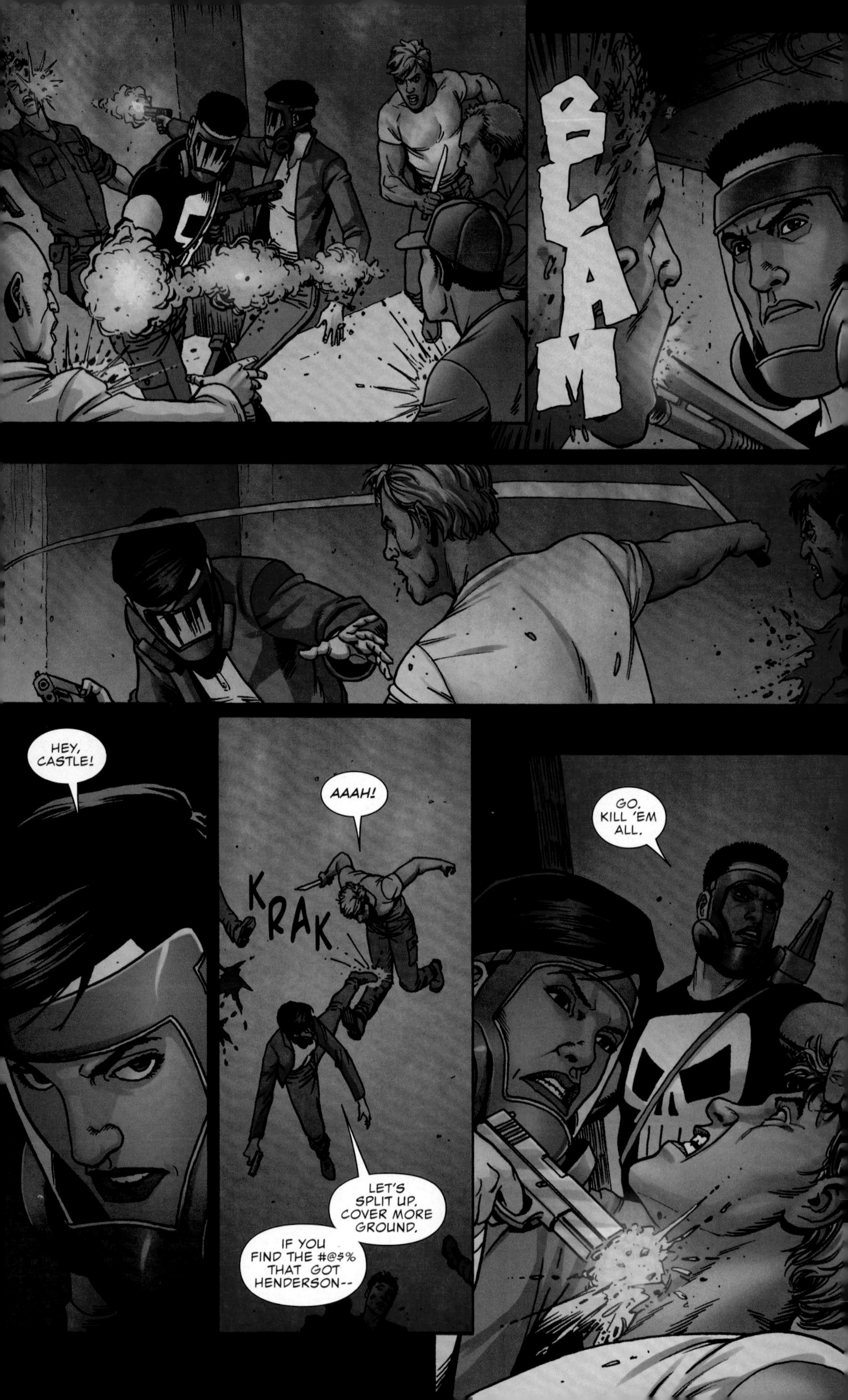

BLAM
HEY, CASTLE!
AAAH!
KRAK
LET'S SPLIT UP. COVER MORE GROUND.
IF YOU FIND THE #@$% THAT GOT HENDERSON--
GO. KILL 'EM ALL.

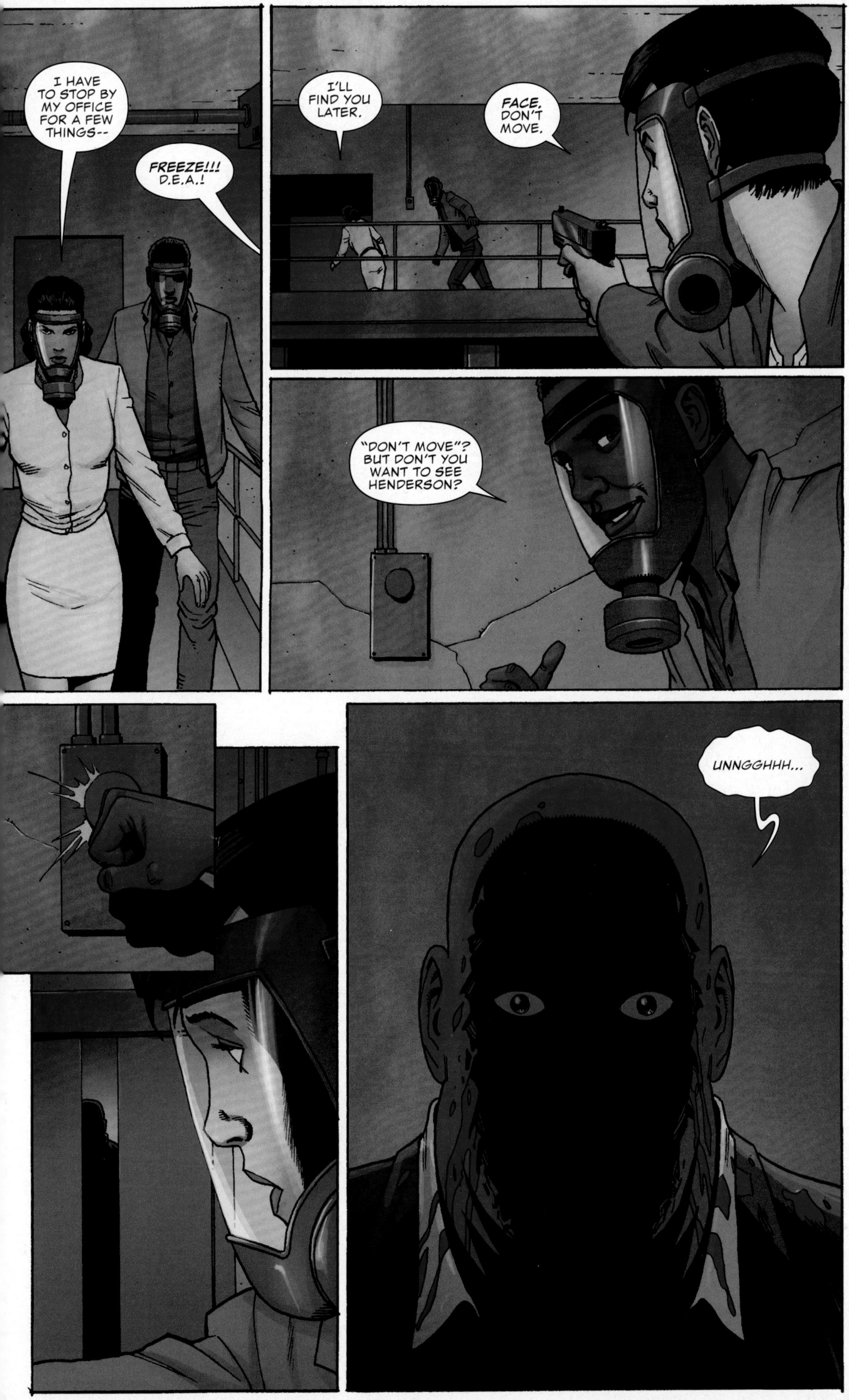
I HAVE TO STOP BY MY OFFICE FOR A FEW THINGS--
FREEZE!!! D.E.A.!
I'LL FIND YOU LATER.
FACE. DON'T MOVE.
"DON'T MOVE"? BUT DON'T YOU WANT TO SEE HENDERSON?
UNNGGHHH...

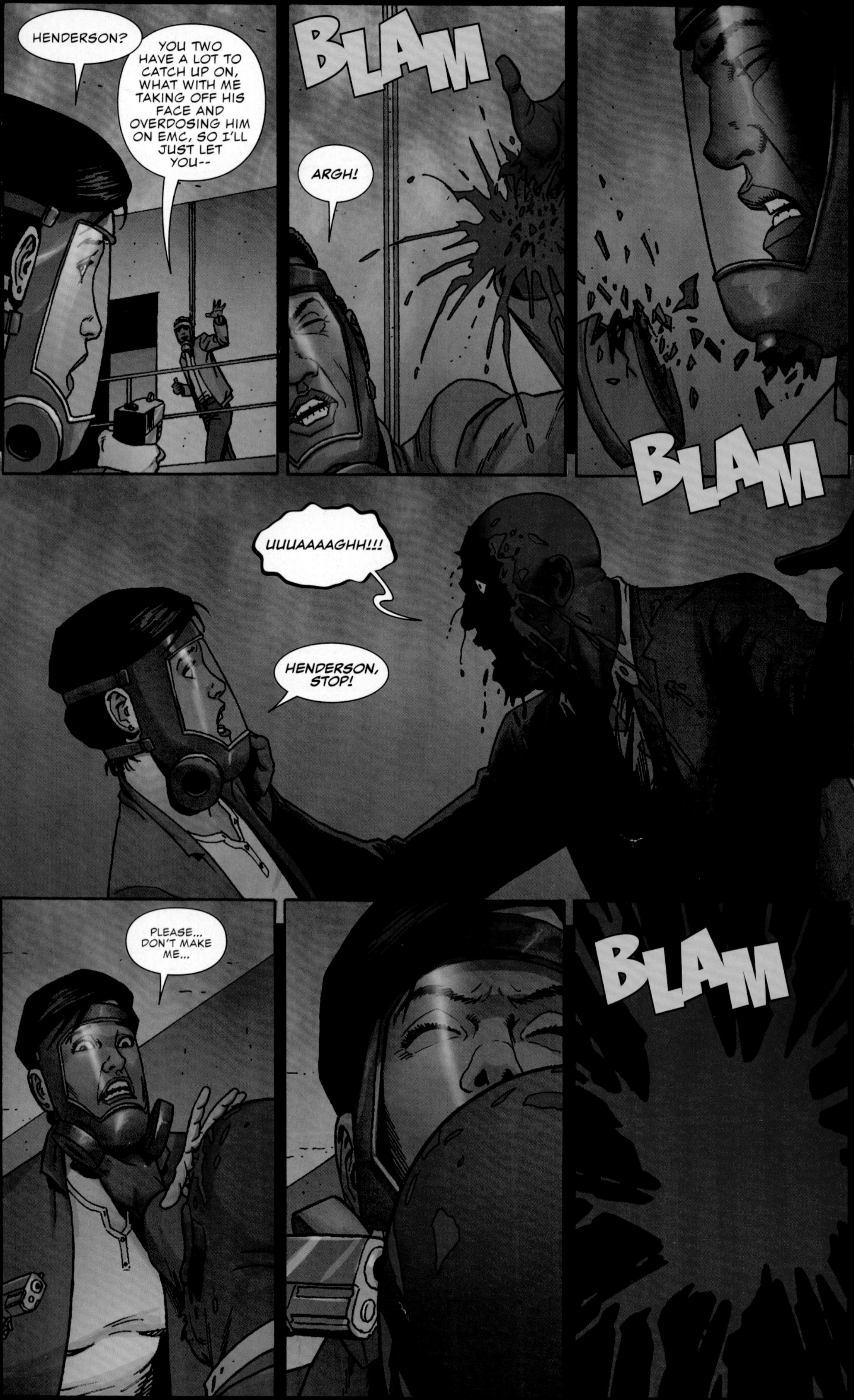
HENDERSON?
YOU TWO HAVE A LOT TO CATCH UP ON, WHAT WITH ME TAKING OFF HIS FACE AND OVERDOSING HIM ON EMC, SO I'LL JUST LET YOU--
BLAM
ARGH!
BLAM
UUUAAAAGHH!!!
HENDERSON, STOP!
PLEASE... DON'T MAKE ME...
BLAM

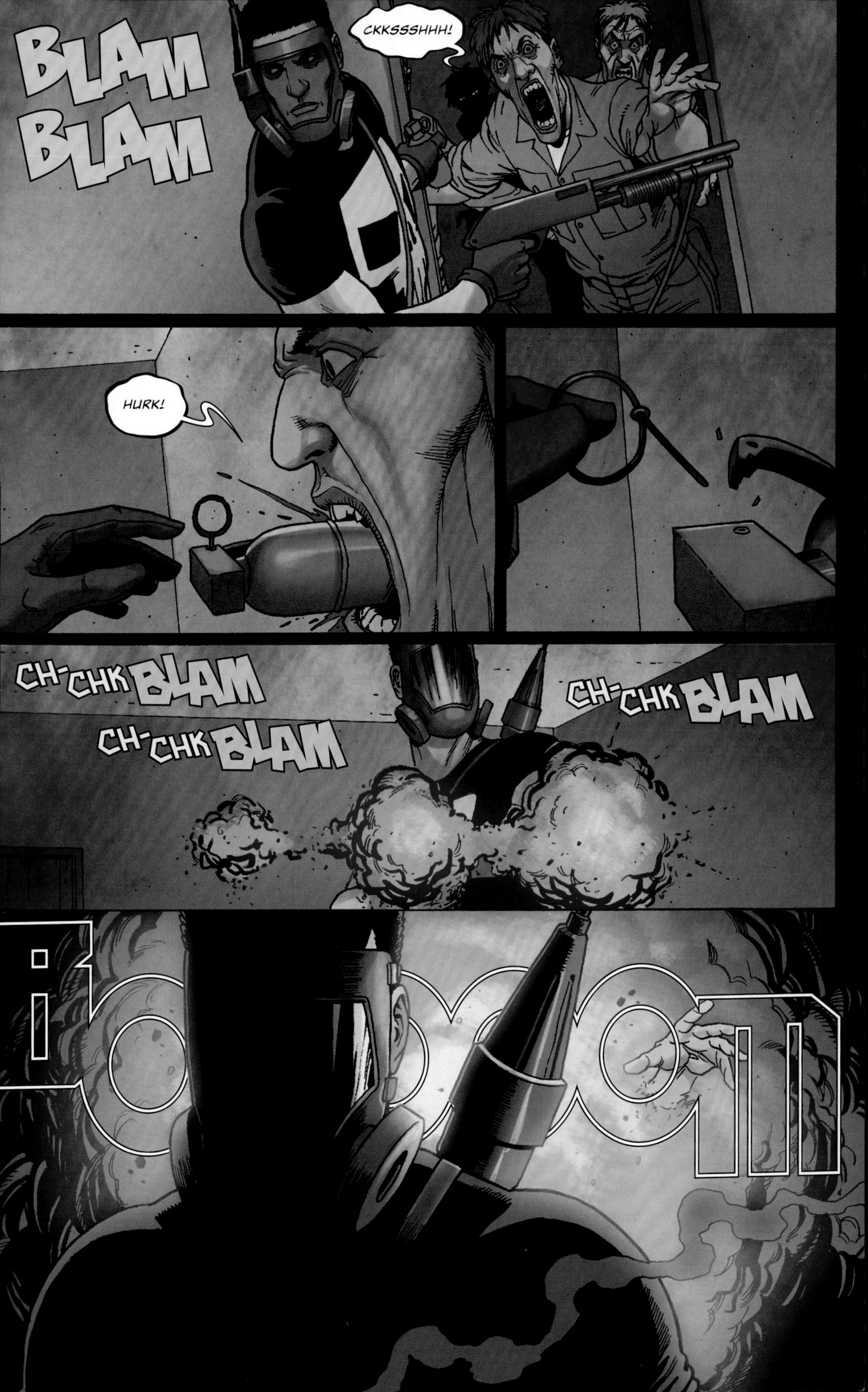
BLAM
BLAM
CKKSSSHHH!
HURK!
CH-CHK BLAM
CH-CHK BLAM
CH-CHK BLAM

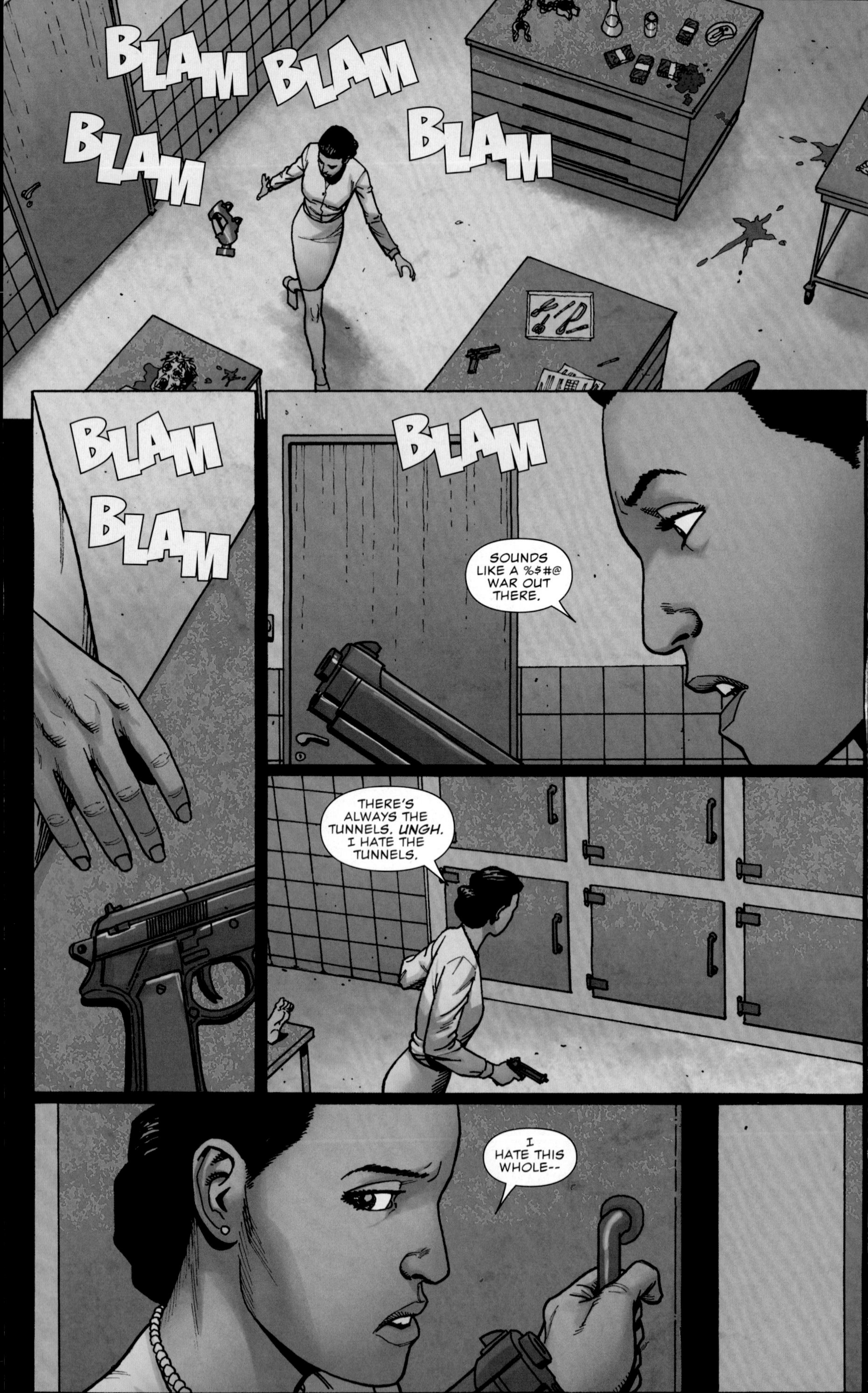
BLAM BLAM
BLAM
BLAM
BLAM
BLAM
BLAM
SOUNDS LIKE A %$#@ WAR OUT THERE.
THERE'S ALWAYS THE TUNNELS. *UNGH.* I HATE THE TUNNELS.
I HATE THIS WHOLE--

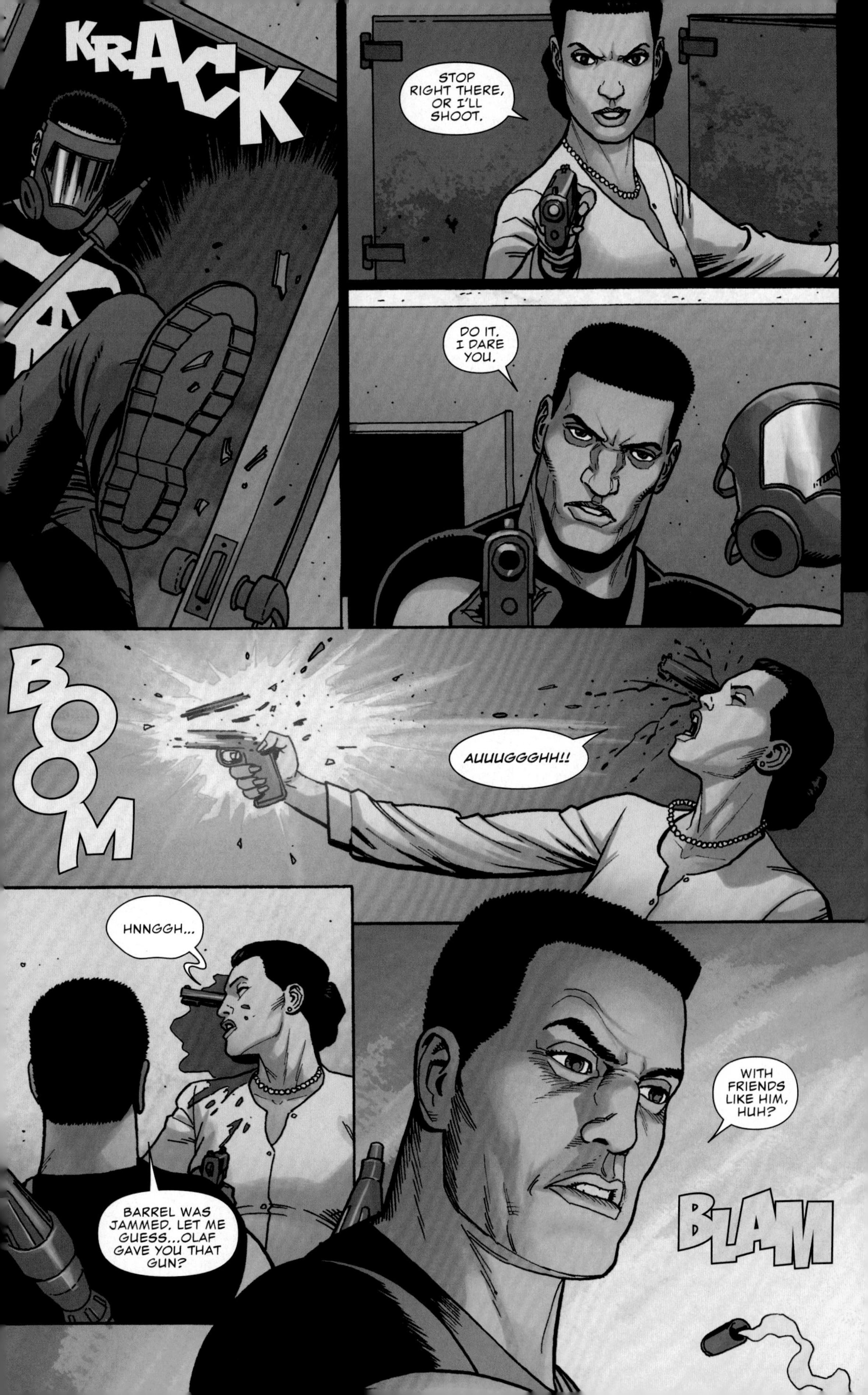
KRACK
STOP RIGHT THERE, OR I'LL SHOOT.
DO IT. I DARE YOU.
BOOM
AUUUGGGHH!!
HNNGGH...
BARREL WAS JAMMED. LET ME GUESS...OLAF GAVE YOU THAT GUN?
WITH FRIENDS LIKE HIM, HUH?
BLAM

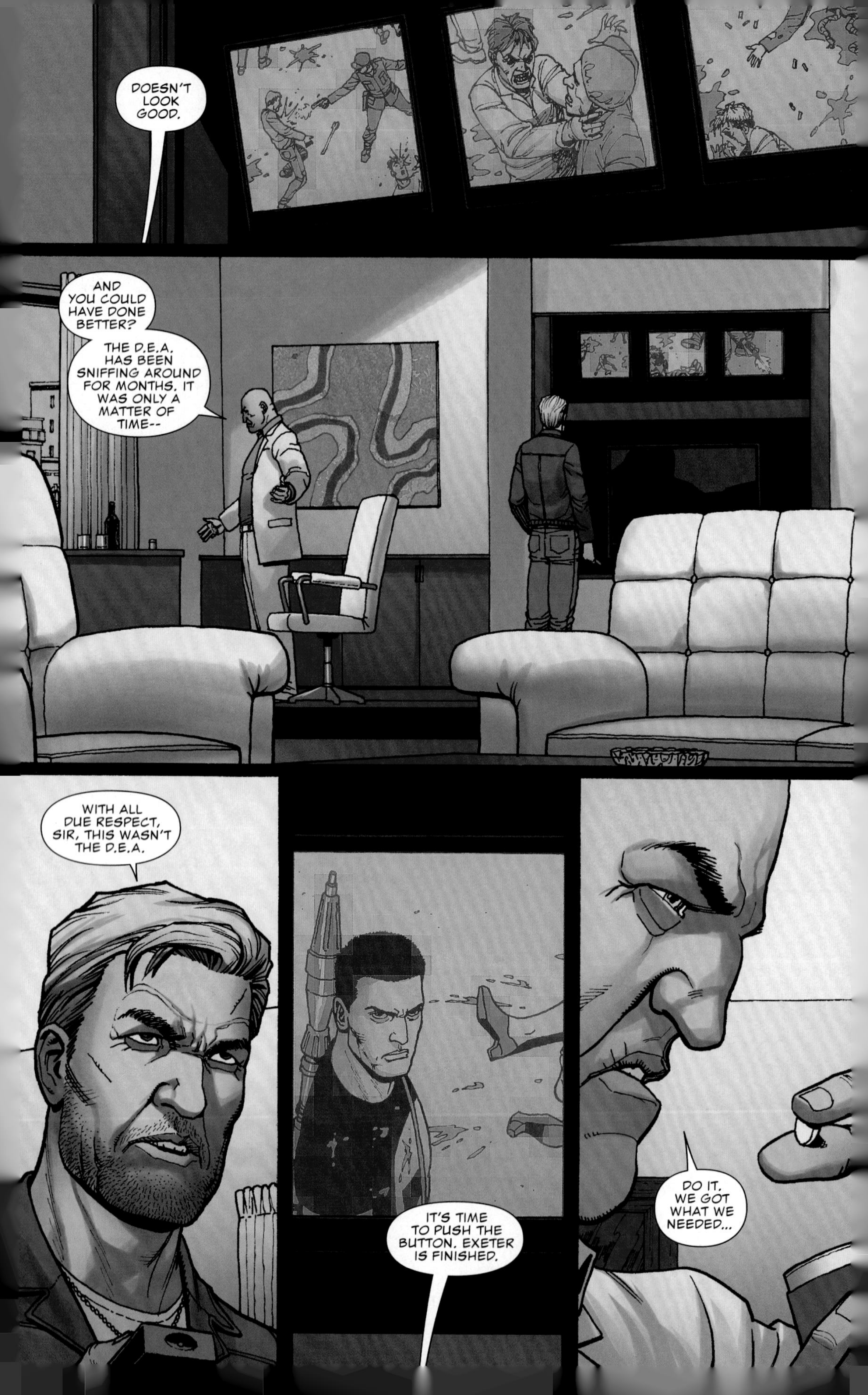
DOESN'T LOOK GOOD.
AND YOU COULD HAVE DONE BETTER?
THE D.E.A. HAS BEEN SNIFFING AROUND FOR MONTHS. IT WAS ONLY A MATTER OF TIME--
WITH ALL DUE RESPECT, SIR, THIS WASN'T THE D.E.A.
IT'S TIME TO PUSH THE BUTTON. EXETER IS FINISHED.
DO IT. WE GOT WHAT WE NEEDED...

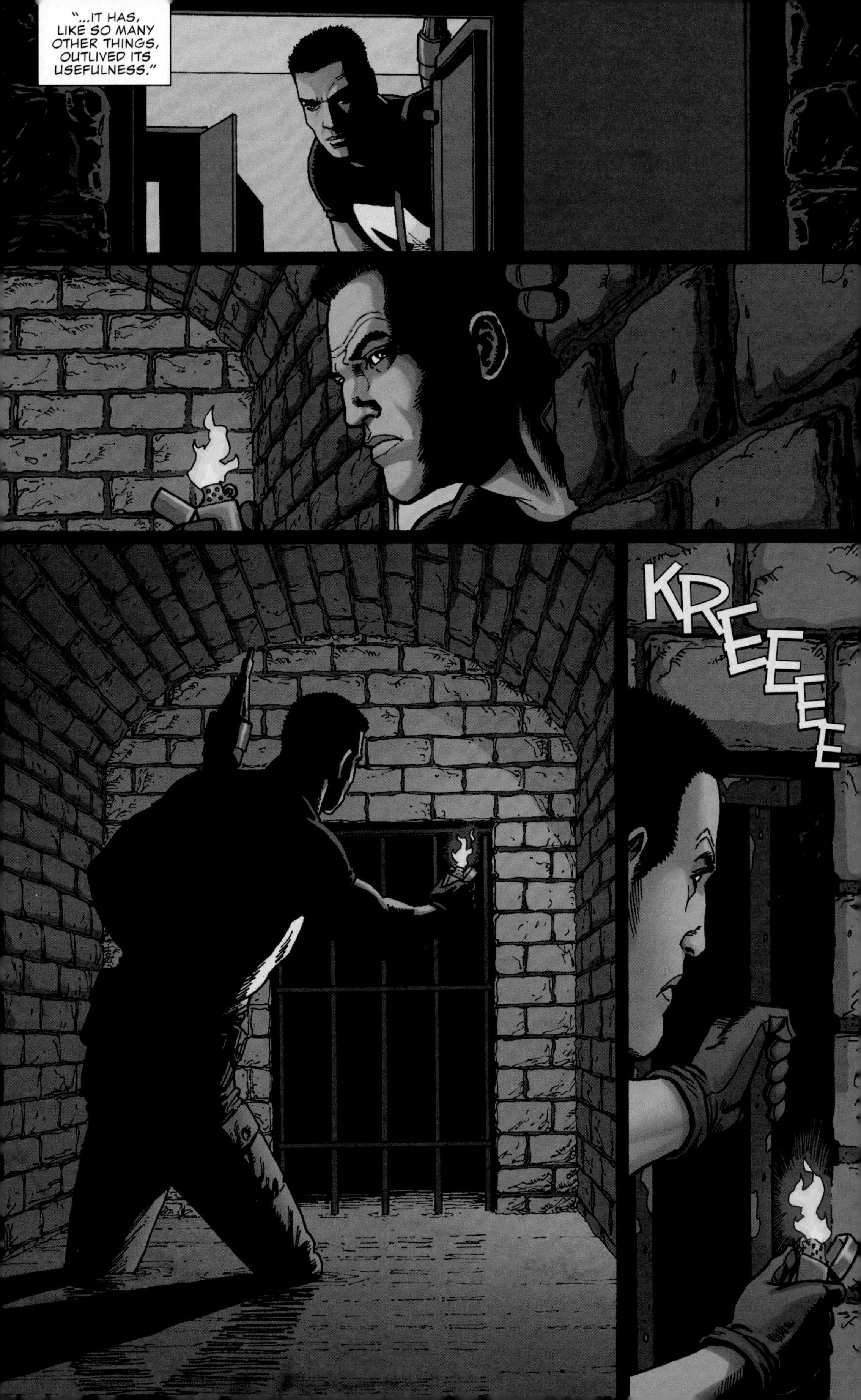
"...IT HAS, LIKE SO MANY OTHER THINGS, OUTLIVED ITS USEFULNESS."
KREEEEE

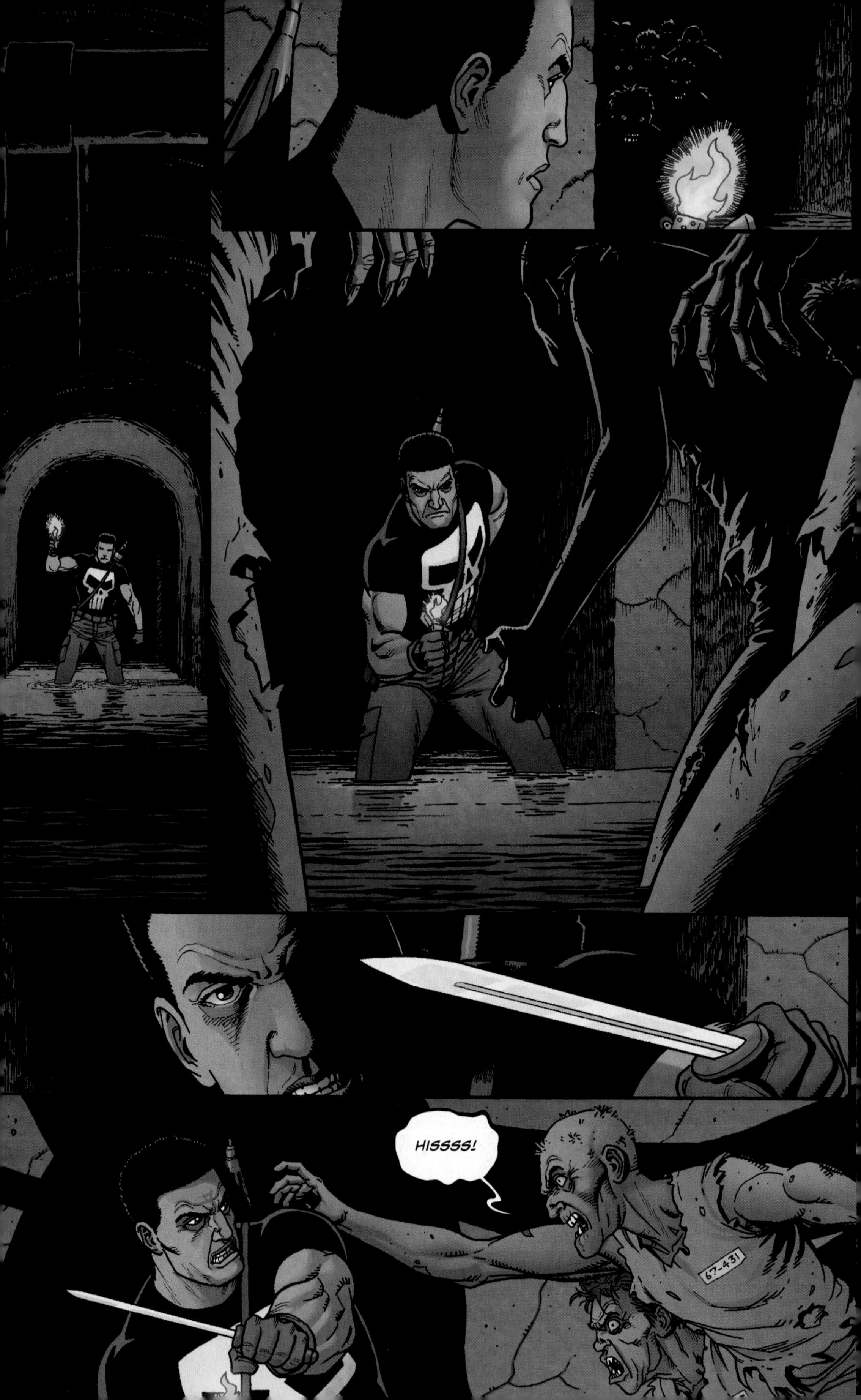
HISSSS!
67-431

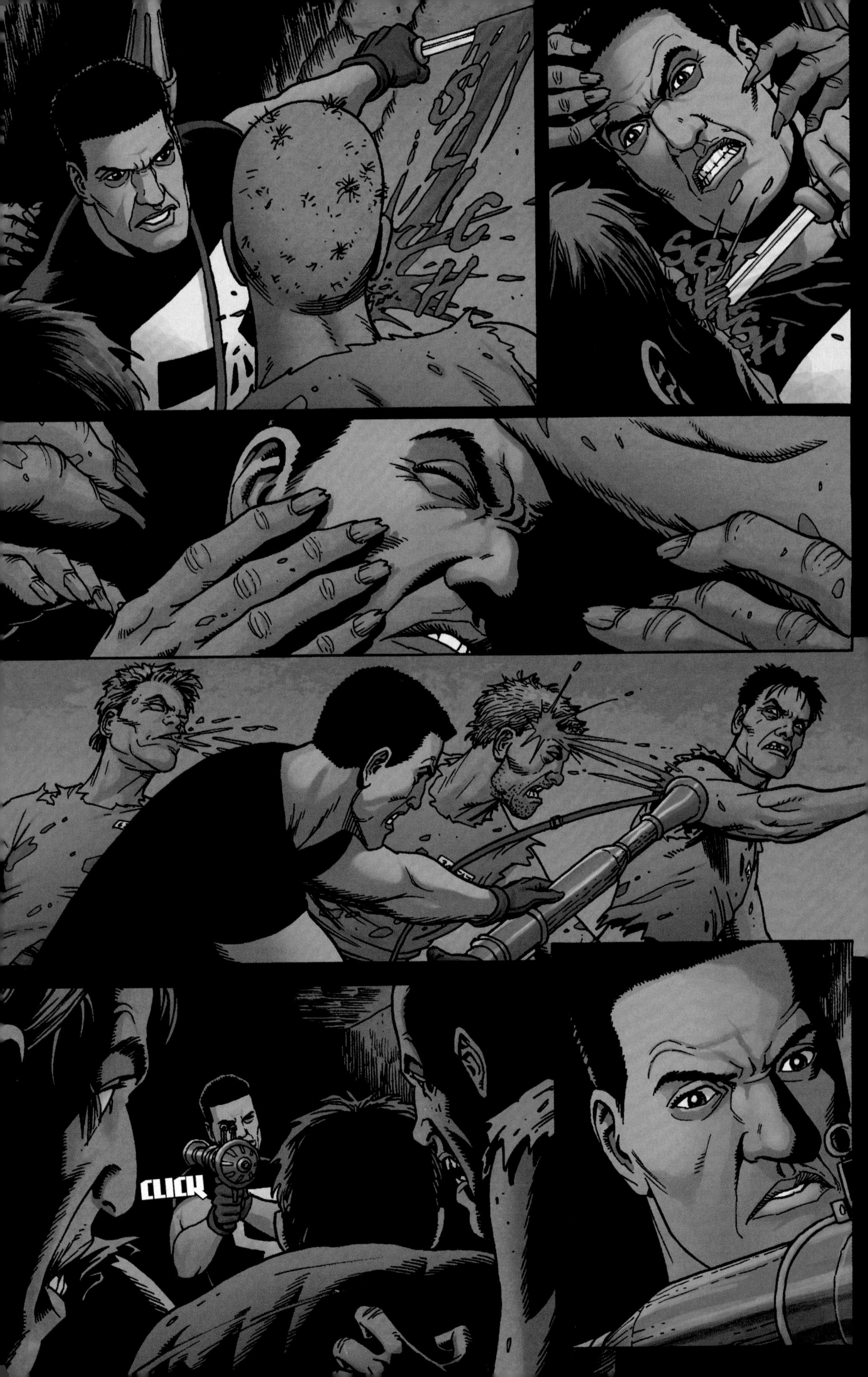
SQUISH
CLICK

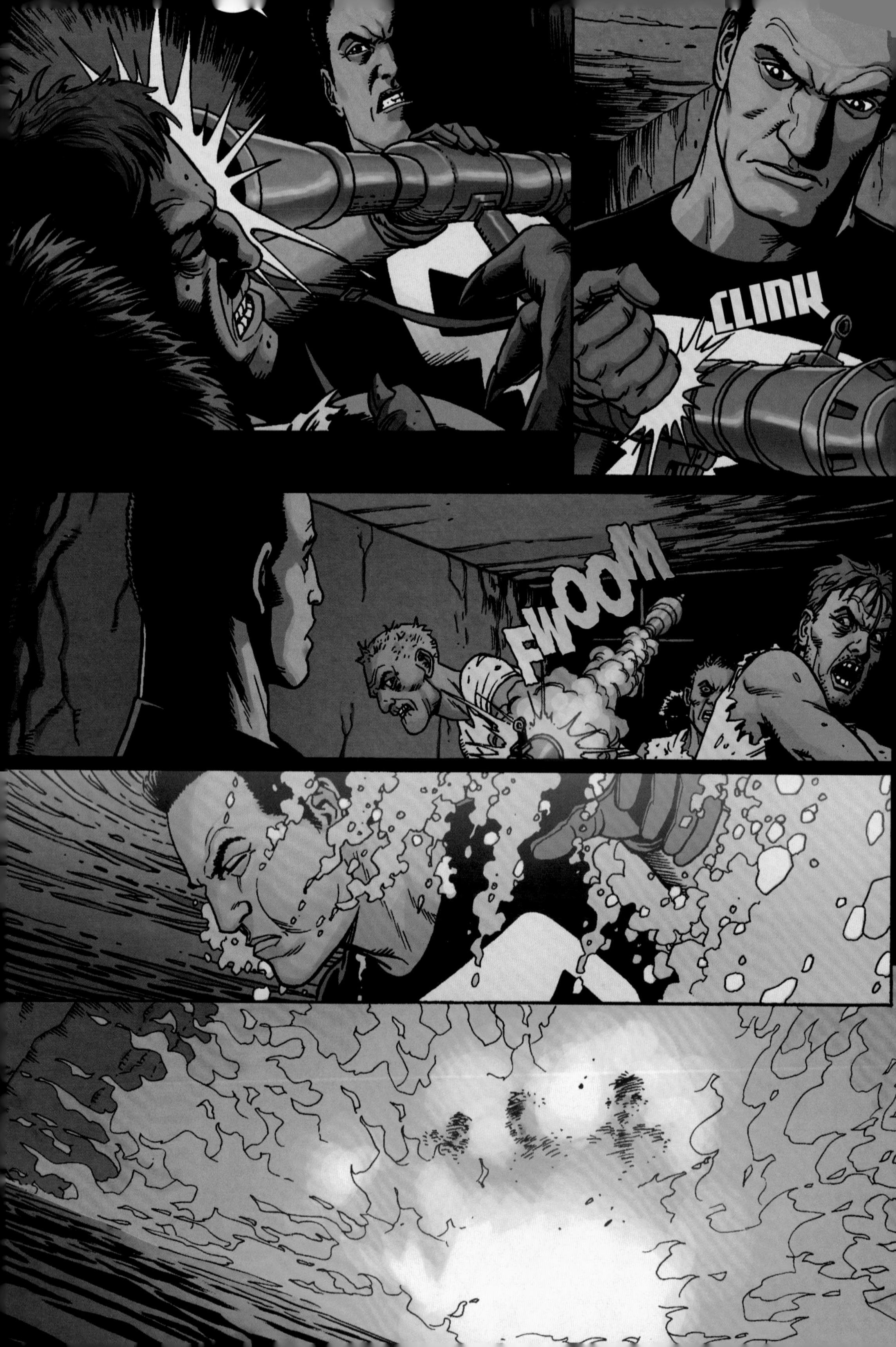
CLINK
FWOOM

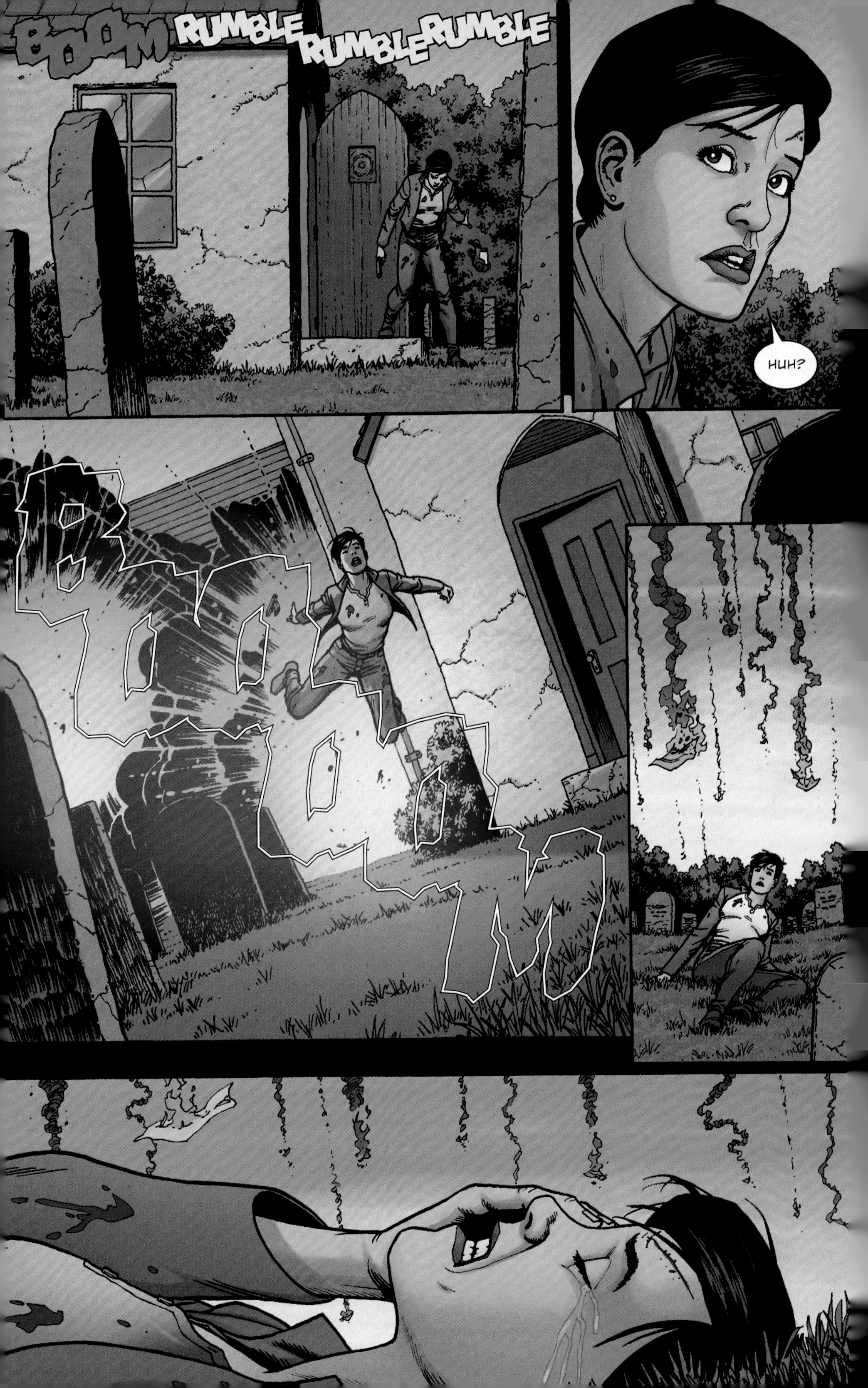
BOOM
RUMBLE RUMBLE RUMBLE
HUH?
BOOOM

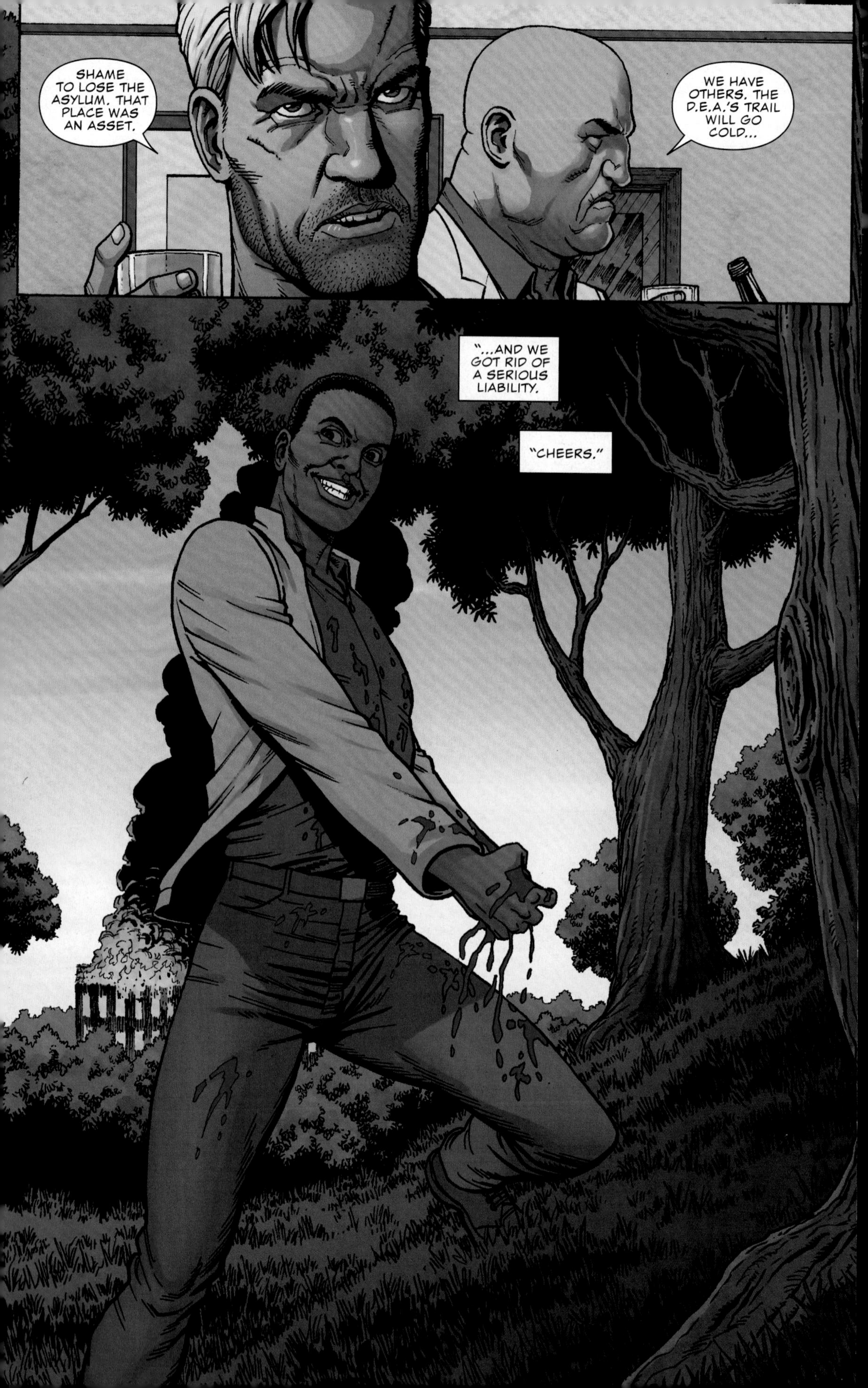
SHAME TO LOSE THE ASYLUM. THAT PLACE WAS AN ASSET.
WE HAVE OTHERS. THE D.E.A.'S TRAIL WILL GO COLD...
"...AND WE GOT RID OF A SERIOUS LIABILITY.
"CHEERS."

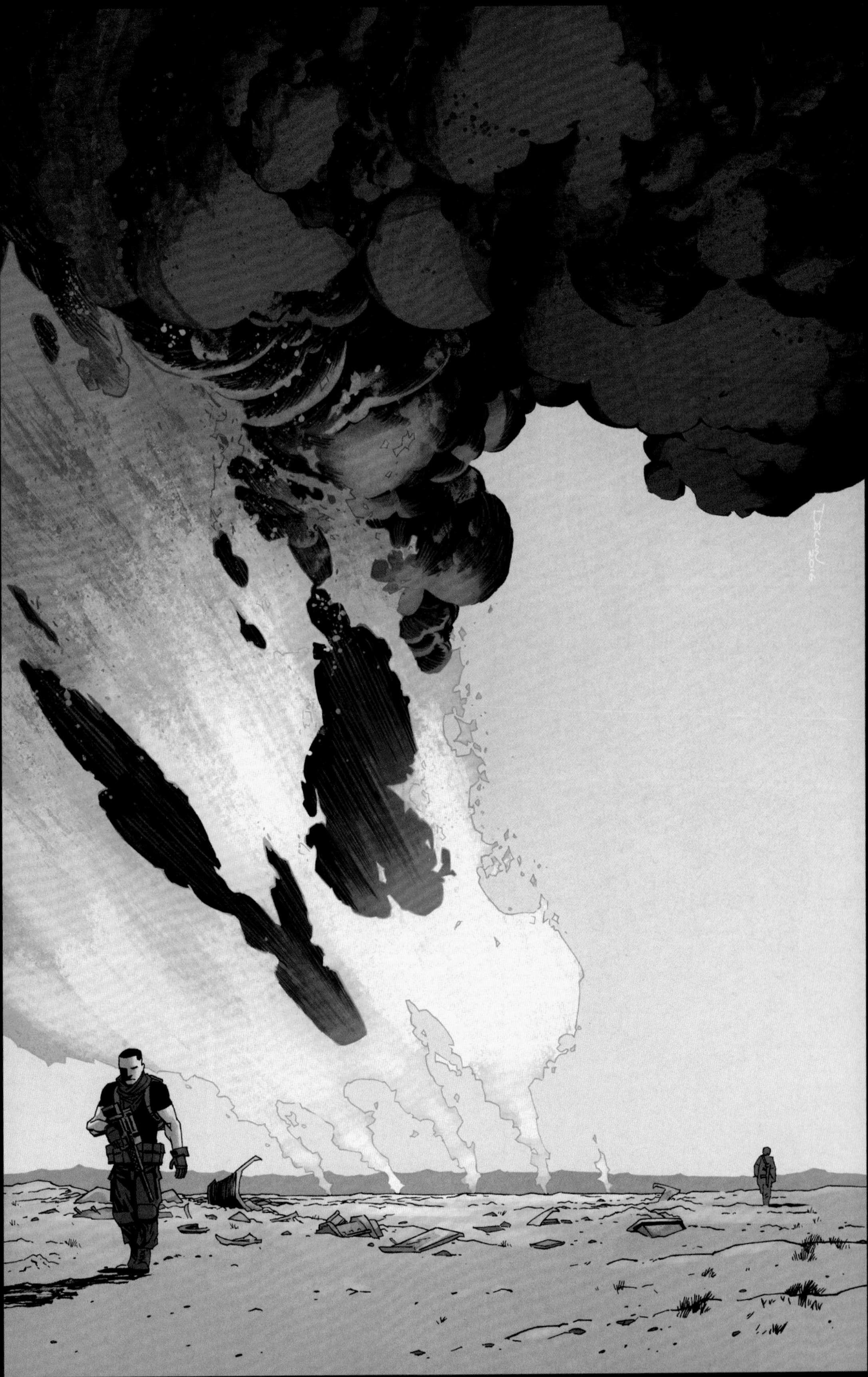

6

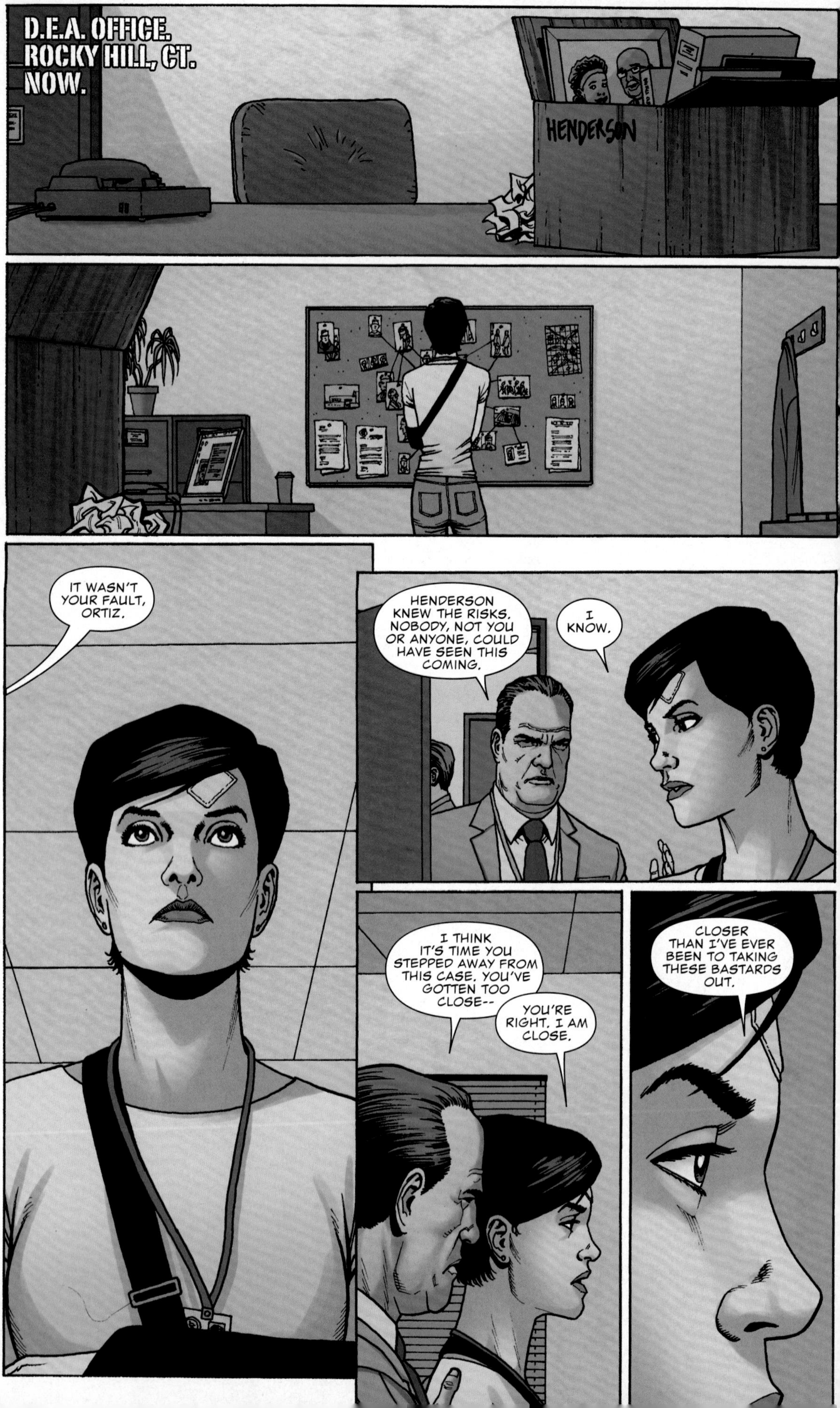
D.E.A. OFFICE. ROCKY HILL, CT. NOW.
HENDERSON
IT WASN'T YOUR FAULT, ORTIZ.
HENDERSON KNEW THE RISKS. NOBODY, NOT YOU OR ANYONE, COULD HAVE SEEN THIS COMING.
I KNOW.
I THINK IT'S TIME YOU STEPPED AWAY FROM THIS CASE. YOU'VE GOTTEN TOO CLOSE--
YOU'RE RIGHT. I AM CLOSE.
CLOSER THAN I'VE EVER BEEN TO TAKING THESE BASTARDS OUT.

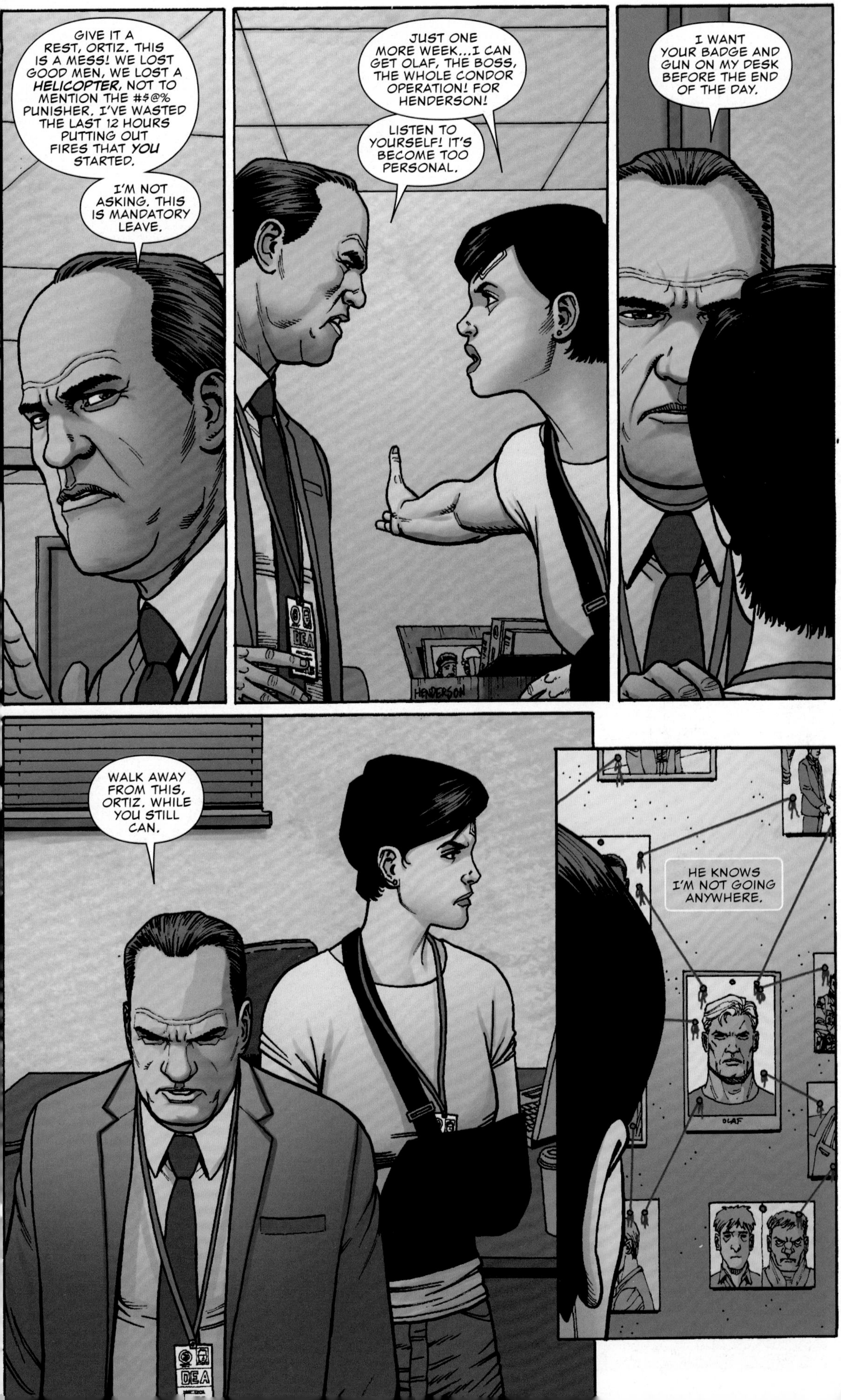
GIVE IT A REST, ORTIZ. THIS IS A MESS! WE LOST GOOD MEN, WE LOST A HELICOPTER, NOT TO MENTION THE #$@% PUNISHER. I'VE WASTED THE LAST 12 HOURS PUTTING OUT FIRES THAT YOU STARTED.
I'M NOT ASKING. THIS IS MANDATORY LEAVE.
JUST ONE MORE WEEK...I CAN GET OLAF, THE BOSS, THE WHOLE CONDOR OPERATION! FOR HENDERSON!
LISTEN TO YOURSELF! IT'S BECOME TOO PERSONAL.
DEA
HENDERSON
I WANT YOUR BADGE AND GUN ON MY DESK BEFORE THE END OF THE DAY.
WALK AWAY FROM THIS, ORTIZ. WHILE YOU STILL CAN.
HE KNOWS I'M NOT GOING ANYWHERE.
OLAF
DEA

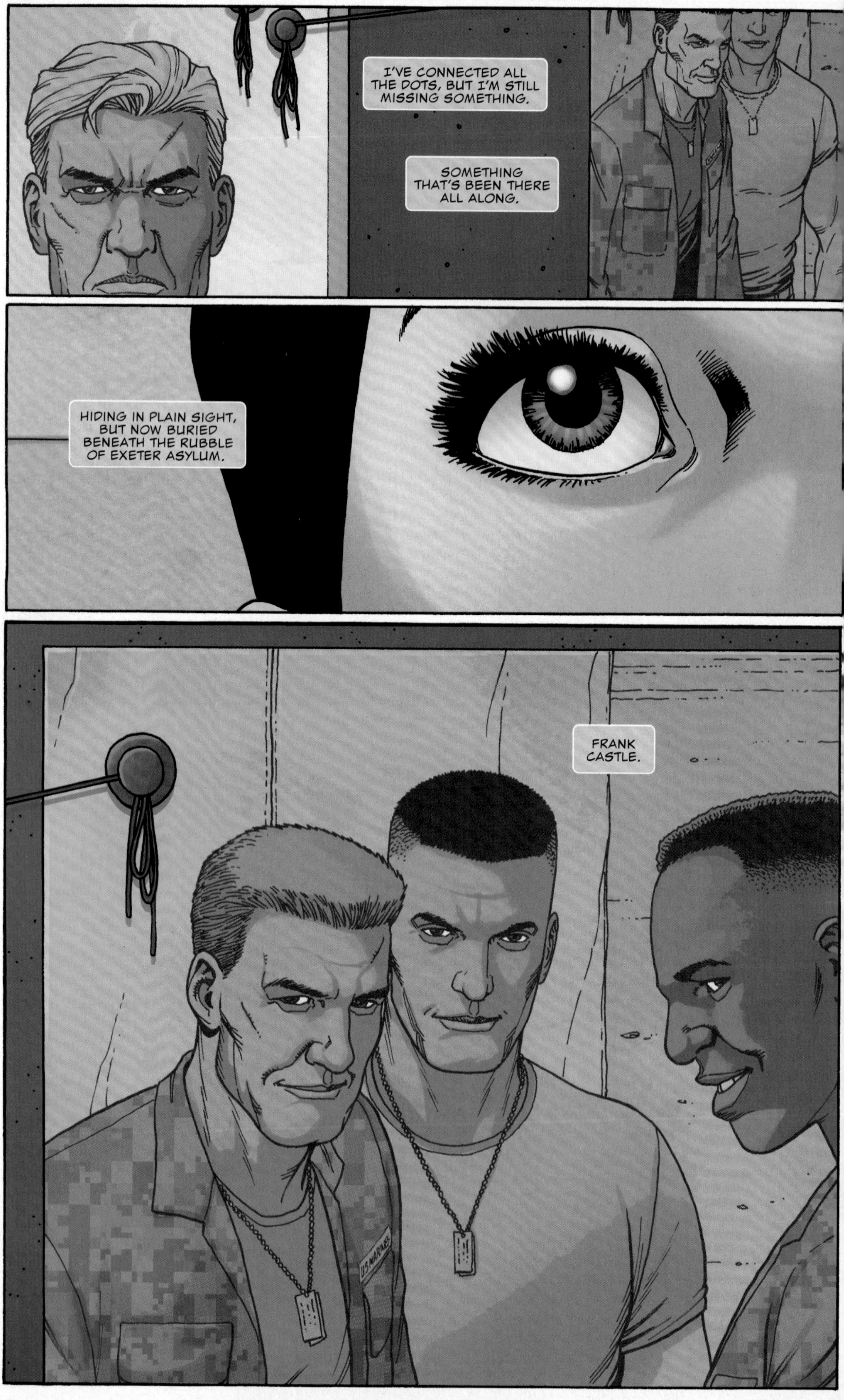
I'VE CONNECTED ALL THE DOTS, BUT I'M STILL MISSING SOMETHING.
SOMETHING THAT'S BEEN THERE ALL ALONG.
HIDING IN PLAIN SIGHT, BUT NOW BURIED BENEATH THE RUBBLE OF EXETER ASYLUM.
FRANK CASTLE.
U.S. MARINES

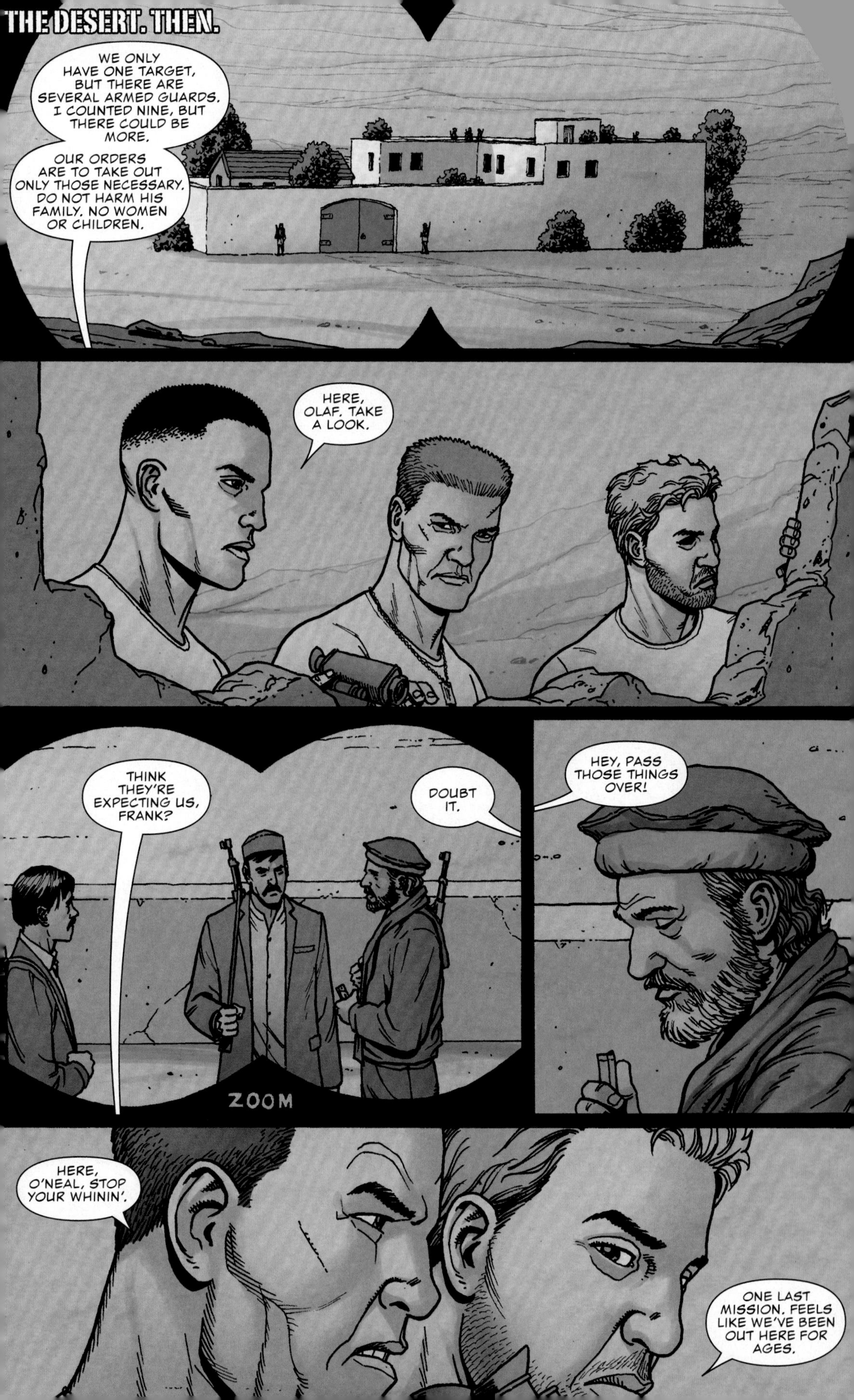
THE DESERT. THEN.
WE ONLY HAVE ONE TARGET, BUT THERE ARE SEVERAL ARMED GUARDS. I COUNTED NINE, BUT THERE COULD BE MORE.
OUR ORDERS ARE TO TAKE OUT ONLY THOSE NECESSARY. DO NOT HARM HIS FAMILY. NO WOMEN OR CHILDREN.
HERE, OLAF. TAKE A LOOK.
THINK THEY'RE EXPECTING US, FRANK?
DOUBT IT.
ZOOM
HEY, PASS THOSE THINGS OVER!
HERE, O'NEAL, STOP YOUR WHININ'.
ONE LAST MISSION. FEELS LIKE WE'VE BEEN OUT HERE FOR AGES.

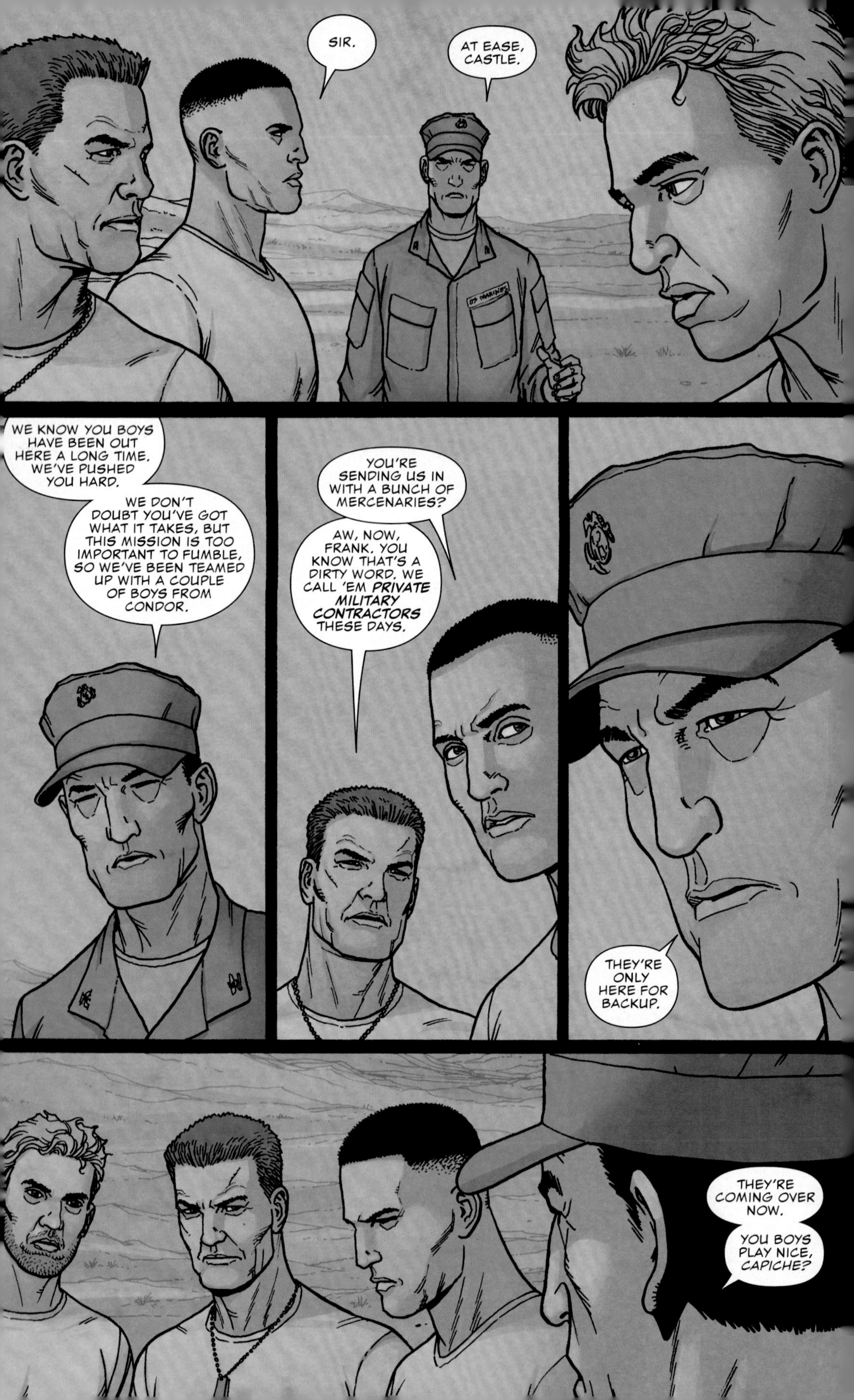
SIR.
AT EASE, CASTLE.
WE KNOW YOU BOYS HAVE BEEN OUT HERE A LONG TIME. WE'VE PUSHED YOU HARD.
WE DON'T DOUBT YOU'VE GOT WHAT IT TAKES, BUT THIS MISSION IS TOO IMPORTANT TO FUMBLE, SO WE'VE BEEN TEAMED UP WITH A COUPLE OF BOYS FROM CONDOR.
YOU'RE SENDING US IN WITH A BUNCH OF MERCENARIES?
AW, NOW, FRANK. YOU KNOW THAT'S A DIRTY WORD. WE CALL 'EM PRIVATE MILITARY CONTRACTORS THESE DAYS.
THEY'RE ONLY HERE FOR BACKUP.
THEY'RE COMING OVER NOW.
YOU BOYS PLAY NICE, CAPICHE?

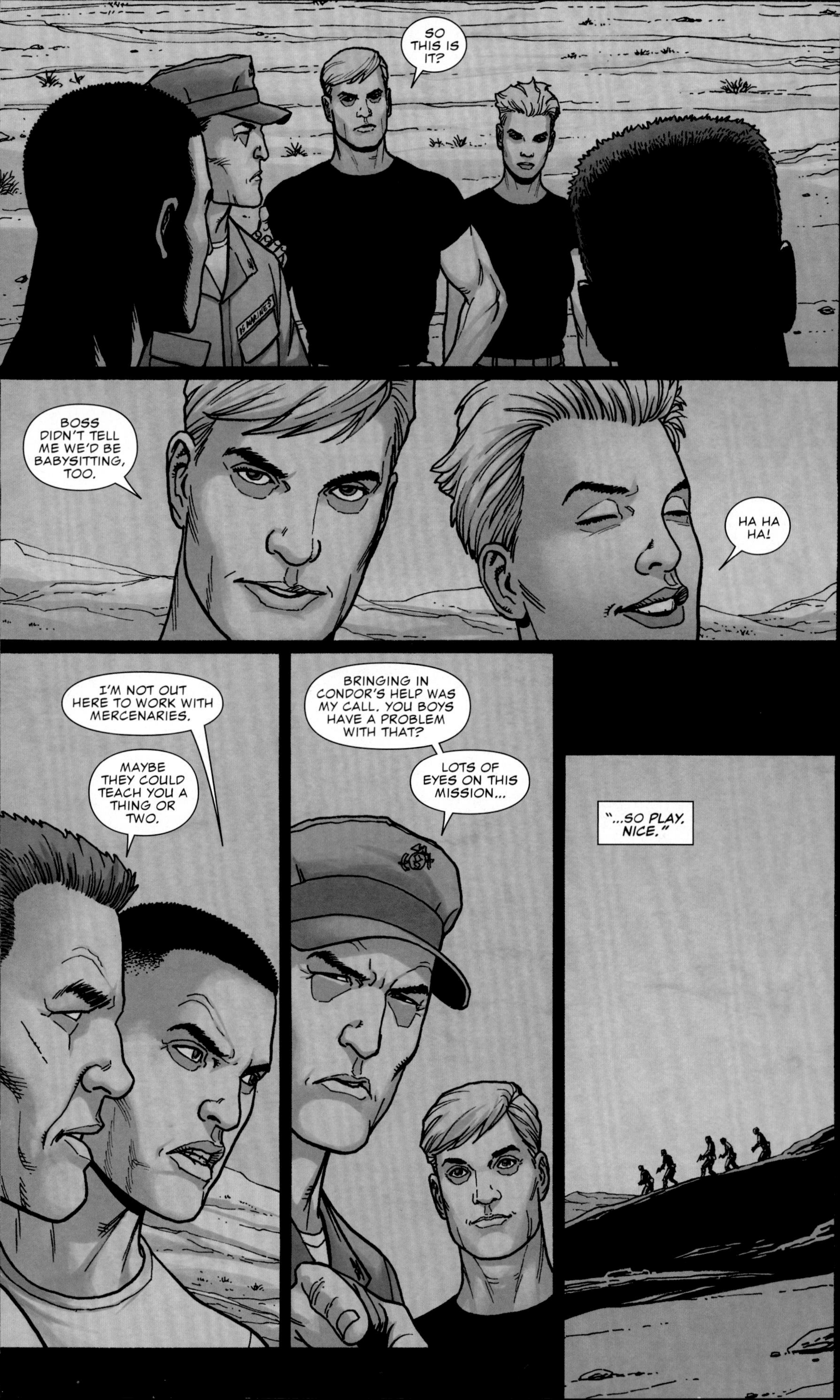
SO THIS IS IT?
BOSS DIDN'T TELL ME WE'D BE BABYSITTING, TOO.
HA HA HA!
I'M NOT OUT HERE TO WORK WITH MERCENARIES.
MAYBE THEY COULD TEACH YOU A THING OR TWO.
BRINGING IN CONDOR'S HELP WAS MY CALL. YOU BOYS HAVE A PROBLEM WITH THAT?
LOTS OF EYES ON THIS MISSION...
"...SO PLAY. NICE."

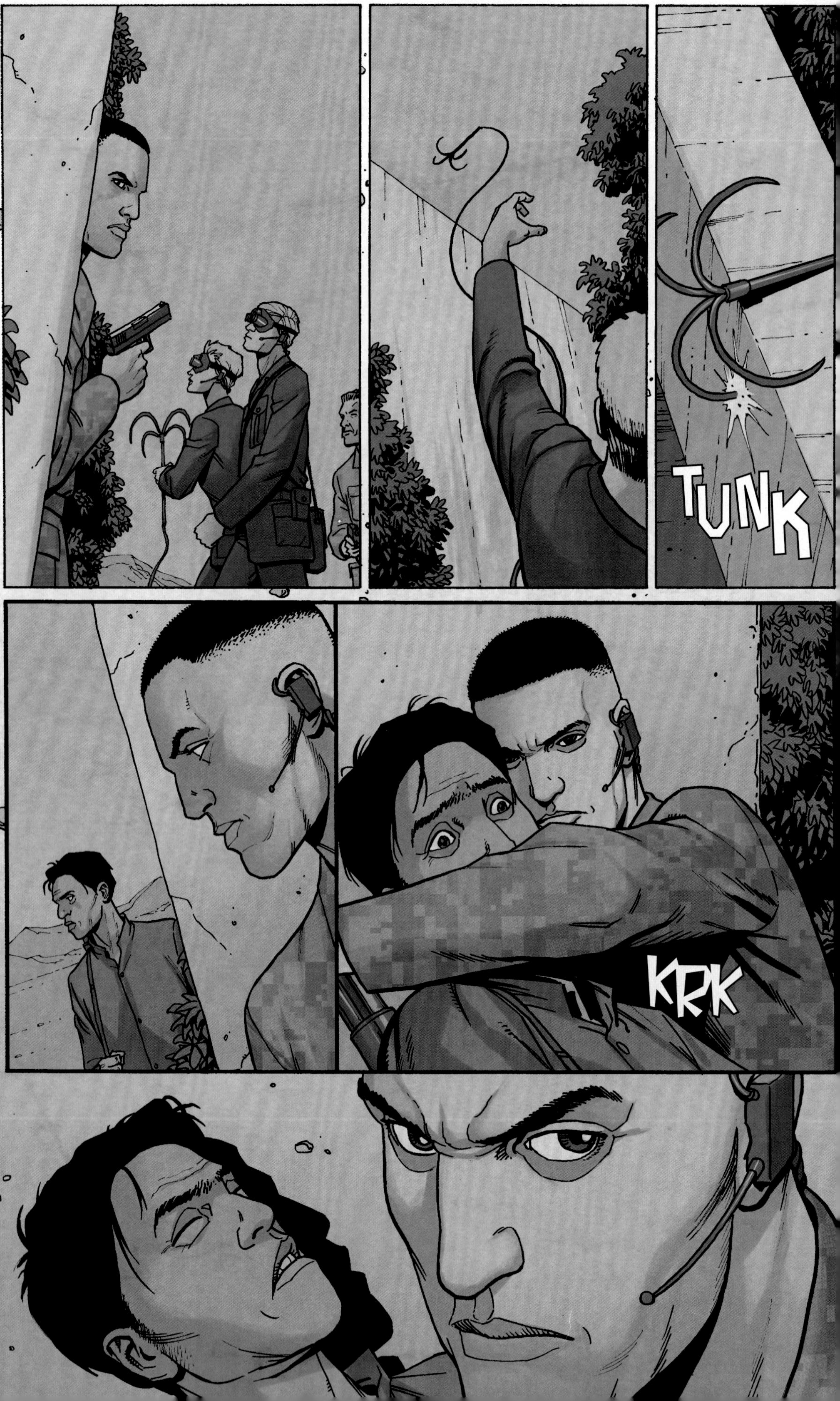
TUNK
KRK

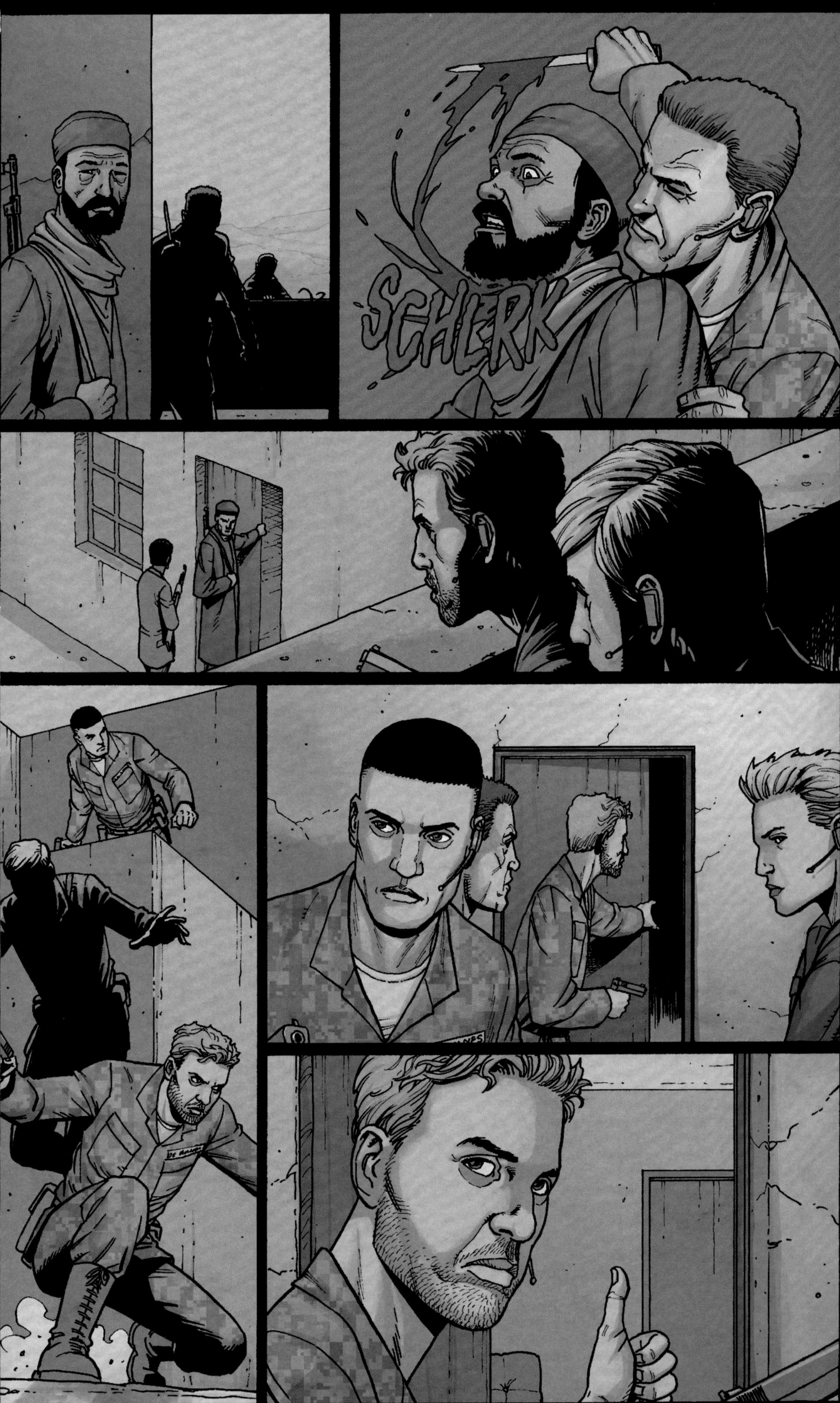
SCHLRK

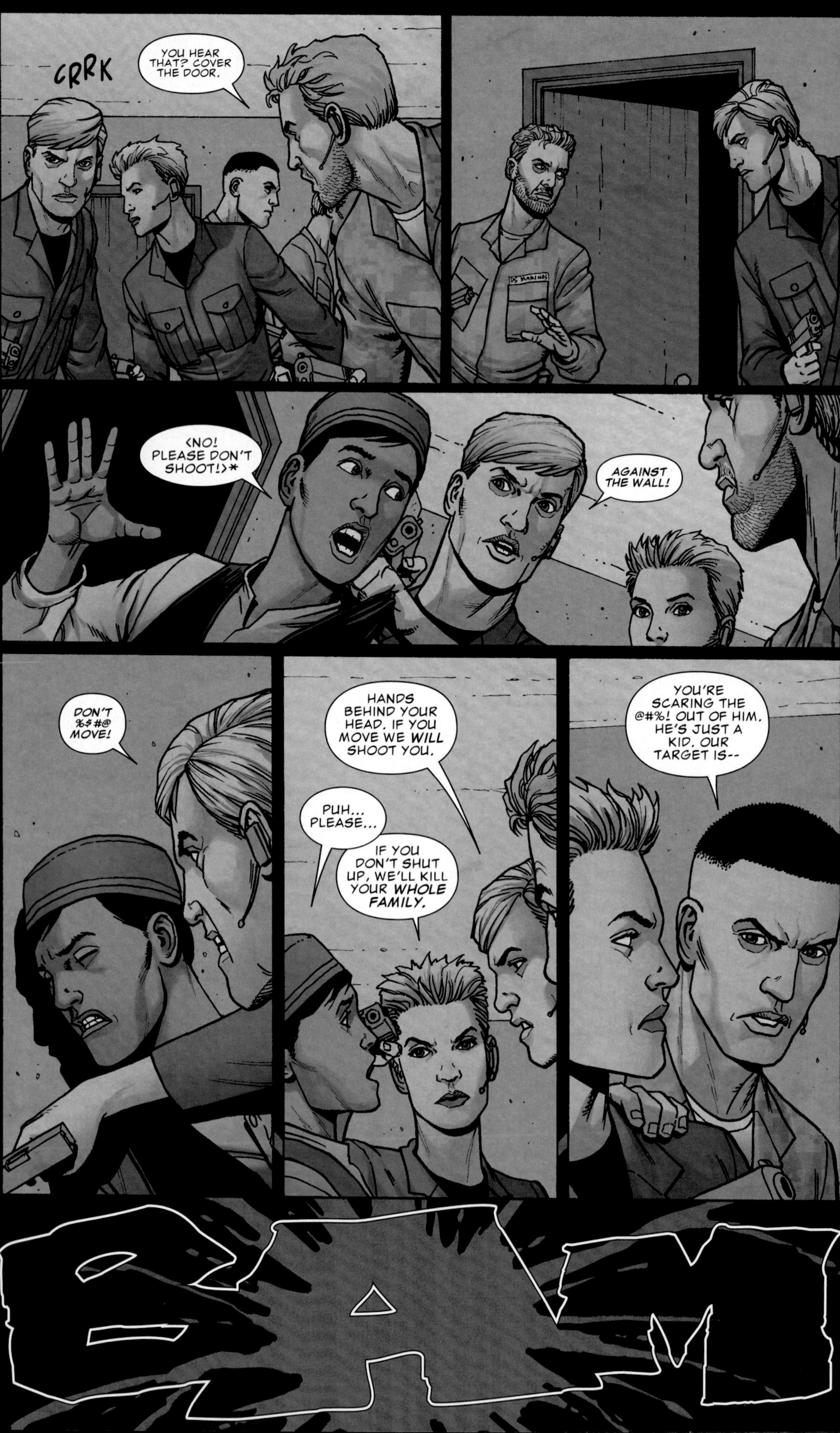
CRRK
YOU HEAR THAT? COVER THE DOOR.
<NO! PLEASE DON'T SHOOT!>*
AGAINST THE WALL!
DON'T %$#@ MOVE!
HANDS BEHIND YOUR HEAD. IF YOU MOVE WE WILL SHOOT YOU.
PUH... PLEASE...
IF YOU DON'T SHUT UP, WE'LL KILL YOUR WHOLE FAMILY.
YOU'RE SCARING THE @#%! OUT OF HIM. HE'S JUST A KID. OUR TARGET IS--
BAM

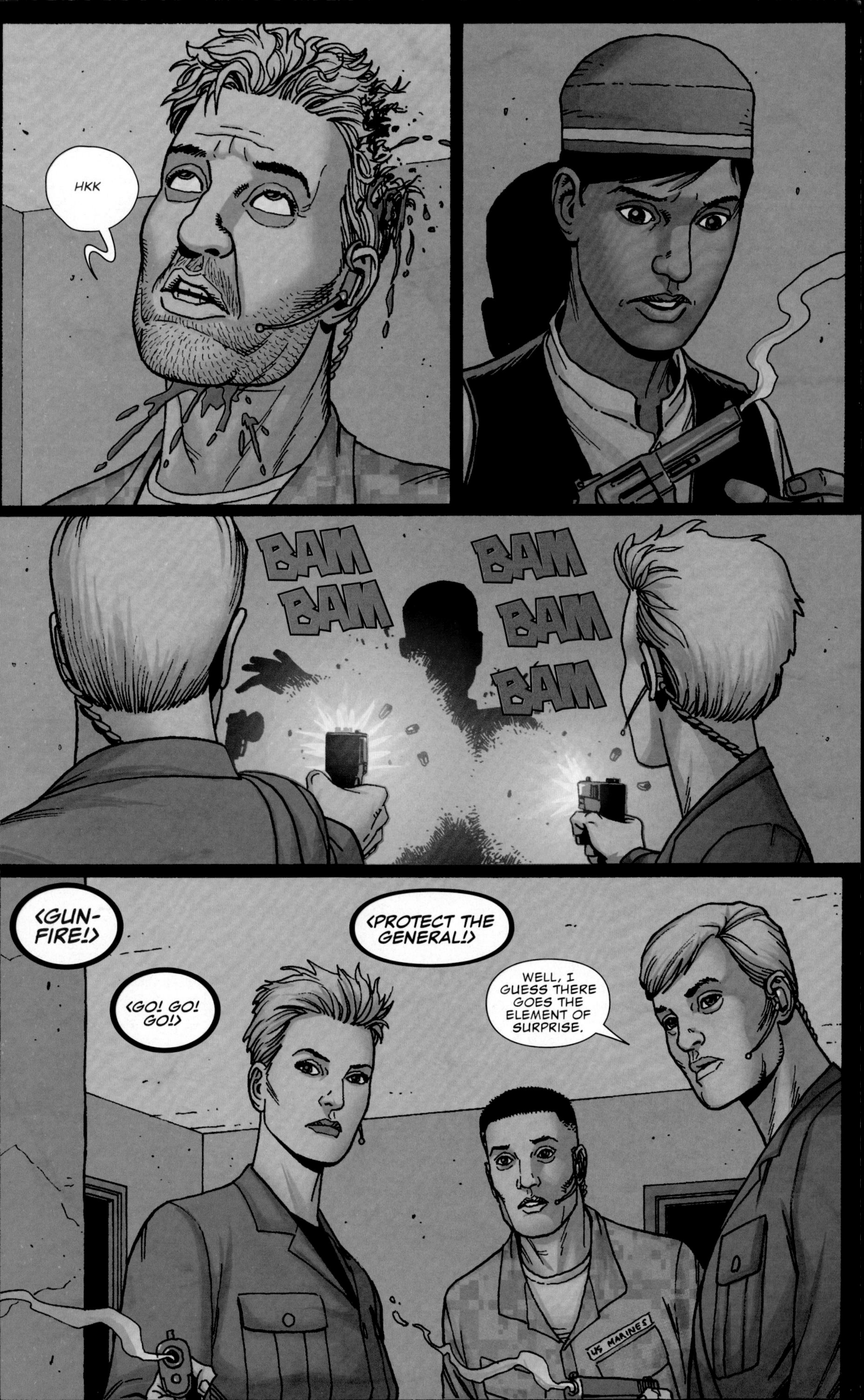
HKK
BAM
BAM
BAM
BAM
BAM
<GUN-FIRE!>
<GO! GO! GO!>
<PROTECT THE GENERAL!>
WELL, I GUESS THERE GOES THE ELEMENT OF SURPRISE.
US MARINES

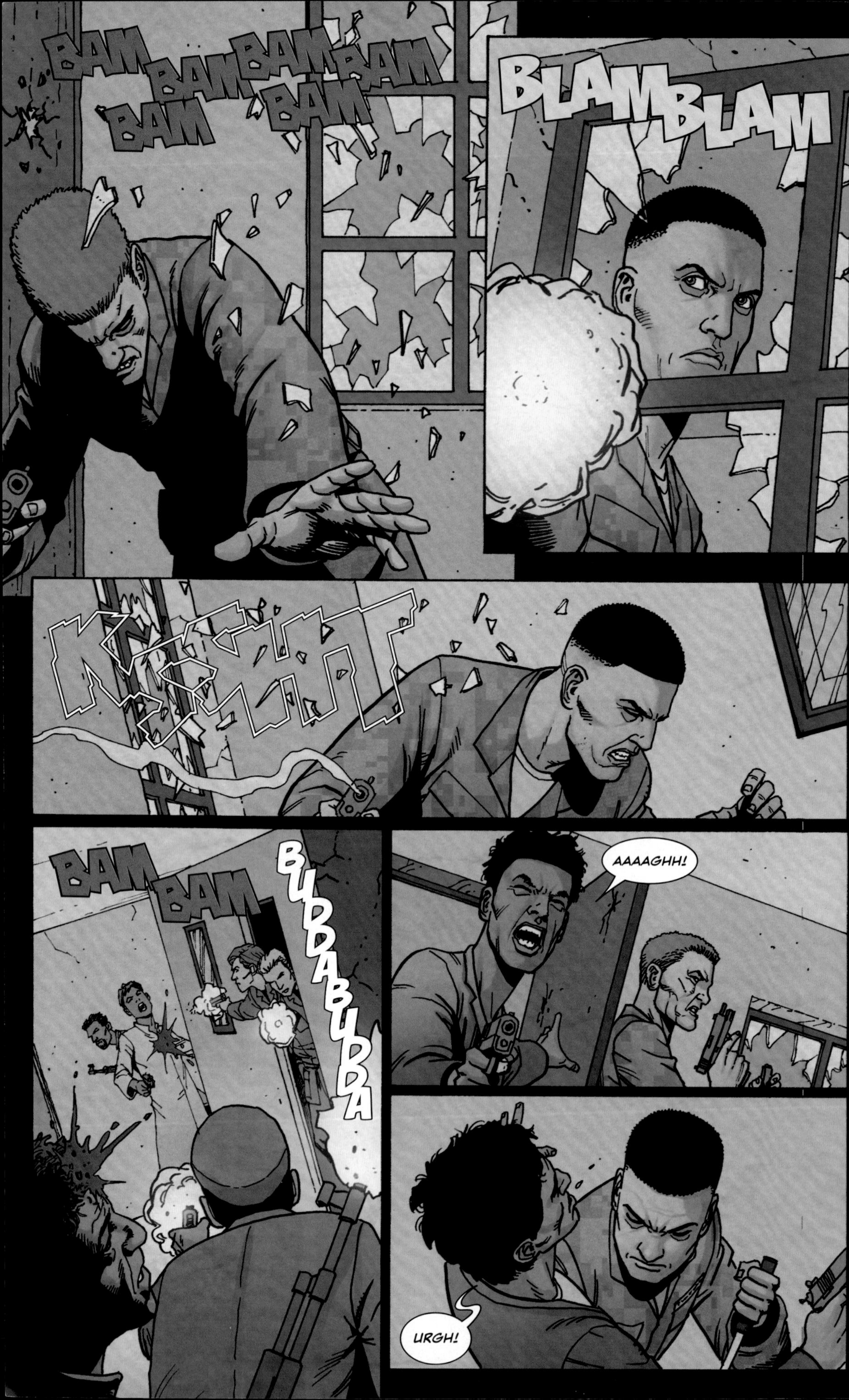

BAM BAM BAM BAM BAM BAM
BLAM BLAM
KRSSHT
BAM BAM
BUDABUDA
AAAAGHH!
URGH!

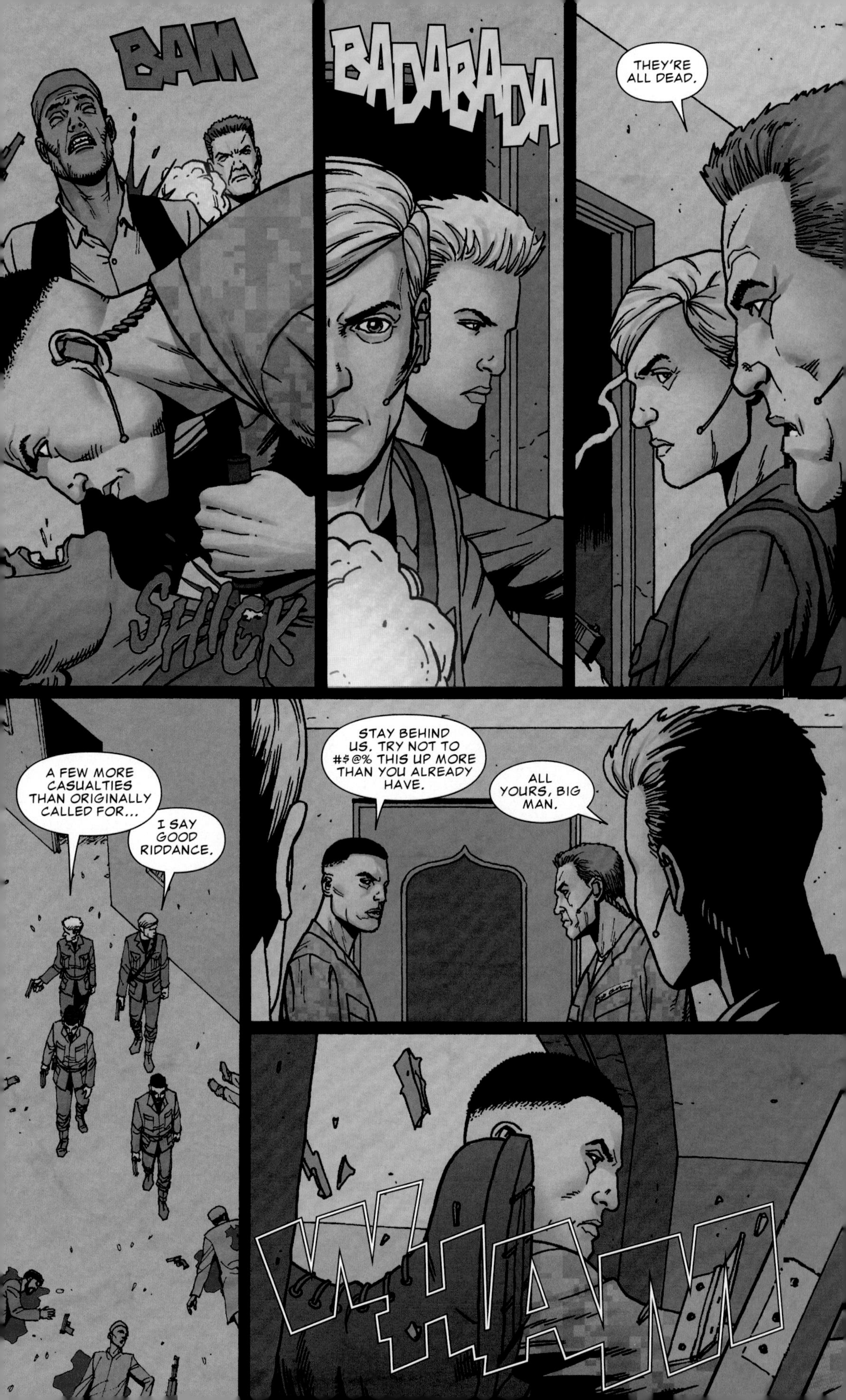
BAM
SHICK
BADABADA
THEY'RE ALL DEAD.
A FEW MORE CASUALTIES THAN ORIGINALLY CALLED FOR...
I SAY GOOD RIDDANCE.
STAY BEHIND US. TRY NOT TO #$@% THIS UP MORE THAN YOU ALREADY HAVE.
ALL YOURS, BIG MAN.
WHAM

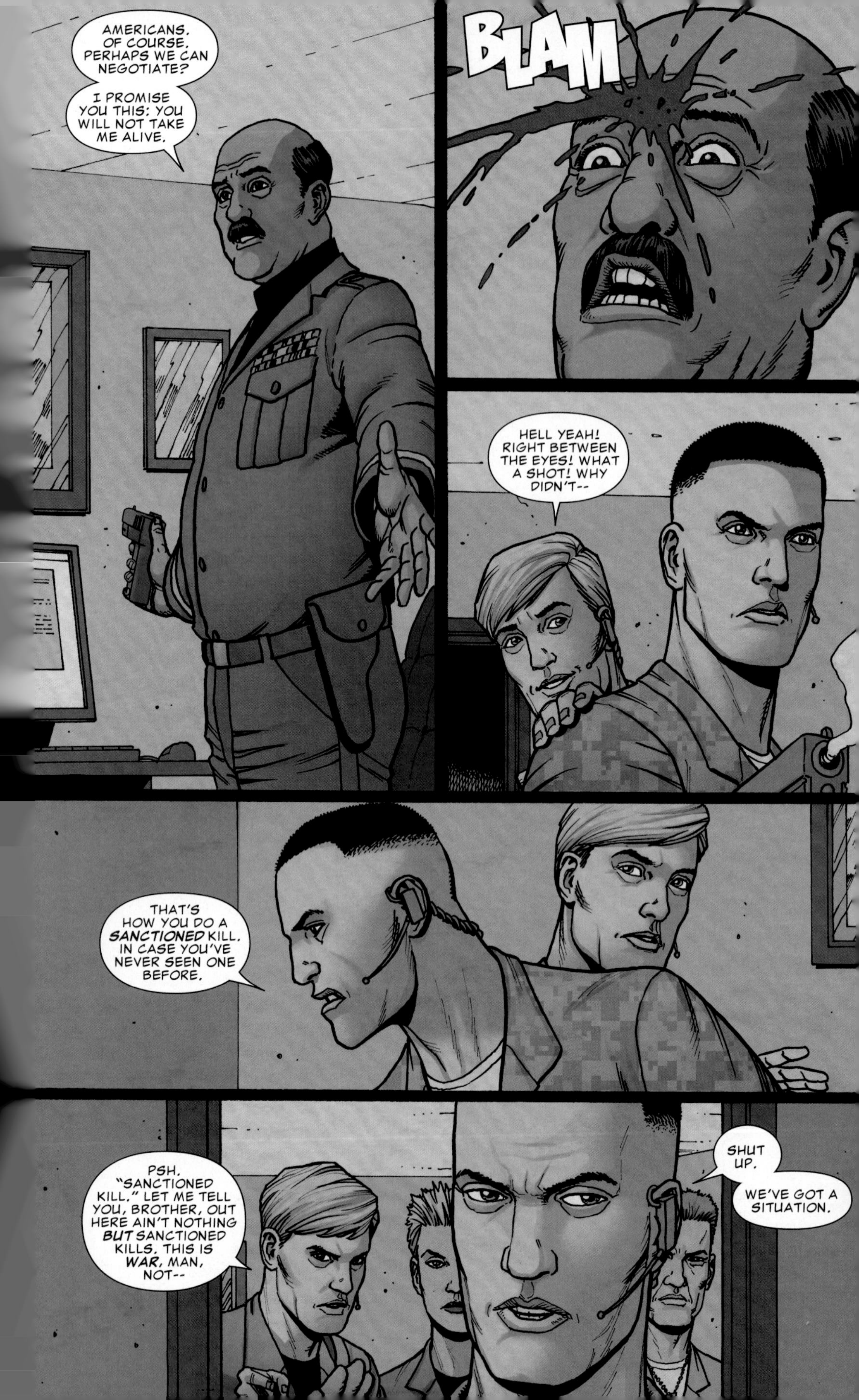
AMERICANS. OF COURSE. PERHAPS WE CAN NEGOTIATE?
I PROMISE YOU THIS: YOU WILL NOT TAKE ME ALIVE.
BLAM
HELL YEAH! RIGHT BETWEEN THE EYES! WHAT A SHOT! WHY DIDN'T--
THAT'S HOW YOU DO A SANCTIONED KILL, IN CASE YOU'VE NEVER SEEN ONE BEFORE.
PSH. "SANCTIONED KILL." LET ME TELL YOU, BROTHER, OUT HERE AIN'T NOTHING BUT SANCTIONED KILLS. THIS IS WAR, MAN, NOT--
SHUT UP.
WE'VE GOT A SITUATION.

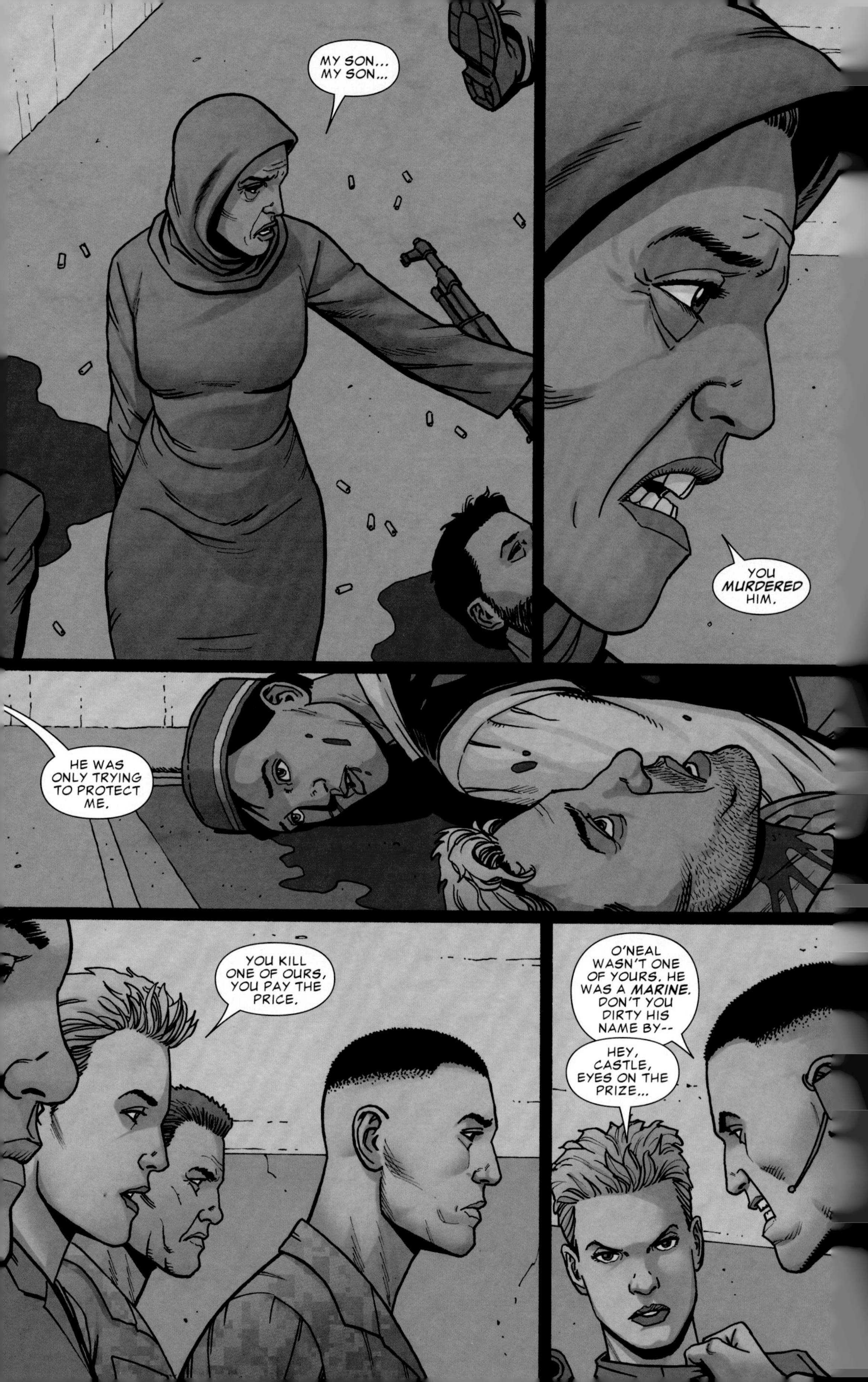
MY SON... MY SON...
YOU *MURDERED* HIM.
HE WAS ONLY TRYING TO PROTECT ME.
YOU KILL ONE OF OURS, YOU PAY THE PRICE.
O'NEAL WASN'T ONE OF YOURS. HE WAS A *MARINE*. DON'T YOU DIRTY HIS NAME BY--
HEY, CASTLE, EYES ON THE PRIZE...

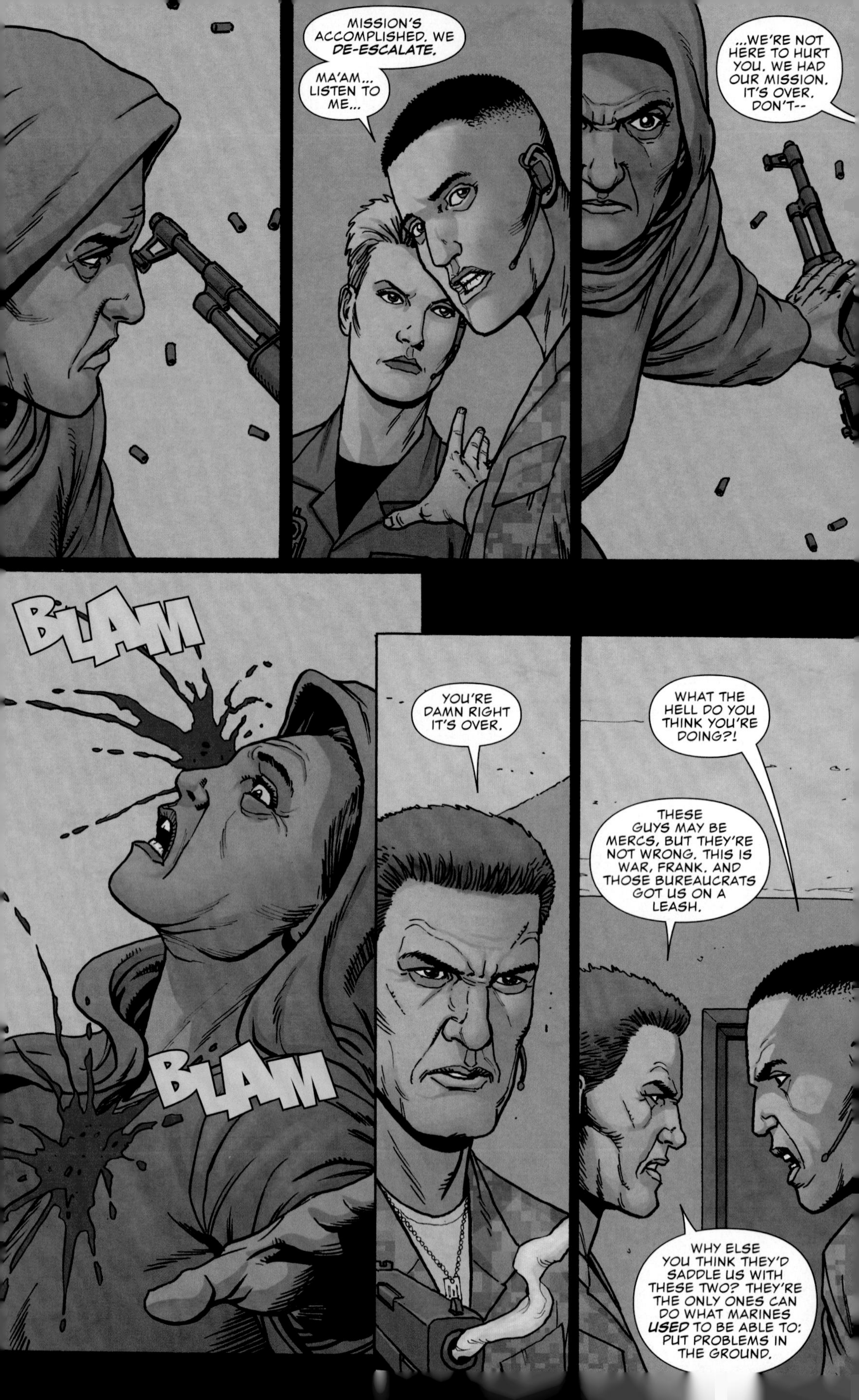
MISSION'S ACCOMPLISHED. WE DE-ESCALATE.
MA'AM... LISTEN TO ME...
...WE'RE NOT HERE TO HURT YOU. WE HAD OUR MISSION. IT'S OVER. DON'T--
BLAM
BLAM
YOU'RE DAMN RIGHT IT'S OVER.
WHAT THE HELL DO YOU THINK YOU'RE DOING?!
THESE GUYS MAY BE MERCS, BUT THEY'RE NOT WRONG. THIS IS WAR, FRANK. AND THOSE BUREAUCRATS GOT US ON A LEASH.
WHY ELSE YOU THINK THEY'D SADDLE US WITH THESE TWO? THEY'RE THE ONLY ONES CAN DO WHAT MARINES USED TO BE ABLE TO: PUT PROBLEMS IN THE GROUND.

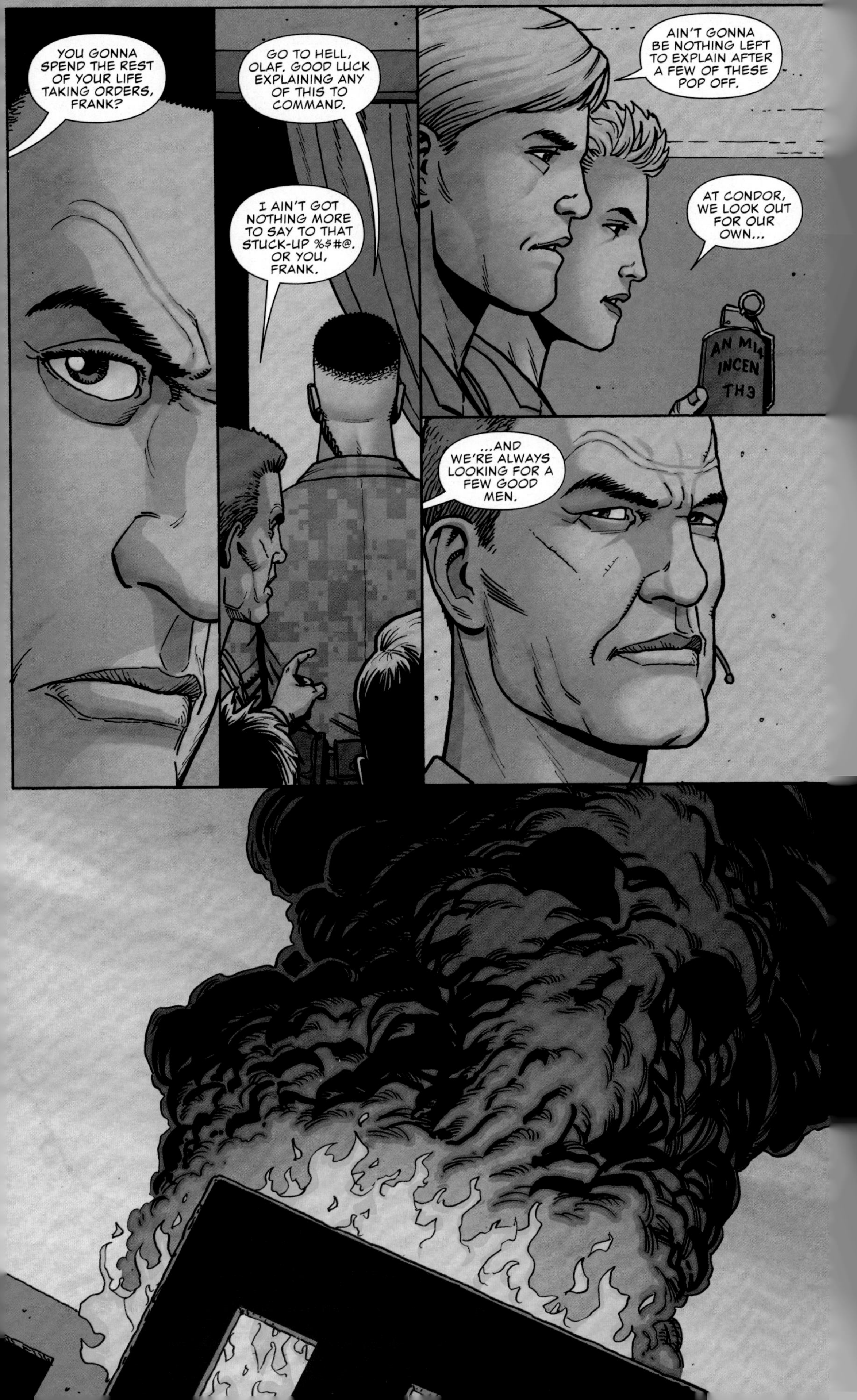
YOU GONNA SPEND THE REST OF YOUR LIFE TAKING ORDERS, FRANK?
GO TO HELL, OLAF. GOOD LUCK EXPLAINING ANY OF THIS TO COMMAND.
I AIN'T GOT NOTHING MORE TO SAY TO THAT STUCK-UP %$#@. OR YOU, FRANK.
AIN'T GONNA BE NOTHING LEFT TO EXPLAIN AFTER A FEW OF THESE POP OFF.
AT CONDOR, WE LOOK OUT FOR OUR OWN...
AN M14 INCEN TH3
...AND WE'RE ALWAYS LOOKING FOR A FEW GOOD MEN.

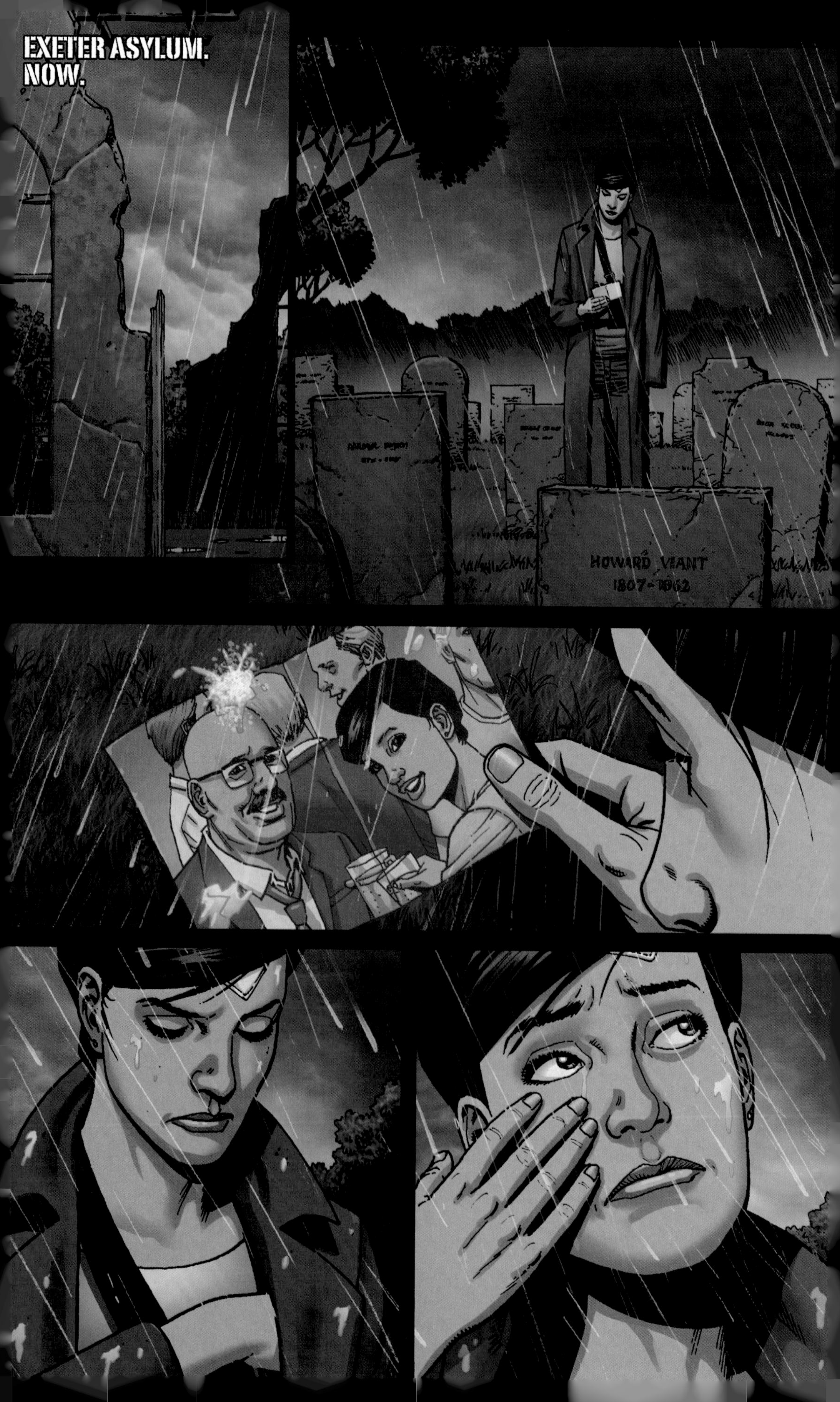

EXETER ASYLUM.
NOW.
HOWARD VIANT
1807-1862

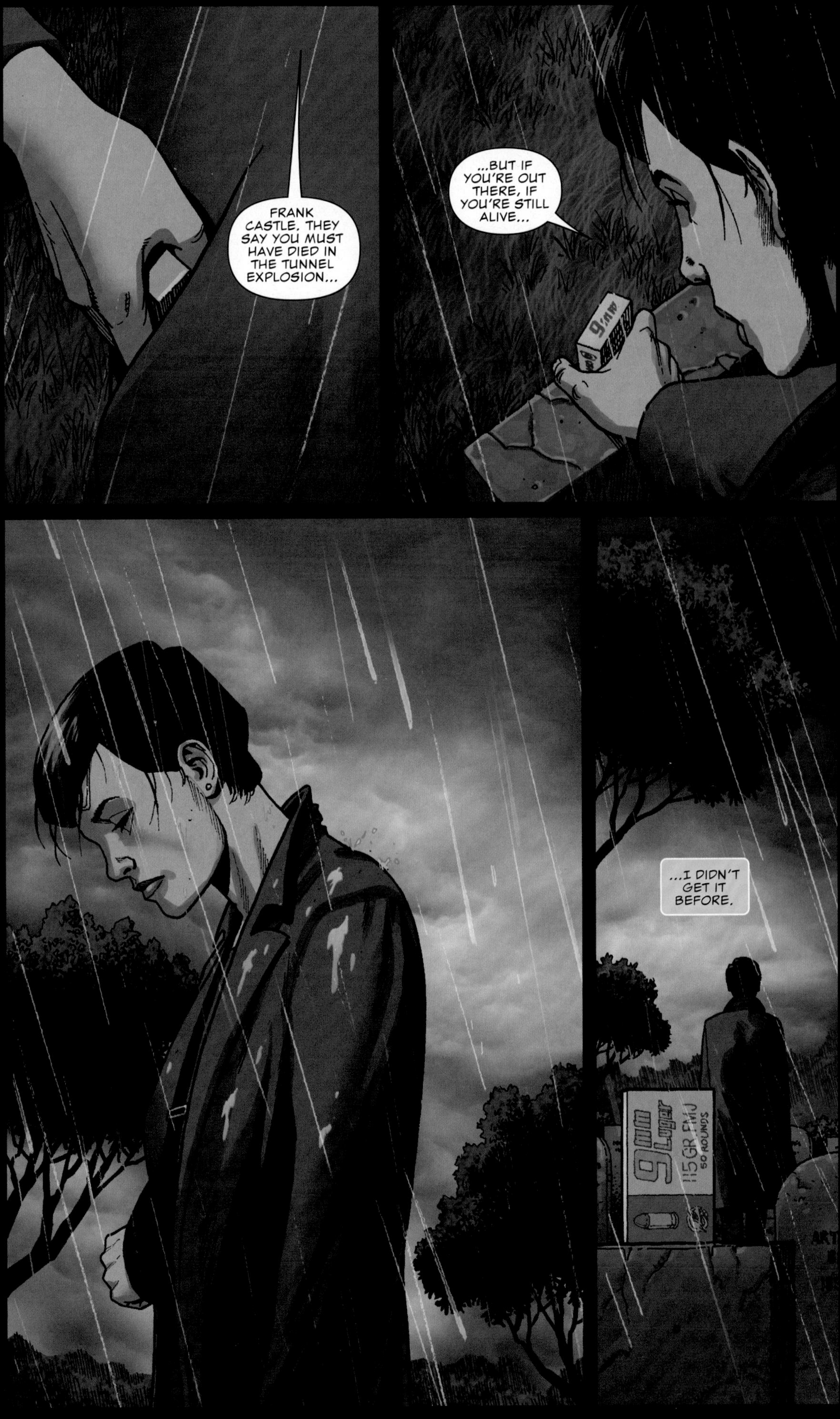
FRANK CASTLE. THEY SAY YOU MUST HAVE DIED IN THE TUNNEL EXPLOSION...
...BUT IF YOU'RE OUT THERE, IF YOU'RE STILL ALIVE...
...I DIDN'T GET IT BEFORE.
9mm Luger
115 GR FMJ
50 ROUNDS

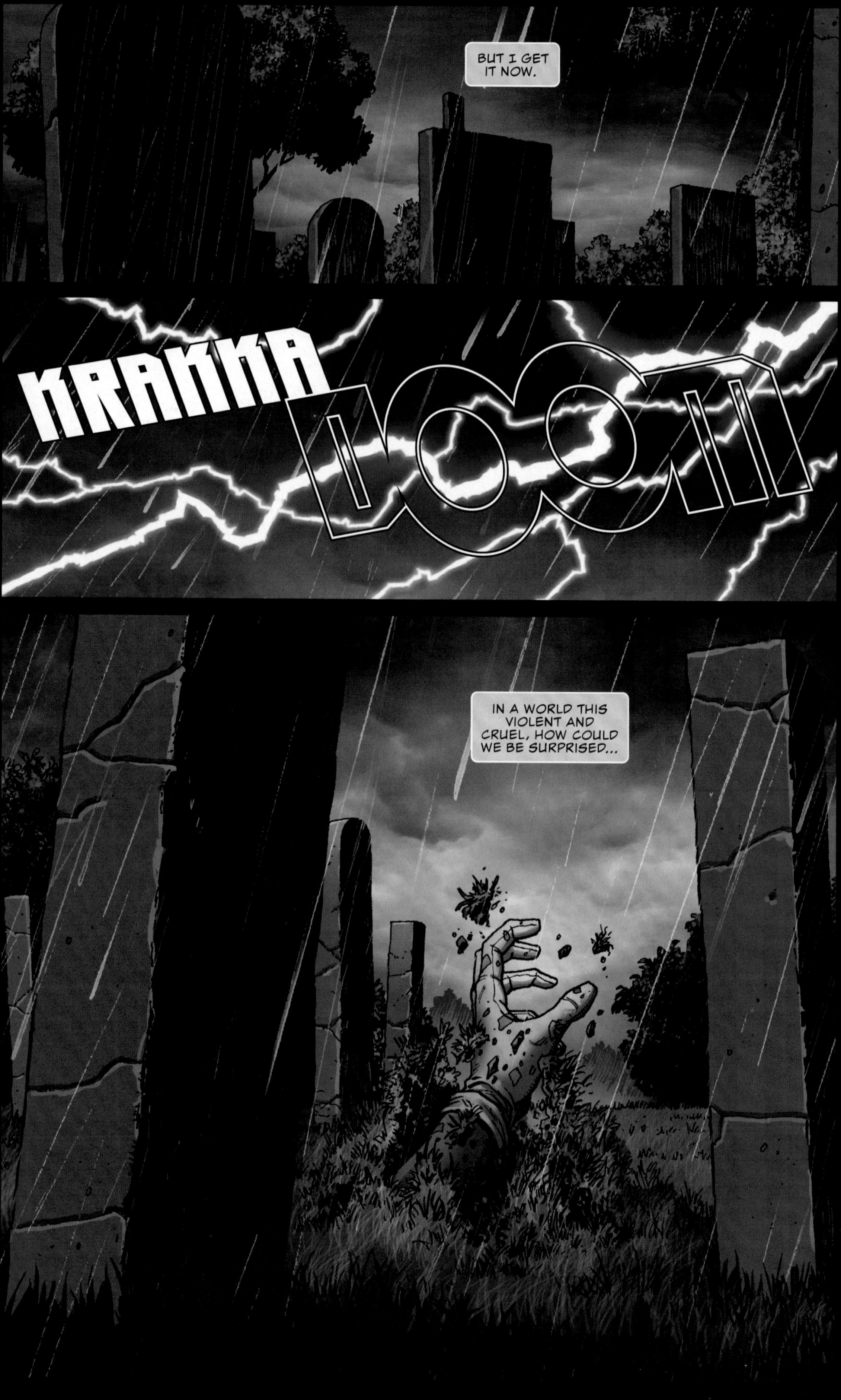
BUT I GET IT NOW.
KRAKKA DOOM
IN A WORLD THIS VIOLENT AND CRUEL, HOW COULD WE BE SURPRISED...

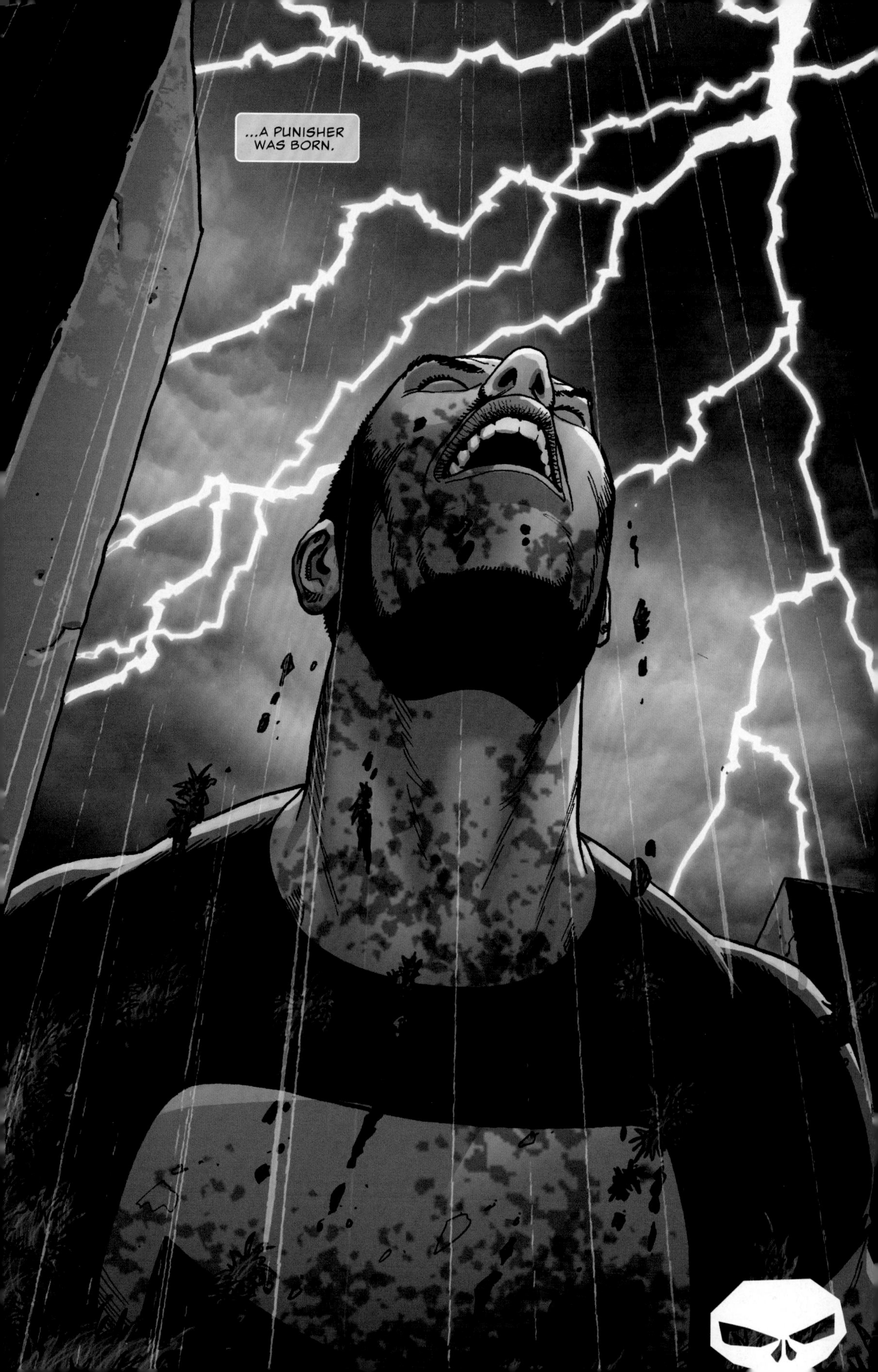
...A PUNISHER WAS BORN.

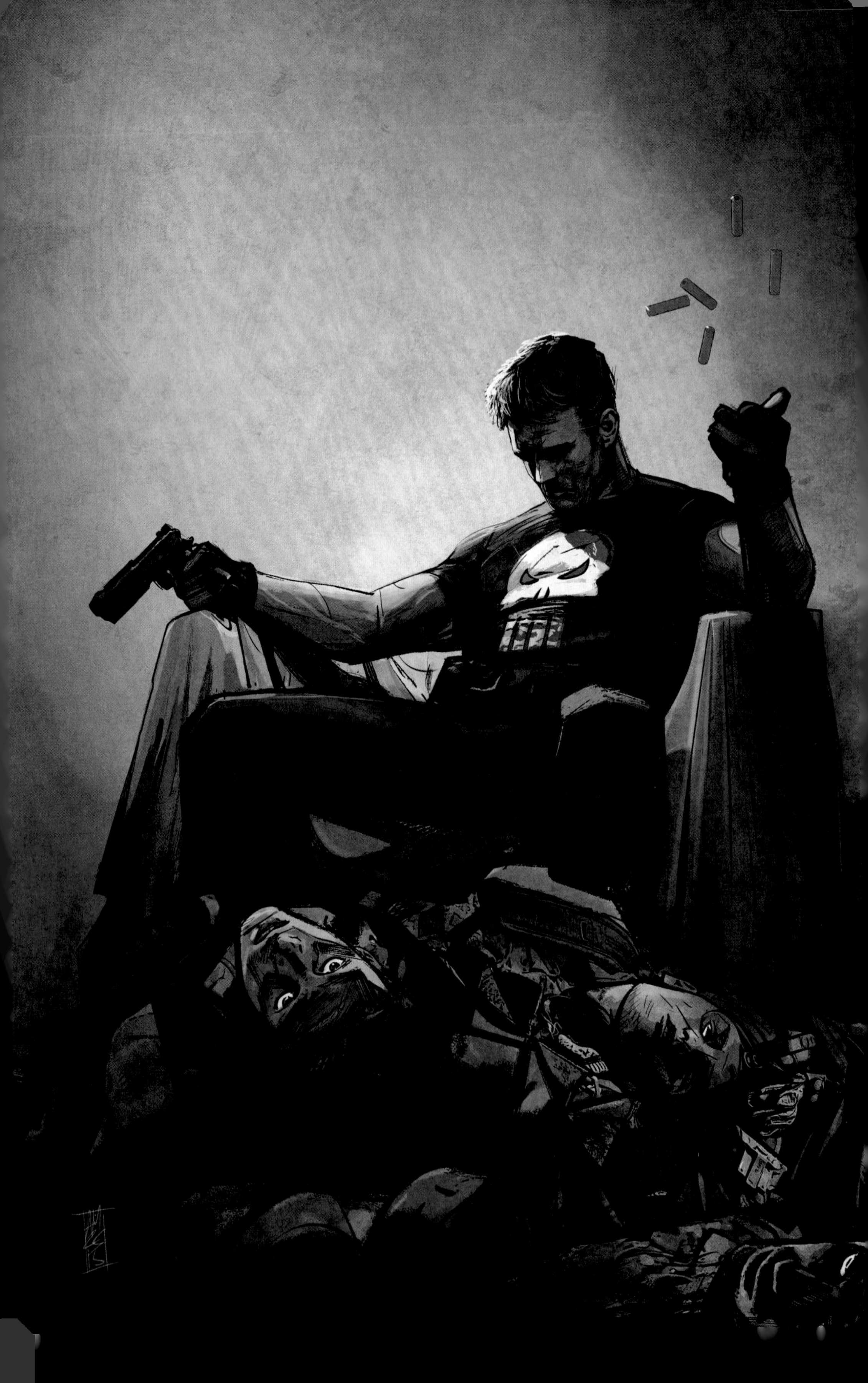

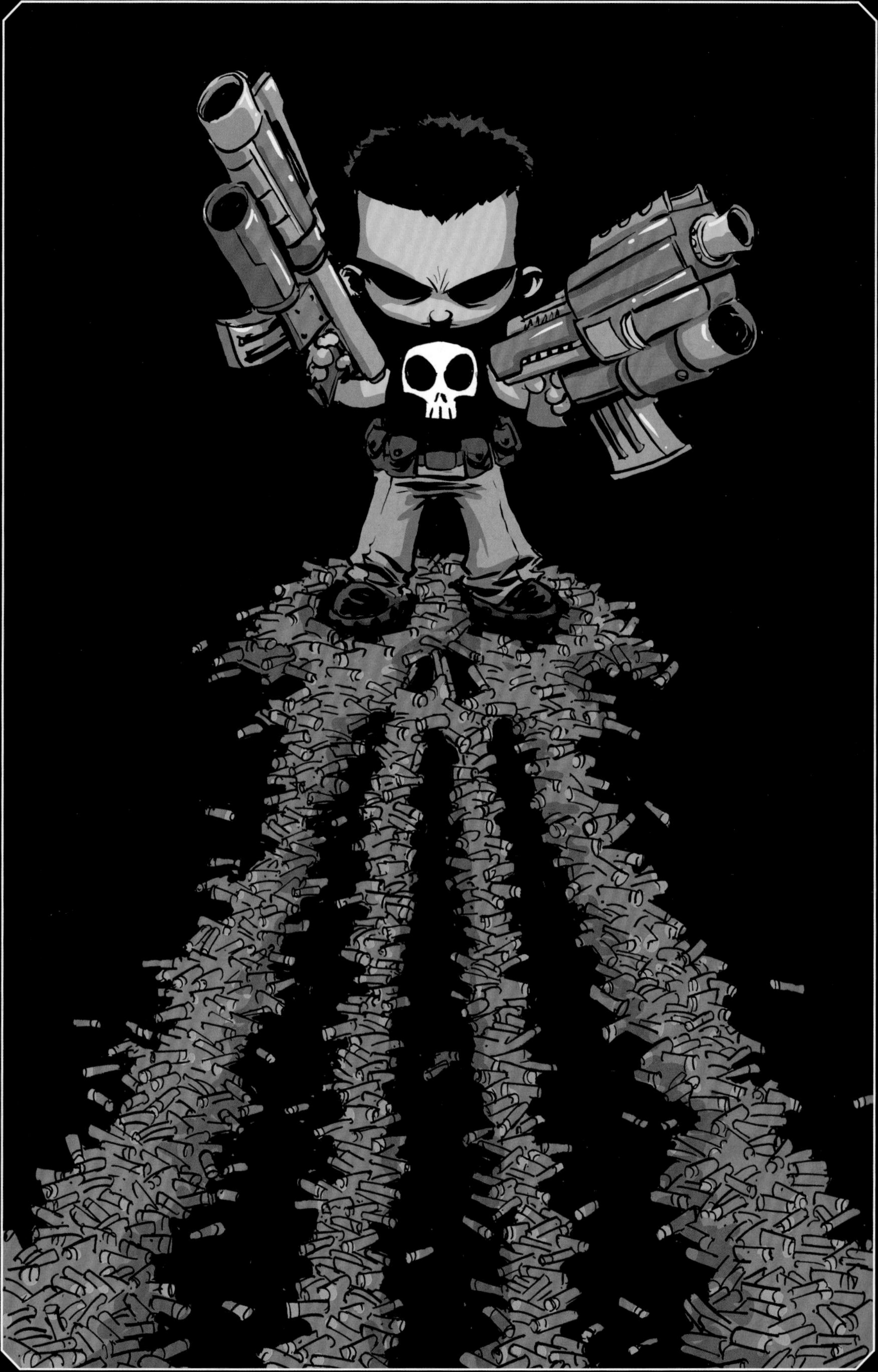

Skottie Young

No. 1 variant

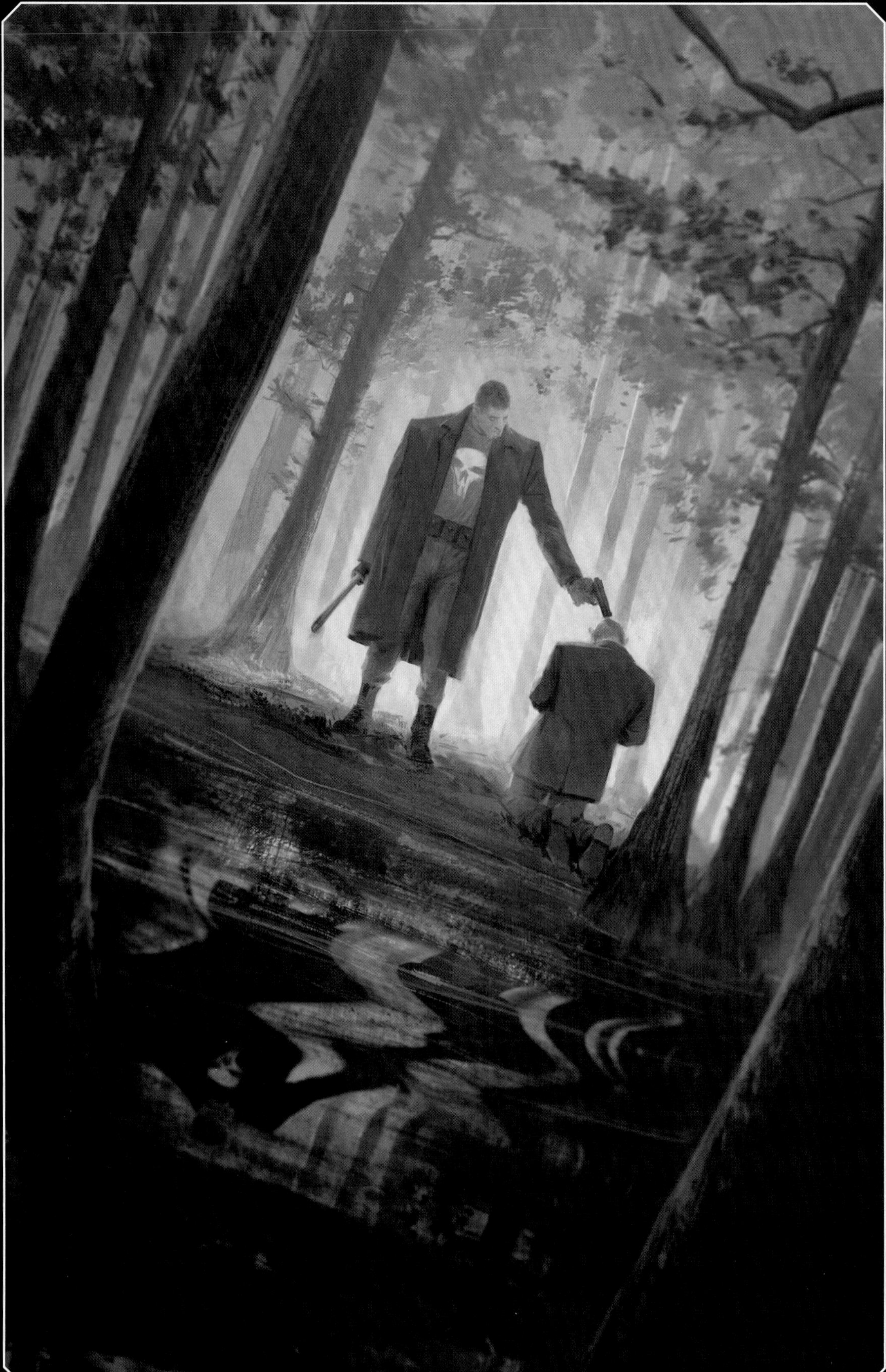

Vanesa Del Rey

No. 2 variant

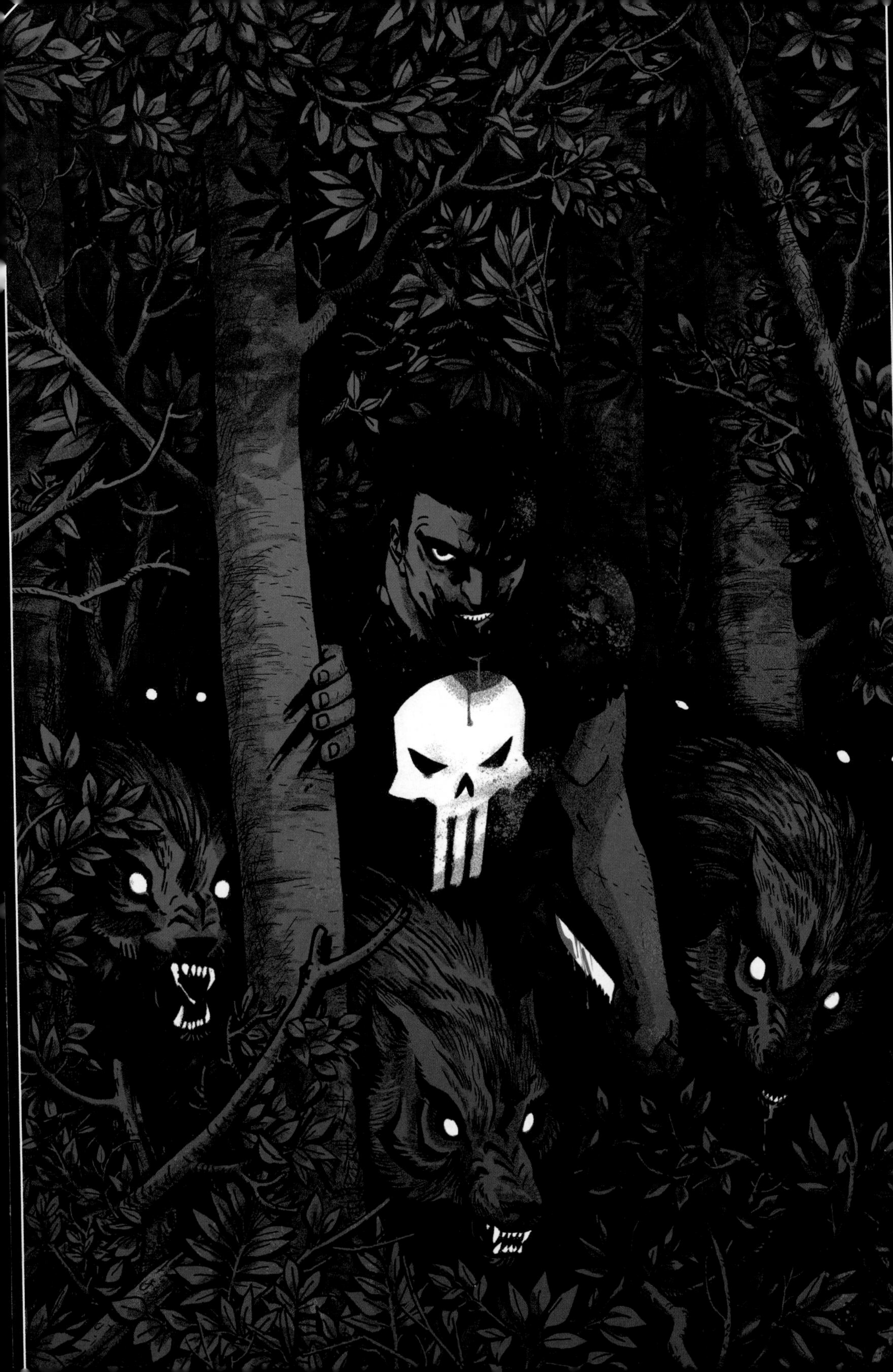

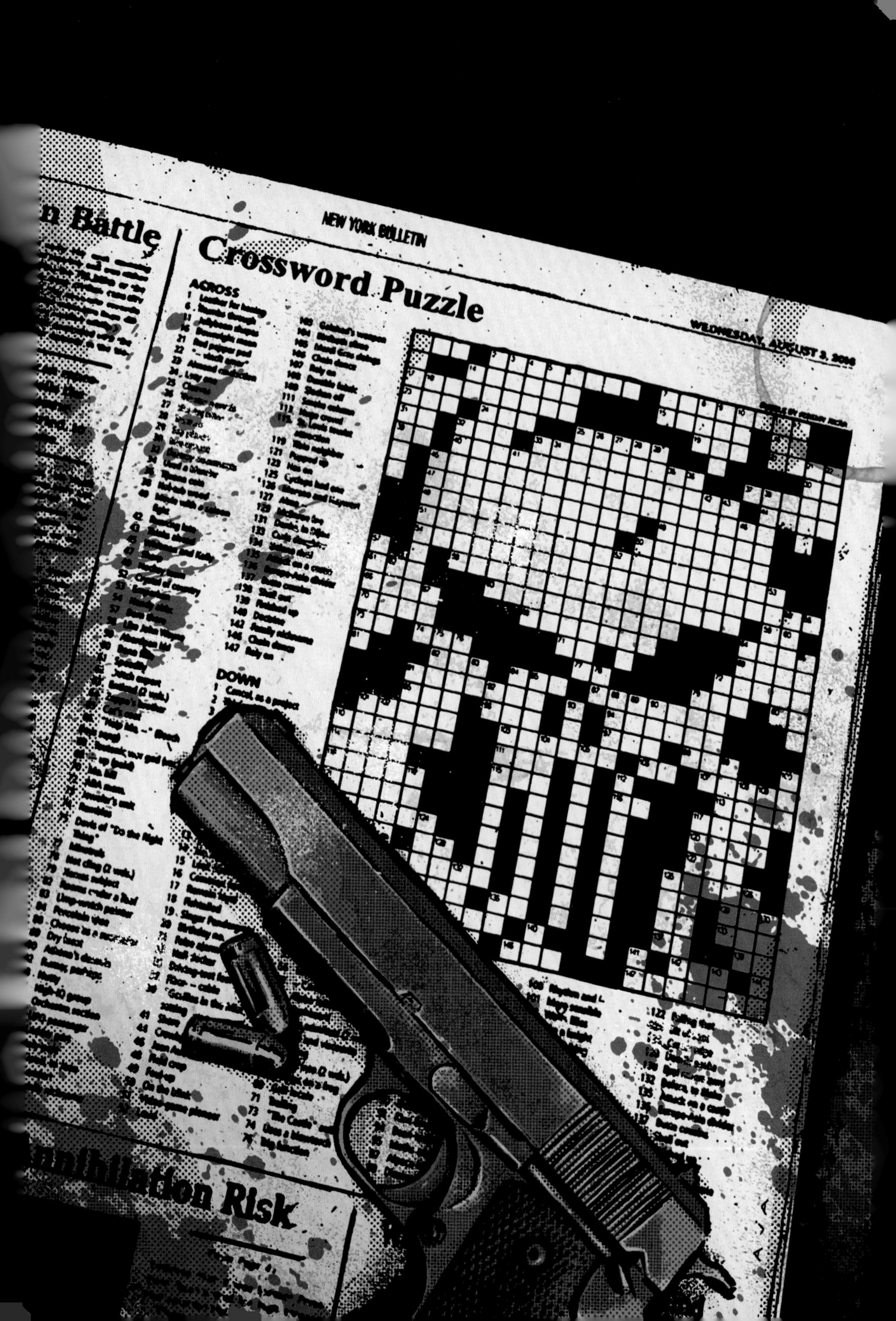
n Battle
NEW YORK BULLETIN
Crossword Puzzle
ACROSS
DOWN
nnihilation Risk

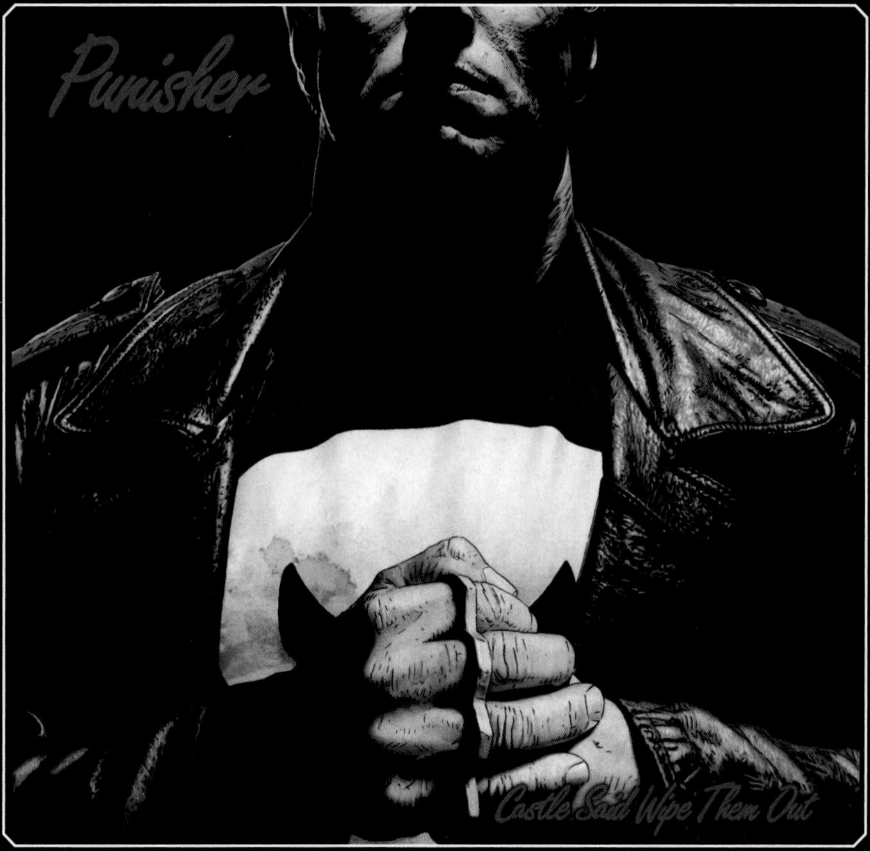
Punisher
Castle Said Wipe Them Out

Tim Bradstreet
No. 1 Hip-Hop variant

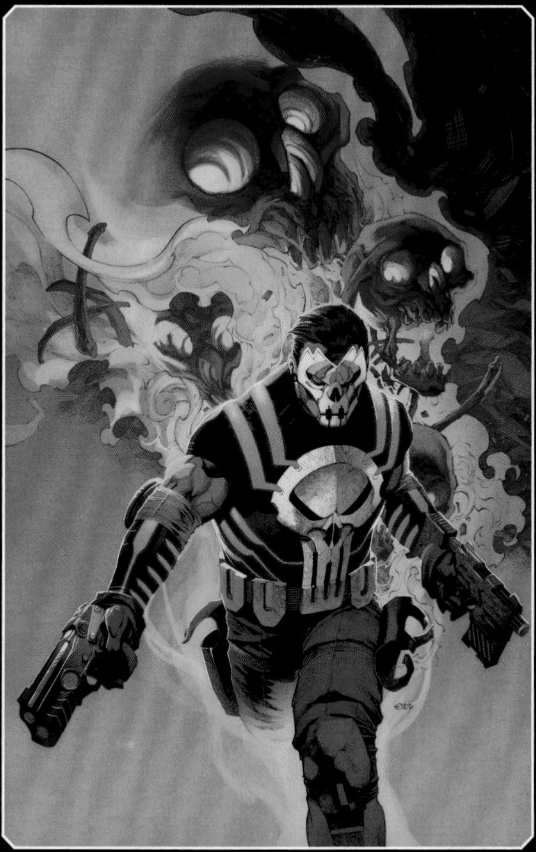

Christopher Stevens & Frank Martin
No. 1 Age of Apocalypse variant

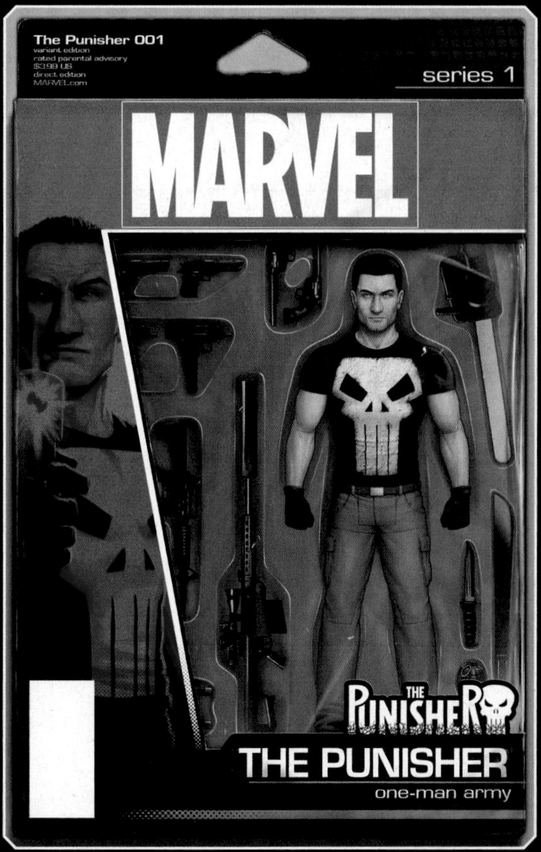
The Punisher 001
variant edition
rated parental advisory
$3.99 US
direct edition
MARVEL.com
series 1
MARVEL
THE PUNISHER
THE PUNISHER
one-man army

John Tyler Christopher
No. 1 Action Figure variant

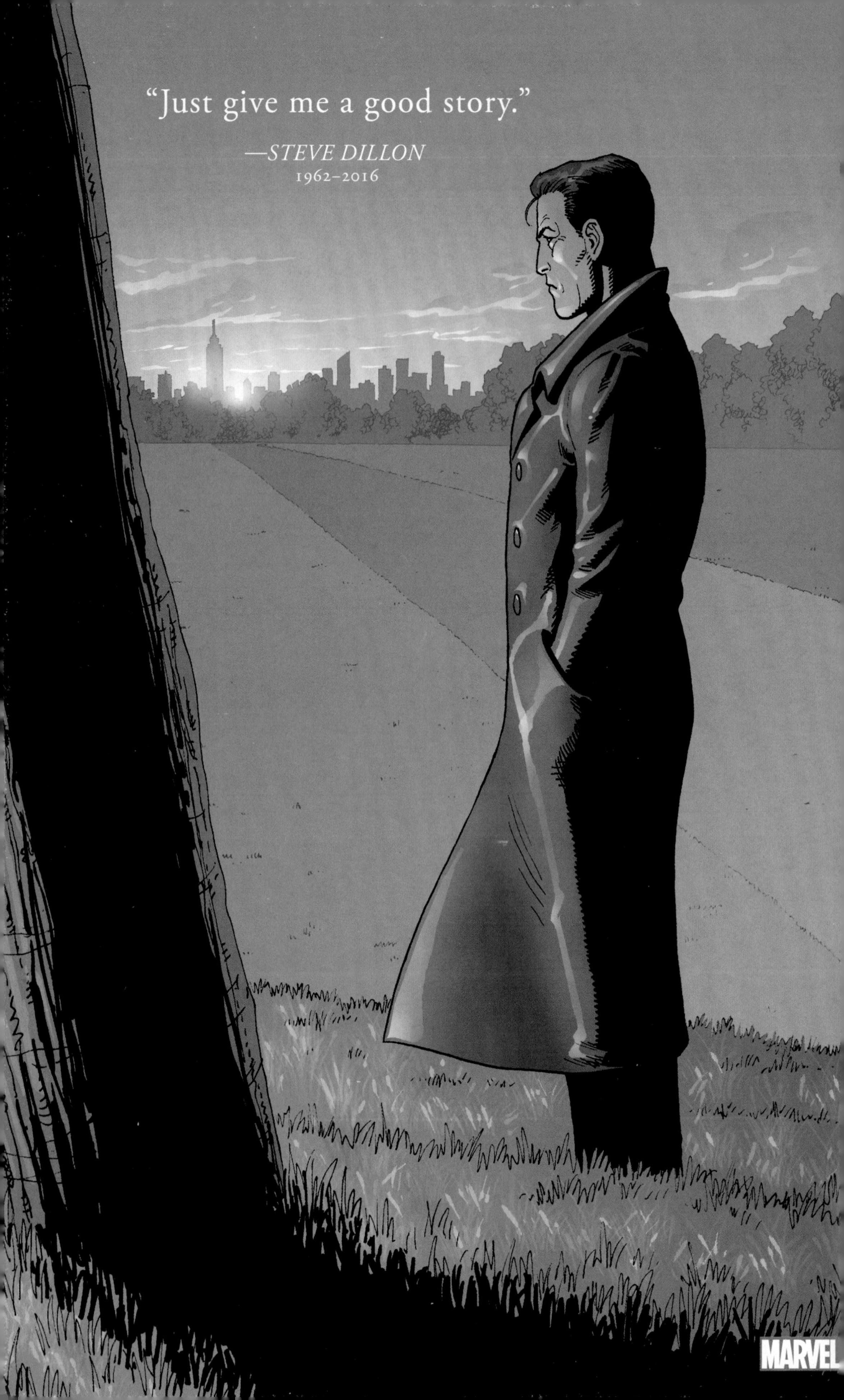
"Just give me a good story."
—STEVE DILLON
1962–2016
MARVEL